"It's my prayer that through Wess Stafford's new book, a passion will ignite in the hearts of Christians around the globe to reach these little ones with his tender mercies and hands-on help."

—JONI EARECKSON TADA, president of Joni and Friends

"*Too Small to Ignore* is a wake-up call for all of us. It speaks to our responsibility to 'the least of these.' If you want to understand children and why they matter to God, you have to read this book!"

—MICHAEL W. SMITH, artist and songwriter

"At last—a book that has to be close to the heart of Jesus, who affirmed the value of children. Read this and get your heart engaged in the priority enterprise of the coming generation!"

—JOSEPH STOWELL, former president of Moody Bible Institute

"Wess Stafford has a heart for children like none I have ever seen. *Too Small to Ignore* is a must-read for anyone whose life touches the lives of children."

—ZIG ZIGLAR, author and motivational teacher

"Wess Stafford has written an amazing book, combining a touching personal story with a very compelling argument for changing the way we view children. This book is both deeply personal and highly provocative on a subject too often left unexamined."

—DALE HANSON BOURKE, author of *The Skeptic's Guide
to the Global AIDS Crisis*

"Weaving a beautiful tapestry of his boyhood adventures in Africa and a lifetime of heartfelt ministry to children, Wess Stafford powerfully defends the cause of God's children and implores us to take action on their behalf. The spiritual impact of future generations simply cannot be ignored."

—TED HAGGARD, president of National Evangelicals Association

"Wess Stafford...is a man of integrity whose heart overflows with love for hurting children and, above all, for our God. You cannot meet this godly man without being challenged and encouraged. Prepare to be moved."
—REBECCA ST. JAMES, artist, songwriter, and author

"Some books are meant to be skimmed, others to be read carefully. Wess Stafford's new book is to be savored, underlined, highlighted, and meditated over. *Too Small to Ignore* is a great book, written with the energy and verve of a man who knows kids and passionately loves them."
—BILL ARMSTRONG, former U.S. senator

"Wess Stafford is a rare and good man, who brings a message for our time straight from the heart of God. His candid book compels us to see and act differently, to enter into God's compassionate heart and move on behalf of his little ones. We *can* have a beautiful impact."
—STASI ELDREDGE, speaker and coauthor of *Captivating: Unveiling the Mystery of a Woman's Soul*

"This book has everything—stories that will moisten your eyes, insight that will stimulate your mind, and proposals that will generate an intense response.... Wess convinces the reader that he or she can make an incredible difference on behalf of the poorest of the poor."
—TONY CAMPOLO, speaker and author of *Speaking My Mind*

"Dr. Wess Stafford has written a compelling book of his own pilgrimage interwoven with the reminder of the importance Jesus placed upon children. It is a must-read that will inspire all hearts to join with Wess to champion the cause of children all over the world."
—JIM GROEN, president of Global Connection International

"Wess's scripturally based perspective and Spirit-authored passion come through. These pages present a powerful message that needs to be heard."
—MATT HEARD, senior pastor of Woodmen Valley Chapel

"Wess has done a remarkable job of helping us to rediscover the value of our most precious resource—our children. This book will move you to compassion and force you to action! Welcome to a front-row seat on what moves the heart of God."
—C. THOMAS DAVIS, president of Children's HopeChest

"Wess Stafford's African upbringing forged in him a passion to declare a long-neglected kingdom truth: our calling as believers is to speak up for those who cannot speak for themselves and to defend the cause of children whenever necessary."
—DR. ALEMU BEEFTU, president of Gospel of Glory

"I have seen these words lived out in the man who wrote them. I have stood beside Wess as he knelt down to love the children of foreign nations, and I have heard his heart break for the 'least of these.'… The real gift of what Wess Stafford writes is that he lives it first."
—BEBO NORMAN, artist and songwriter

"In *Too Small to Ignore*, Dr. Wess Stafford paints a powerful picture of the importance of children.… Wess's story cuts a deep river of compassion for children in the heart of the reader, and his vision for the future creates a broad horizon of hope."
—DENNY RYDBERG, president of Young Life

"This man and his message are for *now*!"
—PATRICK MCDONALD, founder of Viva Network

"Dr. Wess Stafford…has a sensitive, caring, and compassionate heart for the physical, emotional, and spiritual needs of the world's youth. By reiterating their value and reviewing stories from Scripture revealing their integral part in God's plan, he is truly a 'champion' for the children."
—BILLY KIM, president of Far East Broadcasting Company Korea
and pastor emeritus of Suwon Central Baptist Church

"Every page of this spellbinding masterpiece is drenched with the passion of a man dedicated to the cause of children.... I pray that this electrifying read will light a passion for children in the heart of every person—and compel you to action."
        —MRS. JANET MUSEVENI, first lady of the Republic of Uganda

"*Too Small to Ignore* is the ultimate primer on the status of children, their needs, and our responsibility to them. You will see through the eyes of one who has given his life to follow God's heart for these precious ones."
        —CLYDE COOK, president of Biola University

"At last—a powerful voice and message for the children of the world! Wess Stafford's *Too Small to Ignore* makes a case we can't overlook if we want to impact the nations and change our world."
        —DICK EASTMAN, international president of Every Home for Christ

"Wess has provided some incredible insights coupled with personal experiences that have caused me to reflect on every child I come in contact with.... This book has been a long time coming, and I thank God for the courage and lifetime of experiences that he gave Wess to write it."
        —RON CLINE, chairman of HCJB World Radio

"I've known few people who are as committed to a cause so right and close to the heart of God as Wess Stafford. Our world desperately needs to hear and act on the message in *Too Small to Ignore*."
        —JIM MELLADO, president of Willow Creek Association

"Wess Stafford calls us into the world of children in need. Like the organization he leads, this is a compassionate journey into the real world where we are equipped to help those who are truly 'the least of these.'"
        —GEOFF MOORE, artist and songwriter

TOO SMALL
TO IGNORE

Why the Least of These Matters Most

DR. WESS STAFFORD

PRESIDENT & CEO, COMPASSION INTERNATIONAL

WITH DEAN MERRILL

Foreword by Michael W. Smith

WATERBROOK
PRESS

Too Small to Ignore
Published by WaterBrook Press
12265 Oracle Boulevard, Suite 200
Colorado Springs, Colorado 80921
A division of Random House, Inc.

All Scripture quotations, unless otherwise indicated, are taken from the *Holy Bible, New International Version®*. NIV®. Copyright © 1973, 1978, 1984 by International Bible Society. Used by permission of Zondervan Publishing House. All rights reserved. Scripture quotations marked (KJV) are taken from the *King James Version*. Scripture quotations marked (NASB) are taken from the *New American Standard Bible®*. © Copyright The Lockman Foundation 1960, 1962, 1963, 1968, 1971, 1972, 1973, 1975, 1977. Used by permission. (www.Lockman.org). *Italics* in Scripture quotations reflect the author's added emphasis.

To respect the privacy of the author's boyhood friends in Africa, the names "Alezye," "Alezana," "Alebeh," "Kolzana," and "Padubeh" are pseudonyms. Also, the names of the mission boarding school and its various staff members have been changed. However, all events and other descriptions are factual to the best of the author's recollection.

ISBN: 978-1-4000-7392-4

Copyright © 2007 by Compassion International, Inc.

Published in association with the literary agency of Mark Sweeney & Associates, 28540 Altessa Way, Bonita Springs, FL 34135.

The Library of Congress cataloged the original hardcover edition as follows:
Stafford, Wess.
　　Too small to ignore : why children are the next big thing / Wess Stafford with Dean Merrill. — 1st ed.
　　　　p. cm.
　　Includes bibliographical references.
　　ISBN 1-4000-7043-0
　　1. Child rearing—Religious aspects—Christianity. 2. Parenting—Religious aspects—Christianity. 3. Christian education of children. I. Merrill, Dean. II. Title.
　　BV4529.S79 2005
　　259'.22—dc22

　　　　　　　　　　　　　　　　　2005014148

Printed in the United States of America
2008

10 9 8 7 6

Dedicated in loving memory of my father,
Kenneth Stafford
(1925–2003)

This book was a journey begun together
on Wednesday mornings over mugs of coffee
at his kitchen table in his simple forest home.
I was left to finish it alone.
A humble, wise, and gentle servant of God
who gave himself passionately to the kingdom,
his deep love and respect for the poor
and his compassion for all who suffer
shaped and inspired his little boy.
I am grateful and honored to have been his son
and to walk a lifetime in his footprints.

CONTENTS

FOREWORD

My life isn't defined by my music. Music is my vocation. My life is characterized by my relationship with God and my family—my beautiful wife, Debbie, and our five great kids.

My friend and brother in Christ, Dr. Wess Stafford, is a kindred soul. Since 1993, about as long as I've known him, Wess has served as the president and CEO of Compassion International. But this tender-hearted, deeply compassionate man isn't defined by his vocation either.

Like me, Wess wants to be known as a God-fearing man who loves his wife and kids. I believe his dear wife, Donna, and two daughters, Jenny and Katie, would say Wess's greatest priority and most profound accomplishment are being a godly husband and father.

In *Too Small to Ignore,* Wess builds a strong, passionate, and reasoned case for the cause of God's children. He admonishes us, Christ's body, about committing sins of omission and shirking our responsibilities to defend the children—the most vulnerable among us. And he challenges us to change our ways. Wess's message is as simple as it is profound.

Children, the smallest, weakest members of our human family, often pay the greatest price for our fallen world's sins. Yet they are the lowest priority among big institutions in our world. We must begin today giving our children the time, attention, respect, and commitment they deserve and our God requires.

I believe Wess shares our heavenly Father's broken heart; he grieves over the sins and abuses visited upon the little ones of this world. He reminds us that Jesus saved his harshest words of warning for adults to protect little ones, since he knew this world would wage abuses against them if they are not treasured, nurtured, and respected.

In more than twenty-five years of ministering to children across the world, Wess has come to what I believe is an explosive revelation: the reason children are such a low priority to the great institutions of this world is that there is an invisible battle going on—a spiritual war that rages over each and every child.

And the reason for this raging battle is clear. Research indicates that the vast majority of people who become Christians do so while still children, usually before the age of fourteen. If a person hasn't accepted Christ as a youth, studies tell us that the probability he or she will ever know Jesus is only 23 percent.

Children deserve to know that they are valued, that they matter, and *most important,* that they matter to Jesus!

Clearly though, it is children in poverty, "the least of these" among us, who have captured Wess's heart. And for good reason. The son of missionary parents, Wess grew up in a remote, destitute West African village, which helped him develop a deep respect and love for the poor and their children.

Like Wess, I'm firmly convinced that we have a profound obligation to care for the poor and their children. Our mutual conviction is founded in more than two thousand Bible passages that declare our heavenly Father's love for the impoverished and urge his followers, you and me, to defend their cause.

I also agree that the magnitude of the problem of poverty can easily lead us to despair. We believers often do nothing for one reason: we don't know what to do.

In 1994, Compassion asked me to become a spokesperson for its ministry. At that time, I simply wanted to sponsor a child and observe the work of the organization. So that's what I did.

I'd maintained for years that kids, no matter where they live, have some basic similarities—they play the same, they interact the same, and their desire for approval and love is the same. But their similarities end when absolute poverty is added to the situation. When I visited Compassion's work in Ecuador, it was the first time I'd come face to face with poverty's reality. And it was overwhelming.

I couldn't process all the sights, sounds, and smells I was experiencing. I had gone from holding my own kids, safe and healthy in our home, to holding a baby overseas who was probably not going to live much longer.

Then as I met my sponsored child, Gavi, visited several Compassion projects, and saw the quality of the work, it solidified everything for me. I sensed the spirit of joy in the kids who attended the projects, despite the surrounding poverty. These kids didn't have anything, and they leaned on the Lord for everything. But they were happy.

After my trip to Ecuador, I decided to become a spokesperson for Compassion. And because it's a God thing, I love sharing about the ministry and the children it serves. My family and I have since sponsored three other precious children through Compassion's ministry. What an incredible experience. Each child has touched our lives deeply.

Unlike my profession, which puts me in the spotlight most of the year, kids are rarely in the spotlight. But it's time they were. And because of Wess Stafford and this powerful book, they are. Reading this book will change your heart and help you understand God's position for children in his kingdom.

—MICHAEL W. SMITH

ACKNOWLEDGMENTS

I like the old Southern saying "If you find a turtle on a fence post, you know it didn't get there by itself." That makes me chuckle because it rings so true for my life. I am indebted to God for his path for me and to the many, many people whose input into my life lifted me to my particular fence post, enabling me to write this book.

In these pages I talk about how children learn to stand in line and, unfortunately, how they are usually at the end of the line when it comes to being a priority. So the people I want to put at the head of my line are the two most important children in the world to me—my beloved daughters, Jenny and Katie. Thank you for so unselfishly sharing your "dadoo" with the hurting children of the world. As you have grown into remarkable young women who love God and have developed your own tender hearts for the poor, you have inspired me, shaped my heart, and blessed me beyond measure. I am so very proud of you both. You bring me love and joy, healing and happiness, and a delightful, extraordinary friendship that refreshes my soul. I pray that your many sacrifices will result only in your blessing.

Heartfelt appreciation goes to my precious wife, Donna, without whose faith in me and dedication to Compassion International I could not do what I do. You have patiently loved and encouraged this seriously flawed husband through twenty-six years of marriage, and while I have been so often absent from home, you have selflessly poured your love into our children. A committed Compassion sponsor before you ever met me, you have also devoted your heart, time, and talents to hundreds of thousands of Compassion children over the years in your quiet, behind-the-scenes way. I am so grateful for your immeasurable support in my life, including your generous contributions to this book. You shared the path of this project with me, often amid tears of both sorrow and joy, and you know me so well that you can often tell what is in my heart better than I can myself. I am greatly blessed by our loving partnership—not to mention your writing and editing skills!

I am overwhelmed with love and gratitude for my sister and dearest friend, Carol Deaville, who traveled the journey with me and now cannot do enough to alleviate the suffering of others as a caring nurse and pastor's wife. Gary, her husband, is God's perfect gift to her, and their daughters, Bonnie and Debbie, her greatest joys. What blessings you all are to me!

Sadly, my mother, Marjorie Stafford, who suffers from Alzheimer's disease, will never read this book. But it stands as a tribute to her courage, faithfulness, and love for her Lord. She was one of a great generation of missionary pioneers who left the comfort and safety of home to serve God in the harshest of circumstances in "darkest Africa," and I will always cherish her example and gentle love.

I owe a deep debt of gratitude to the ministry I am honored to lead. I'm not the founder of Compassion International, but had it not existed twenty-eight years ago when I came along, I would have launched it myself—so close is it to my heart and values. My predecessor as president, Rev. Wally Erickson, was an amazing leader. Wally, I will always be grateful that you saw something of worth in a skinny, young field worker in Haiti. Thank you that seventeen years before your retirement, you believed in me, began mentoring me, and patiently guided me into my turn as leader. Compassion's dedicated board of directors, led by Ron Lehmann, has shepherded me for the past thirteen years and would not rest, nor allow me to rest, until I "got the book written." Without your encouragement and support, this book would still be at the top of the to-do list!

Compassion is led by an outstanding team of executives who are passionate about serving their Lord through this ministry. I am honored to serve alongside them. Thank you especially to Senior Vice Presidents David Dahlin and Ed Anderson for holding up my arms and leading brilliantly in my absences. Thanks to Vice Presidents Charlie Dokmo, Mark Hanlon, Larry Lemmon, Paul Moede, Tony Neeves, Dawn Rowley, Jeff Wood, and Mark Yeadon for so willingly and capably carrying a fuller portion of the load to allow me to step away for a time and get this book written. I also greatly appreciate the diligent administrative assistance I received from Angie Lathrop, Charey Neal, and Laurie Struck for keeping my work life organized as I juggled the competing demands of writing and leading the ministry.

I am deeply grateful for Compassion's sponsors and worldwide staff who heard my heart over the years and urged me to "tell it in a book." Special thanks go to Peg and Jon Campbell and Doug and Vee Stepelton, who ministered to me through their gracious hospitality. I cannot adequately express my appreciation for your generous gift of opening your beautiful homes to me—they were perfect oases of peace and refuge in which to write.

Many thanks to Dean Merrill, my cowriter, who listened, prodded, challenged, and used his considerable talent to put it all in order and make sense of it. Thank you for keeping my nose to the grindstone and reminding me that "the ultimate inspiration is the deadline." I appreciate your gentle, patient spirit and your heart for God. I am also grateful to the wonderful staff at WaterBrook Press who caught the urgency and vision for this book in a single lunch hour. Thank you, Don Pape and Bruce Nygren, for your faith in me and your passion to put this book into the hands of people who could make the world a better place for "the least of these."

I can never repay the people of my African village, Nielle. Though all of the adults and most of my boyhood friends have passed on, I will always carry their love, courage, and suffering in my heart. My spirit was shaped by their "pearls of poverty," and everything I need to know to lead Compassion's worldwide ministry, I learned from them.

Likewise, I am indebted to the generation of heroic missionaries who served in West Africa with my parents. You were my "aunts and uncles" in a faraway world. Through you I understood sacrifice, strength, grace under pressure, and what it looks like when godly people pour themselves out in love for others. Thank you for the hugs, prayers, and kindness—you couldn't have known just how treasured they were by little Wesley.

And finally, to my childhood boarding-school friends, you will always be my heroes. You lived brave and compassionate lives with remarkable strength and resolve to silently bear on your small shoulders whatever you had to bear out of love for your parents, their mission, and the souls of the people of Africa. No cry went unheard—our tears broke the heart of God.

Mysteriously and wonderfully, a great reward awaits you. I pray I have told our story well and that through it you will find a measure of comfort and peace that can come only from God. I am grateful for all your kindnesses to me and am proud to be your brother. Years ago I was the first to break down and expose the silence of the lambs. Now half a century later I've done it again—this time not for my own protection but with a deep passion that such a tragic history will never be repeated. May this journey together take you back to your own childhood and then move you forward to join the battle for the children of today.

Introduction

THE GREAT OMISSION

Late one evening D. L. Moody, the premier American evangelist of the 1800s, arrived home from speaking at a meeting. Emma, his wife, was already asleep. As her exhausted husband climbed into bed, she rolled over and murmured, "So how did it go tonight?"

"Pretty well," he replied. "Two and a half converts."

His wife lay silently for a moment pondering this response, then finally smiled. "That's sweet," she replied. "How old was the child?"

"No, no, no," Moody answered. "It was two children and one adult! The children have their whole lives in front of them. The adult's life is already half-gone."

⌑⌑⌑

I have to ask you, what mental image came to your mind when you read "two and a half converts" just now? Did you picture what Emma Moody pictured: two grownups standing at the front of an auditorium with a little child beside them? Be honest.

If you did, don't feel bad—you're in the overwhelming majority. In fact, I'll be honest too. I had worked with Compassion International, a child-focused organization, for ten years when I first heard that story, and even I sat there imagining two adults and one child.

I don't anymore...and that is what this book is all about.

If I say to you, "Fold your arms," you will most naturally place your right hand on your left biceps and tuck your left hand inside the crook of your right elbow. This feels natural to you. Of course, you could place your left hand on your right biceps, but it would feel very strange. (Try it; you'll see what I mean.)

To change your natural pattern is a good example of what is called a paradigm shift. The term means a new and off-stride view of reality—just like D. L. Moody's unique perspective on his world of listeners. He heard the beat of a distant drummer and marched to that cadence. He was clearly out of step with his contemporaries. He would still be out of step with the perspectives, priorities, and practices of today's world, both secular and Christian.

No matter what the setting, children seem to be a second-rate mandate. No matter what the ill of society, it tends to spiral downward and eventually land with its cruelest and most smothering impact on our littlest citizens. Small, weak, helpless, innocent, vulnerable, and trusting, they are the waiting victims for our simple neglect and most evil abuse. No matter what goes wrong, the little ones pay the greatest price.

When hunger and famine strike a nation, adults become weak and hungry, but it is the children who most often starve to death. When disease arrives with all its fury, adults can become very sick, but the first to die are usually the children. When war erupts over ethnicity or boundary lines in the dust, it is the littlest victims who pay the most tragic price. The wars of the last decade killed more children than soldiers.[1] Far more children were injured or permanently maimed by our battles. The tragedies go on for years after the last gunshot or grenade blast, as land mines and booby-trapped toys keep wounding, terrorizing, and killing our innocent ones.

The ritual sacrifice of children has been taboo for thousands of years. Yet tragically it is practiced every day across our world. We sacrifice children on the altars of our most destructive sins. When the sickness of pornography has run to its most evil and destructive end, it takes the form of child pornography. When prostitution reaches its sickest, most depraved form, it becomes child prostitution.

Perhaps a little closer to home is the reality that children are the sacrificial lambs when our homes break up through neglect, anger, hostility, and eventually divorce. Kids frequently blame themselves for the destruction, carrying deep scars on their innocent spirits for a lifetime.

Our most vulnerable citizens have become the world's most disposable commodity. So vulnerable are children to the ravages of poverty that malnutrition causes more than 55 percent of the child deaths in our world.[2] This is all the more tragic when we are told that the earth can produce enough food for every man, woman, and child to have 2,720 calories per day—more than any of us need.[3] So while God has done his part in creating a world capable of providing what we need, we have not done our part in the stewardship of it, in seeing that it gets to the end of the line, to the poorest and neediest—the children.

Statistics as appalling as these can overwhelm us. We become paralyzed by the sheer magnitude of the problem. It's a bit like looking at children from the wrong end of a telescope. They appear vague and otherworldly. But do you remember the shock and heartache you felt when you watched the World Trade Center towers crumble to the streets of New York, taking nearly three thousand innocent lives with them? It was one of those historic moments that will live in infamy. We will all be able to tell our grandchildren exactly where we were when that tragedy of tragedies occurred. The whole world staggered to a halt that day. Nothing else seemed to matter.

Now imagine with me for a moment. What if a catastrophe of equal devastation had happened at noon, just three hours later, at the Sears Tower in Chicago? Suddenly the people behind the microphones and lenses would have scrambled to cover this new disaster. And what if in the midst of their gathering that Chicago story, reports had come in saying that three thousand *more* innocent people had died in a nightmarish attack on Denver? Wouldn't that have brought all else to a stop? Wouldn't our national and world leaders have declared that nothing else mattered on the planet until we brought an end to this carnage? Enough is enough!

But if, as the world kept turning that dark September 11, the same level of human loss had continued to occur every three hours—Los Angeles...then Honolulu...Tokyo...Bangkok...Calcutta...Moscow...finally London—the world would have shuddered to a grinding halt, never to be the same again.

Well, something similar did happen on a worldwide scale that tragic day. *Thirty thousand of our little innocents under age five were taken from us.*[4]

Sadly, this level of loss also happened on September 10 and again on September 12 and every single day since. The microphones, cameras, and satellite dishes don't bring this shocking reality into our living rooms as they did on 9/11. But it happens nonetheless. Without power or voice, these little children keep silently slipping away into the arms of their grieving heavenly Father, lost from a world that is unworthy of them, a world that has lost its heart.

∽∾∽

Because children have no political clout or even voice in global affairs, they can become marginalized. Since they don't vote, they have little effect on the political powers that should act on their behalf. Every segment of society seems to have figured out how to protest, march, and agitate for its individual and collective rights. But have you ever seen children holding a protest? Ever seen their placards going down your city streets? I thought not.

They have much to legitimately protest, but they are voiceless and powerless. Our selfishness and greed cause them to pay the greatest price, but they suffer silently.

In all my world travels, I have never come across a Children's Hall of Fame to honor the champions and heroes of the young. It should come as no great surprise that very little gets handed down on their behalf by the powers that be.

But is it really true that children have nothing to offer? Ask any mom or dad who puts little ones to bed at night. Ask any teacher who gets a Valentine's Day card made with construction paper, glitter, and way too much glue.

Children may not have much to give materially, but they generously give all they have to those they love and believe in: hugs at bedtime that require both arms and legs; full-body squeezes amid giggles and laughter that are beyond value; a storm of sloppy kisses on your cheek; a squeeze of your hand that confides, *I'm afraid, but I trust you;* pudgy little fingers folded in simple, sincere prayer that rises up like perfume to the very heart of God. These things are priceless and more than enough.

Few gifts on earth are as wondrous as the love of a child. Advocates for children know deep in their hearts the truth of the saying "You never stand so tall as when you stoop to help a child."

∾∿∾

Sadly, the church cannot claim exemption from the neglect and abuse of children. The church may have avoided overt sins of commission (tragically, not always), but we are equally guilty of the covert sins of omission. I have rarely attended a major church or mission conference that focused on children. Have you?

Several years ago I attended an international conference for sharing vision, strategies, programs, and priorities to bring the world to Christ by the year 2000. I was not one of the scheduled speakers; those slots were reserved for a very select group of mission and denominational heads. Each was given just fifteen minutes on the platform to share the most essential priorities in which they were engaged. So precious was the time of this three-day conference that a bell was actually rung when time was up, to keep things moving.

I went enthusiastically, notebook in hand, to glean from the very best what all of us could do in this great effort to reach the world for Christ. What strategic role could my child-focused organization play in this exciting movement? I sat there, pen poised, as the first few speakers made their case for what they were doing and why.

By the third speaker, I realized I had written nothing down. Not one Christian leader had said anything about children and how to evangelize them in this final hour of human history. I began to keep a tally of how many times I actually heard speakers mention "child" or "children" in their strategic presentations. As the hours passed, I became more and more discouraged. Children were not on the minds of any of these great leaders.

By the end of the conference, I had heard the words "child" or "children" only twelve times—and never in the context of a specific strategy to reach them. They were instead lumped into the broader group of "every man, woman, and child." I was filled with despair and bursting to speak up for the children—those who cannot speak for themselves. The printed program said that in the final session there would be open microphones for "additional questions or comments." I could hardly wait for the chance to make a speech about this great omission from the Great Commission.

To my dismay, the conference had gotten behind schedule (despite the ringing bell), and that final session had to be cancelled. What I had hoped to say, if given a chance that final day, was this:

> People, humor me for just a brief moment. All of you close your eyes and picture this great harvest of humanity you have been talking about so passionately. What does that vast sea of people actually look like? You have spoken eloquently about the needs of "the 10/40 Window." Who are these individuals who stretch across Asia and Africa, knowing nothing of Christ's atoning work and needing to hear the message of salvation? If, in your mental image of that vast sea of humanity every other person is not a child, you don't know what the harvest looks like!

Fully half of the world, and especially the developing world, are children and teenagers. Yet they were not even a miniscule part of the conference strategies. Believe me, D. L. Moody would have gone ballistic about this.

What portion of your church budget is dedicated to children's ministry? If it is more than 15 percent, yours is an exceptional church. What portion of your denomination's mission budget is spent on worldwide children's ministry? Again, if it is more than 10 percent, that is very rare.

Have you ever heard a major radio or television program or even a single broadcast advocating children's ministry? Ever seen an edition of your favorite Christian magazine focused exclusively on children? Who are the hardest volunteers to recruit in your local church? Often it's the nursery workers and children's Sunday school teachers.

Can you name a single evangelical leader who is known as an outspoken champion for children, a D. L. Moody of today? I can't. No, the church simply cannot wash its hands of the great omission.

What makes all this so urgent is that missiological research indicates that almost two-thirds of the people who give their lives to Christ do so before the age of eighteen.[5] In other words, line up any twenty Christians, and thirteen of them will have accepted Christ as their Savior while a child or youth. In fact, researchers tell us that if people have not accepted Christ by age twenty-one, the probability that they ever will is only 23 percent. Yet we spend a pittance on the more open and strategic part of the harvest.

Every major movement in world history has recognized the strategic importance of mobilizing children. The Nazis had their Hitler Youth bands. The Chinese Communists had their Red Guards. The Taliban in Afghanistan had their madrasah schools to instill extremism in the young. The great omission seems to be unique to Christians.

One of the first things children are taught their first day of school is how to stand in line. Eager to please, they become good at it. The tragedy is that all too often they find themselves at the end of society's line. And that is where they stay, while others with more size, influence, and resources jump in front of them. Most of us can remember the class bully who would push us aside with a sneer because we could do nothing to stop him. That is what happens to children in today's world all the time. Something has to be done on their behalf!

⌒ᴄᴄ⌒

We cannot claim that the Scriptures are unclear on how precious children are to God Almighty. He not only loves them with a love we cannot begin to understand, but he respects and believes in them. The Bible tells more than a few stories in which God had such an important task to be done that he simply could not entrust it to an adult. Only a child would do! Jesus uttered a powerful and terrifying warning to protect little ones from the kind of stumbling and abuse that humanity can impose upon them if they are not treasured, nurtured, and respected enough. His disciples never got a more enraged tongue-lashing than when they tried to keep children away from the Master.

Neither can we say that today's societies and cultures do not innately love their children. Nowhere do mothers fail to mourn the loss of a child or to sacrifice all they have in time, effort, and resources on their children's behalf. What parent has not experienced that amazing flood of love that finds its way into your heart as you hold your newborn child? You are captivated by love in just moments.

Then what is the problem? I have spent more than twenty-eight years ministering to children across the world. Some of them suffer in great poverty, while others are smothered in the lap of luxury. Deep down, I have come to the conclusion that the reason they are such a low priority to the great human institutions that seek to control this world, both secular and Christian, is that an invisible battle, a spiritual war, rages over each and every child. It is above us and beyond us and engages the full fury of the hosts of both heaven and hell. Children may be ignored by government, church, and mission—but not by Satan or God Almighty.

First, we must understand that Satan knows the heart of God. It is Satan's greatest joy and highest priority to do all in his power to break the heart of *Elohim,* the creator of heaven and earth. Remember that, as Lucifer, Satan was a witness to the process of creating the world. I can imagine heaven's one-time chief angel watching with great interest as the Spirit of God hovered over a dark and formless world. He saw the dazzling advent of light. He watched amazed at the creation of land and sea, plants and animals—all the creative work of Jehovah. It frustrated and angered him to see the great joy and satisfaction God was getting from the emergence of this wondrous work of his hands.

Ever watchful for an avenue of attack, Satan found it in the moment God fashioned a man in his own image from the dust of the earth and then breathed his own breath into the man's nostrils. Something about this crowning part of the Creation moved God deeply with a profound love. Satan saw it and knew he had found an inroad. All he had to do was attack and hopefully destroy mankind. He began his strategy as a serpent in the Garden of Eden, and he has been doing it ever since.

At the moment of birth, all heaven stands in breathless anticipation and breaks into shouts of joy and praise. Each child is born into the world loved and full of potential to bring joy to the heart of God. A little flame flickers deep in the child's being. It reflects a dignity and worth, made in the image of God Almighty.

Meanwhile Satan and his evil hosts stand ready to pounce and destroy that life as quickly and completely as possible, knowing how that will break the heart of God. All of heaven and hell are present and focused on the newborn life—for vastly different reasons. Both have strategic designs for this little one.

Given this frightening warfare between heaven and hell, it is all the more ironic that children are seemingly so unimportant to us adults. While all of heaven stands and cheers whenever a little one is born, and all of hell hurls itself at its destruction, we glibly go about our lives and ministries oblivious of the raging battle or the strategic importance of the children around us day by day. What is to be done?

❦

It begins now, here, and with you! It begins with the very next child God brings across your path. Every child you encounter is a divine appointment. With each one you have the power and opportunity to build the child up or tear the child down.

A life can be launched with as little as a single phrase, an uplifting word, or an act of kindness. The spirit of a little child is a lot like wet cement. When a child is young, it takes little effort to make an impression that can last a lifetime.

If you are a positive, productive member of society, I'm willing to bet you owe that to someone long ago. Take a moment to reflect on your childhood. Who believed in you before you believed in yourself? Was it your mom or dad? Was it a teacher? Your Little League coach? Your grandmother?

Who said, "My, but that's a beautiful picture you drew," and now you make your living as an artist?

Who said, "You have a beautiful voice; I loved your song," and now you sing for a living or get great joy from singing for others?

Who said, "You were the best Joseph in the Christmas play I've ever seen. I thought you were really him!" and now you make your living as an actor?

The source of my sense of worth was my parents and the people of a little African village in northern Ivory Coast. Though poverty-stricken in many ways, these tender people took me in as one of their sons and nurtured me when the cement of my soul was wet. I'll tell you throughout this book about growing up in that village. There, daily, this adage was lived out: "It takes a village to raise a child."

Sadly, the opposite is also true. All it takes is a single unkind word, an isolated act of cruelty or abuse to destroy a life! Again, Satan knows this all too well. As I have shared these thoughts with people over the years, I have often seen their eyes well up with tears. They can remember exactly who almost destroyed them as a child.

Tragically, it is usually easier to name this destructive person than someone who impacted your life positively. Someone somewhere looked at you and said you were ugly. Someone said you were stupid, clumsy, worthless, or naughty—and the words made an impression on your soul with which you still struggle.

You probably have done one of two things with the hurt in your spirit. You have either accepted it as true, allowing it to define you, and resigned yourself to expect less than the best for your life. Or you have made it your life's crusade to prove them wrong. You have become a superachiever, driven, competitive, although perhaps deeply unhappy in the process. It all sprang from that one person's act of cruelty. If you are such a person, some of the most profound questions you can ever ask yourself are, what am I trying to prove? to whom? and why? This mental process may help you know the truth—and perhaps set you free.

Believe me, nothing thwarts the efforts of Satan to destroy little lives more than a caring adult's timely intervention to build up their self-worth and assurance of being loved. The path of destruction can end with you. You can decide, as I have, that you will be an instrument of grace in the hands of God. Every child who crosses my path in the grocery line, at church, or at the ballpark I consider a divine appointment, an opportunity to lift that child up—if only for a brief moment. It may just be the moment that will launch a life or restore one that needs kindness today.

You won't know until eternity, but your single act of kindness might not only change the little life standing before you; it might resonate for generations. A dear friend of mine named Danny Cook knew from family tradition that his ancestors came to America on the *Mayflower* as part of that courageous band of Pilgrims in 1620. Today, nearly four centuries later, his family includes a number of dedicated ministers of the gospel.

One time Danny decided to research his family tree to discover what had been accomplished. He was expecting a glorious path of outstanding men and women that led right to his doorstep. But as he followed the trail into the seventeen hundreds and eighteen hundreds, the downward spiral shocked him. He discovered criminals, suicides, imprisonments, and even insanity. He began to wonder how on earth this family had ever returned to its God-fearing roots.

Then Danny came across the life of his great-grandmother. He learned from her obituary that, despite her conditions, she had accepted Christ as her Savior at the tender age of eight. She became known for her love of Jesus and for singing hymns wherever she went. She was a woman of earnest prayer and brought up her children to love the Lord. From that point onward, the story of the generations changed. That one woman's life of faith and joy a century ago changed the entire course of the Cook family, right up to the present time.

I wonder who led that little girl to Christ? The person who knelt with a child so long ago had no idea that this would be a pivotal moment in the life of an entire family. The dark decline would be reversed through that simple prayer.

Your small pebble in the pond of one child's life may send out ripples that eventually transform many others. I'm convinced that heaven will be full of such delightful surprises for those who were quietly faithful and sensitive.

If God places a child before you, and you are too busy to wield either a positive or negative influence…you just did the latter! You communicated that the child doesn't matter and isn't important.

I have never met anyone who truly believes in children who does not have a powerful story behind that perspective. I am no exception. In the chapters that follow, I will tell you the story of my childhood, of growing up in a remote, poverty-stricken African village, of surviving the boarding-school nightmare, of managing the shock and challenge of returning as a teenager to a very different place called America...and of ultimately taking up a life as a champion for children.

PART
ONE

NOT SOMEDAY...TODAY

Childhood—we get only one pass at it, and yet it dictates the quality of the rest of our lives. What we think, feel, experience, and endure in this earliest phase is the single most important indicator of what the rest of life is going to be like.

Yet as we mature, our first few years almost totally fade from our memory. Like the adults in the Peter Pan stories, we find that adulthood seems to expunge all traces of memory of what it was like to be a young child. Life recycles itself completely with each succeeding generation. When the delivery room nurse places that little bundle of joy into our arms that first magical minute, it seems we have to learn anew what childhood is about. Why do babies cry? What makes them learn the liberating joy of crawling? Why do they fight so desperately not to give in and go to sleep? So little we know. So much we have forgotten.

Too many of us tend to treat childhood as a preamble to actual life, a vulnerable period of time merely to be survived in order to get on with the real business of being a valid, contributing member of the human family. This is the mind-set that causes us to speak of children as "tomorrow's world" or "the church's future." As noble as those phrases sound, they are all about pushing off the value of children to the Realm of Someday. Someday they will add value. Someday they will make a difference. Not today.

Our excuse, perhaps, is that no creature in the animal kingdom begins life more vulnerable and more in need of constant protection and nurture than the newborn member of *Homo sapiens*. Within an hour of birth, the baby antelope can dart about and outrun all but the swiftest of its predators. Even during those first dangerous sixty minutes, the fawn's perfect camouflage and virtual lack of odor protect it. Thereafter, the antelope can manage.

A new hatchling crocodile fresh from the egg has all the features of its fearsome parents as well as all the instincts and life skills needed to find its way to the marsh and immediately begin a lifelong hunt for prey. Most birds within a month of hatching in the nest are full feathered and have taken wing. Babies of predators such as the lion, cheetah, or hyena had better be completely on their own within a year, before mom gives birth to the next generation, and they suddenly find themselves alienated, attacked, and driven away. They have to grow up fast!

But not so the human child. The creature destined to be the smartest, most cunning of all the animals is a helpless infant at birth. The child passes through several long years of vulnerability, needing absolutely everything. Food, protection, hygiene, sanitation, warmth, and shelter must be provided. What was God thinking? Even baby monkeys have the strength and survival instinct to cling tenaciously to their mother's fur as she runs, jumps, and swings from branch to branch high above the jungle floor. I never once saw a little monkey fall off its mother's back.

While children are born in the same condition all over the world, I have always been intrigued with how every society holds strongly to its own perception of childhood. Each frames different answers to such questions as, What is a child? How long is childhood? What roles do children play at different ages?

As already mentioned, my own childhood placed me in two of the most radically opposite societies on earth. At one end of the spectrum was the remote little village in Ivory Coast, West Africa, where life was simple, primitive, unchanged for centuries, just a step removed from the Stone Age. But with just a few days' travel, I was suddenly uprooted and transplanted to the other extreme of human society—the fast-paced, ultramodern Western world. Not just anywhere in that world, but its epicenter of frenzy, materialism, and competition: New York City!

I'm not looking for sympathy, mind you. I learned a great deal from both extremes. In fact, let me invite you to journey back with me to my first hours as a teenager in the "land of the free and the home of the brave." It was a hot, humid midsummer day…

COKE BOTTLES AND TEDDY BEARS

"Hey, kid, whaddya say?" With a grandiose gesture, the greasy little Coney Island barker with the droop-down mustache presented his carnival stand. His beady lizard eyes glared out from behind wire-rim glasses.

I understood every word of his question but didn't have a clue what he meant. In the village where I had grown up with my missionary parents and older sister, the word *kid* most often referred to a baby goat. And "What do I say?" I was mystified. In this country, so far from what I had assumed was the center of the earth, were kids each assigned something to say? Was this some kind of branding to keep track of so many children in this vast city they called New York?

"I don't know what I say," I finally stammered, embarrassed.

This man was only the second American I had met since disembarking the day before from the SS *Rotterdam*. His gruffness reminded me of the first American, a Manhattan taxi driver. In a fifteen-minute ride, he had assaulted everything I held dear—lessons learned around the campfire in the evenings from the wise village chief and his elders, not to mention my parents. As we careened through crowded streets lined with skyscrapers, the driver's frustrations with life cut deeply into the tender spirit of America's newest fourteen-year-old. His horn didn't honk in friendly greeting, and as I later learned, that wasn't a warm salute he gave with his left hand out the window. The traffic light changing from green to red brought a flurry of what I thought was English, but they were words I had certainly never picked up from the missionary community. My instincts told me to tread lightly here. There was much about this place I didn't understand.

Now on the Coney Island midway I was still moving with caution. The obnoxious man snapped, "Don't know what ya say? Yo, stupido, ya want one o' these colossal teddy bears or not? All ya gotta do is break the bottles. It's easy!"

I looked him over, as if sizing up prey in the jungle. Was he dangerous? He wore a cocked beret just like the French officials whose convoys occasionally stormed into our dusty village in their Jeeps, barking orders and demanding answers to perplexing questions. I didn't like this barker, didn't understand him, and didn't trust his shifty eyes and raspy voice. I backed away as I would have from a showdown with a panther.

At a safe distance I began studying the gaudy carnival stand. It was painted in loud, clashing colors. Behind the counter, about fifteen feet back, were three rickety shelves lined with Coke bottles. On the ground were glass shards that crunched as the man swaggered back and forth, harassing all who passed by. On the front railing lay half a dozen slingshots and a large jar of colorful marbles.

I did a double take, my eyes riveting on the slingshots. Finally! In this noisy, glitzy, crowded city, here was something familiar. Since I was six years old, a slingshot had hung every night from the post of my cot. It was the first thing I picked up every morning, draping it around my neck. To the boys in my village, slingshots were not just toys; they were homemade weapons, status symbols, and, yes, clothing. I smiled as I remembered that for some of my poverty-stricken African buddies, their slingshots around their necks were *all* they wore.

"Three shots! Twenty-five cents! Step right up!" The barker's staccato eruptions snapped me back to the reality of New York. Flashing between these radically different worlds would become a way of life for me in the months to come. Such sudden transitions would often leave me speechless as I tried to determine which of my four languages to use. Dyoula? Senari? French? No, it had to be English, which was my weakest.

High on both sides of the carnival stand were the most beautiful teddy bears I'd ever seen. I had read Winnie-the-Pooh books in Africa at noon rest, and these were just as I envisioned Pooh Bear to be. They were huge and impressive, like full-grown male baboons. The man may have been repugnant, but he clearly knew what he had: the biggest and best prizes on the midway.

A group of boys about my age came by and got the full treatment from my tormentor. They eyed the huge prizes, fingered the slingshots awkwardly, and huddled near the counter. They pointed at the prizes, punched each other on the arm, and speculated about whether to take the chance.

Finally one little guy was pushed to the front and hesitantly plunked down his quarter. The second he picked up the slingshot, I could didn't have a clue what he was doing. As he gripped the handle in his left hand, I could see his nervousness. With contorted face and squinting eyes, he pinched the leather pouch with his right hand and shakily pulled the rubber bands back.

I cringed, not sure if the next action would be the marble flying or the slingshot crotch planted firmly in his nostrils. Luckily, he let go of the proper end first. The marble limped forward pitifully, thudding softly against the canvas backdrop. The next two marbles were equally futile. Amid laughter and insults, the boy retreated into the group. I smiled.

Another boy tried, then a third. The booth man taunted them mercilessly. "Three lousy bottles. What's so hard about that? Come on, ain't any of ya man enough?" I thought of that same taunt from the giant Goliath just before his downfall. The boys shook their heads. With shoulders slumped, they slunk away. This was not only not fun; it obviously couldn't be done.

With the crowd gone, my camouflage disappeared, and there I stood once again, exposed. Just me and this pint-sized Goliath with the big mouth and the big prizes.

"Hey, you! Skinny kid! What ya scared of? C'mon, give it a try!" I could take all of his insults except for the insinuation that I was scared. In my village that dare would provoke any of us young warriors to do absolutely anything.

I approached him and pointed to the prizes overhead. "What do I have to do?"

"You take this slingshot and three marbles out of the jar. You shoot; you break three bottles; you win the prize!"

Now who is the stupido? I thought. Back in my village every kid was a slingshot virtuoso. We prided ourselves on driving baboons out of the cornfields, herding cattle, killing poisonous snakes, and shooting the eye out of any lizard foolish enough to poke its head over a mud wall—all with stones aimed with surgical precision. I wasn't up to the skill level of my African friends, but I could pretty much hold my own.

As I surveyed the booth's challenge, I thought, *What's the problem?*

There must be a trick to make this hard. The bottles are no more than fifteen feet away. They aren't even swinging on a rope or anything—they're stationary! Maybe they're unbreakable.

But then why all the glass on the ground? This is simple.

On our ocean crossing I had practiced recognizing American coins. I now pulled a quarter out of my pocket. I remembered when coins and paper money had come to our village to take the place of cowrie shells. We weren't sure the new currency could be trusted. How could anything be valuable if you could burn it or melt it?

Surrounded by the buzz of the amusement park, I picked up the slingshot. It felt comfortable and familiar in my hand, like a long-lost friend.

"Do I have to hold it like the other guys did?" I asked. Maybe that was the catch.

"Naw, hold it any way ya want, kid. Just pull it back and break the bottle. Is that too hard?"

I began wrapping my left thumb and forefinger around the two prongs of the slingshot, burying the handle deep into my palm the way I knew would guarantee steadiness. Engulfed, the slingshot was an extension of my arm.

The man snickered. "Never seen anybody hold it like that before. If ya hurt yourself, I'm not responsible!"

I picked a shiny marble out of the jar. This was going to be even easier than I thought. Unlike the irregular stones we had to use in the village that required an extra calculation before firing, these totally smooth and perfectly spherical marbles were guaranteed to fly straight and true.

I raised the slingshot, pulled back the rubber, and with one flashing flick of my wrist, *splink!* went a bottle on the far end. A shower of glass exploded in all directions. The man stared at me while brushing bits of glass from his hair and clothing.

"Whoa, beginner's luck, huh?" he growled hopefully.

"Well, maybe not," I replied as I picked up another marble. *Blam!* Down went the second bottle. A crowd was beginning to grow behind me.

"I'm guessin' you've done this before, kid," the man hissed.

"Well, yeah, we do this where I come from," I answered. With that, I picked up my third marble and pulverized the third bottle. The crowd cheered. Little Goliath winced.

Success—my first in America! My village buddies would have doubled over with laughter at my having won such a huge victory with so little challenge.

"Okay, I'll have that big brown bear with the black nose, way up there!" I said, pointing.

"Not so fast, not so fast!" the barker sneered. "That's not how it works. I said you'd win *a* prize, not the *grand* prize." With a sarcastic flare, he pulled from under the counter a fuzzy little bear about four inches tall.

I felt foolish. He had conned me after all. "Well," I stammered, "what do I have to do to win the grand prize?"

"Oh, you've got to work up to that. Another quarter, three more marbles. This goes in stages, don't ya know that, kid? Where ya from?"

Fine. I had seen this kind of trickery among the Dyoula craftsmen from the village down the road. I plunked down another quarter. *Pow, pow, pow.* Three more Coke bottles shattered.

"Okay, now I want that big one," I announced with a slight edge in my voice.

The man threw back his head and guffawed. "Well done, hotshot. Now ya get *this* one." He pulled out a ten-inch bear. But when I disgustedly plunged my hand into my pocket to fish for another quarter, he paused.

"Wait just a darned minute. You're gonna keep on bustin' all my bottles, ain't ya, kid?"

I nodded, glaring at him through eyes that were now slits of determination.

Reality set in. The guy could see a pattern developing. This skinny little kid was going to shatter all his pop bottles. If he made me work through all four prize levels of his little game, he might earn a lousy buck from me, but he'd lose more than that in bears and bottles. And if I decided to keep playing, he'd have a severely reduced inventory with which to swindle his next victims.

He got out his stick and unhooked my teddy bear—the huge brown one with the black nose. "Look, kid, just take this miserable bear and get outta my face!" he snapped.

I smiled as I walked away with my prize. The crowd was silent for a moment, then relished the drama that had just played out in front of them. Good had triumphed over evil. They broke out in wild cheers and applause.

What a strange and wonderful country, this United States of America. I came; I saw; I conquered.

BEST FRIENDS

As I strode back to the nearby church where my parents were attending an all-day reorientation-to-America mission meeting, I carried my massive prize on my shoulders piggyback style. I might as well have been a mighty hunter returning to feed an entire village.

My mom rolled her eyes and gave me a *Now what have you done?* look. As the meeting droned on, my mind wandered five thousand miles across the Atlantic to my little village of Nielle. The hot, dusty town was five hundred miles inland, about as far as anyone dared venture on the washboard-riddled path we called a road. Trucks were so rare that to have one grind through our cluster of mud huts was the highlight of the day. We children used to run alongside it in a jubilant troop, waving and cheering, until the truck rumbled on, leaving us engulfed in a billowing cloud of red dust that would settle over us and everything else for the next hour or so.

For most of the time my sister, Carol, and I had been the only white children within a day's drive in any direction. Color didn't much matter. We sang with great gusto, "Red and yellow, black and white—they are precious in his sight. Jesus loves the little children of the world." Actually, for much of a typical day, we were all basically the same—very red with dust.

My mother had told us once that, as a young woman, she had begged, "Lord, please don't call me to be a missionary. But if you do, please don't let it be in Africa!" Well, this was not only Africa but the most remote, undesirable outpost one could imagine. A typical day for six months of the year was 110 degrees Fahrenheit and bone-dry. To step outside the house felt like opening the oven door to see if the cookies were done. The waft of heat could stop you in your tracks like a fiery wall. Then came the rainy season, which meant a tropical downpour, turning the dust into a sea of sticky mud every day for the next six months.

When we first arrived in Nielle, I was just six years old. There was no electricity or running water. The two-hole outhouse was at the end of a scary, snake-infested trek that required foot stomping to scare off all manner of scorpions and things that go bump in the night. In short, this place was a city girl's worst nightmare—but a little boy's paradise.

Here in this God-fearing missionary home, in the remote heart of Africa, among the poverty-stricken children whom I would later serve as an adult, my heart was shaped, filled, and tenderly nurtured. As I mentioned earlier, we truly thought Nielle was the center of the world. It wasn't that we were remote; it was that everything else on planet Earth was terribly far away. The dirt road brought trucks from afar; radio programs wafted in from exotic places; France, the home of our colonial masters, was (thankfully) on a whole different continent. None of the villagers had ventured far, even though the dirt road ambled north another twenty miles to the border of the Republic of Mali, across the wide, grassy savanna, and then dead-ended in the vast Sahara Desert.

Shifting restlessly in my chair at the New York church, I knew exactly what my friends were doing that day back at the center of the earth. It was the end of the rainy season, and the animals would be in abundance. I could see Padubeh, bent double, gracefully slipping through the ten-foot-tall elephant grass as he stalked a gazelle. He was the handsome one all the girls admired. He had a great sense of humor and was always joking.

Padubeh had jet black skin, so black that it had a bluish hue. When he smiled, his dazzling white teeth were like a beacon in the night. He was a great hunter and always seemed to be in the right place at the right time; he could think like his prey. It was often Padubeh who strode confidently into the village in the evening, a rabbit tossed over his shoulder.

Kolzana would be nearby. He, like all the other boys, had three horizontal scars on each cheek, like cat whiskers, etched when he was very young to mark him as a male member of the Senufo tribe. They were scars of honor, and Kolzana's were perfect on his handsome face. I wished I had them too. In my mind I was a Senufo.

In fact, I used to pray every night, "Lord, if you love me, let me wake up black like everyone else." I was tired of being teased by the others for scaring away the game when we hunted. "The monkey saw your white skin and took off!" they would scold. Morning after morning I'd check my arm first thing, only to be disappointed to be white for yet another day.

I remember one time in the cab of our pickup truck sitting between Kolzana's spread knees. We both had our elbows hanging out the passenger window. I looked at the color of his arm and then at mine, now darkened by the tropical sun. To my great joy, they were almost the same color. That night I thanked God for working in mysterious ways his wonders to perform. Now if I could just get Senufo scars!

While all of the village boys were my brothers, Alezye was more than that. He was my hero, my soul mate. I admired everything about him, wanted to be just like him, and would do anything for him. His brothers were Alezana and Alebeh. Their names, following the tradition of the Senufo culture, were drawn from their mother's name, Ale. The suffix "-zye" indicated the "firstborn son of Ale," while "-zana" pointed to the second born, "-beh" to the third born, and so on.

It was not unlike the biblical pattern of "Joshua the son of Nun" or "David the son of Jesse," only in our case the name was tagged to the mother instead of the father. This made a lot of sense in Nielle's polygamous culture. It was like having a better address; you knew precisely who your friends' mothers were, not just their fathers.

Alezye, with his muscular build, was always the strongest among us. He could carry a full bucket in each hand to water the young trees my father had planted for shade, while I waddled along like a duck straddling just one bucket, straining and putting it down with a slosh just as I thought my fingers were going to snap off.

I'm not sure how much older Alezye was than I, but it must have been five or six years. No one really knew. Precise birthdays went untracked in our village, much to the chagrin of the French officials who hounded us ceaselessly for details like that. No one had so much as a birth certificate. To ask one of my friends how many years old he was would be as silly as asking you how many times you ate carrots last year. You would simply have to reply, "Well, quite a few, but I have no idea how many." So it was with years of life among the Senufo people. They could only tell you they were born "before the big flood" or "after the great locust plague came through."

If anybody from our village was going to be successful in life, here or anywhere else, we all knew it would be Alezye. He was one of the very first to accept the gospel message and "take the Jesus road," as the Africans put it. He sat with my father day after day in the hot tin shed with Bible translations stacked all about, sweating profusely and helping Dad translate the Scripture into the Senari language. He was so smart. Before Dad learned the tonal complexities of the language, it was Alezye who ventured courageously with him to new villages to translate the stories and Dad's messages of God's love and salvation.

Being a tonal language, Senari was a minefield of faux pas. Mispronunciations could be funny or devastating. The word for "mother" and "cow" were virtually identical. So were the words for "father" *(naàwì)* and "scorpion" *(náwa)*. Alezye no doubt kept our family out of more embarrassments than we ever knew.

He was always kind and generous. Together we built a tree house in one of the few trees big enough to support such a structure out there on the savanna plains. When we hunted, I followed him, placing my feet exactly where he had placed his as we stalked our prey across field and swamp. He taught me how to identify and track animals. He was an expert with the slingshot and taught me carefully to fire the weapon. How he would have laughed and patted me on the back after my carnival victory!

He was one with nature; he understood it, loved it, and respected it. He used his skills to protect the village from dangerous animals, to guard against the destructive ones, and to harvest those that could feed his family. He taught me to hide in the grass or a tree and call to various birds as they passed by. If a hornbill flew over, Alezye would match its call perfectly, and I'd watch the bird immediately make a sweeping circle and come land in the tree just over our heads. If a fruit dove flew by, the sound would be different, but the result would be the same.

It was Alezye who first figured out how to mix a concoction of lime juice and the white milk that oozes from a cut in the rubber tree, making an amazingly sticky, tenacious sort of glue we termed *la gum.* So long as you kept your fingers wet, it was as harmless as clay. But the minute anything dry touched it, it would stick fast, coming off only when it was again made wet.

We would lick our fingers and stalk the fields with la gum. We would study the bushes and trees to see which twigs and branches were favorite perches of certain birds. Licking our fingers again, we would spread the mixture on that twig, then hide and wait. Within minutes the unsuspecting master of the perch would return and alight. We would count to ten, then come charging out of our hiding places to capture bewildered creatures glued to their perches, flapping wildly and wondering what had happened to their flying ability. We would clean up their feet with our saliva. Little birds were studied, admired, and set free. Some birds just couldn't figure the whole thing out; we could catch them on the same branch day after day. Bigger birds weren't so fortunate; they wound up in the evening soup pot over the fire. We lived close to nature, giving to it and taking from it as naturally as breathing.

BABOONS, BEWARE

I knew that by now the corn and millet would be tall and ripening in the fields surrounding the village. At the beginning of the rainy season, the whole village had cultivated the fields with short-handled hoes called *dabas.* Men, women (with babies tied to their backs), and even children had taken their places in the long lines, rhythmically turning the soil. Resting spectators swayed or danced in the shade of the baobab trees as they set a musical pace with drums and balaphones (similar to xylophones, but with resonating gourds instead of metal pipes underneath). Older men sat and chanted encouragement to some for their outstanding efforts and lighthearted harassment to others whom they deemed to be slackers. In time the elephant grass was painstakingly beaten back, and a cultivated field emerged.

As the months passed, the fields were planted, weeded, watered, and watched. Now the harvest was approaching, and the rewards for the hard work could almost be tasted. It was time to send in the boys and their trusty slings! Every plant was precious, and our very lives depended on bringing an adequate harvest into the little thatched-roof mud silos beside our huts. We loved this time of year because it allowed us boys, even very little boys, to do something for our people that nobody could do better: protect the harvest from marauding troops of baboons and monkeys that could destroy an unguarded field in a single night. This was dangerous work, since a full-grown, fanged male baboon can weigh more than fifty pounds. In large troops, baboons fear almost nothing, certainly not a little boy—unless he is lethally armed and skilled!

We used two kinds of *lance-pierres,* a French term that simply means "stone-thrower." One was the traditional slingshot, or catapult, made from the fork of a tree branch, to which we attached a half-inch strip of rubber cut from an inner tube. In the middle of the strip was a leather pouch where the rock would go.

Then there was the higher-caliber sling like the ones shown in Bible picture books. Made of rope woven together from sisal plants we kids had cut down and beaten on rocks to extract the pulp, it had a loop at one end to fit over the index finger and a leather pouch in the middle to hold rocks as big as a fist. The remaining strap was held lightly in the palm of the hand. After placing a smooth, round rock in the pouch, we would whiz the sling in a circle, building up velocity with several revolutions, and then turn loose the end of the rope at precisely the right moment to nail the target.

The bigger boys could get off a powerful shot with just one revolution if they were in a hurry, but for most of us, the longer the windup, the more power we could deliver. The release exploded with a crack as loud as a shot from a high-powered rifle.

We village boys never went anywhere without our lance-pierres hung around our necks. In the intense heat, we rarely wore much else, except maybe a pair of shorts as age and civilization imposed itself on us. My mother insisted that I wear sandals, although all my friends went barefoot. The soles of their feet were tougher than my shoes!

Grown men, when needing to dress up for an occasion, would wear rubber sandals made from the tread of truck tires, with inner-tube straps. That seemed like such a waste to us kids. Inner tubes were best cut into strips and made into the business end of lance-pierres.

At the edge of the fields, we built surveillance platforms about five or six feet high so we could visually patrol the entire area. With razor-sharp machetes we chopped down brush, stripped off the leaves and bark to make poles for framing, tied them together with strips of the bark, and then spread elephant grass on top to make a relatively comfortable platform. At the crack of dawn or in the fading light of evening, you could hear the baboons swishing through the grass, heading for the ears of corn. As they crossed the cleared strip between grass and cornstalks, we had a split second to get off a shot with our slings.

Perched on our stilted posts, we stood watch until the corn was harvested. We often just sent warning shots at the rustling sounds in the elephant grass. If a big baboon still dared to trespass into our field, he was met with a hailstorm of rocks. If a whole troop of thirty or forty baboons invaded, we took no prisoners. Any baboon we hit and killed became instant lunch. We'd build a small fire at the base of our platform and roast it on sticks. Yum! Tradition dictated that the smallest child involved in the hunt got the most delicate part of the beast—the hands. In fact, it was a great honor; the little guy would sit there proudly chewing on a hand that looked just like his own except bigger and now roasted over the fire.

Nearly every evening we dragged "supper" home to the village. The men would pat our heads, their eyes filled with pride for their sons. The women would start the fires, and the feast would go way into the night. We felt so good that, even as children, we could make a real contribution.

If for some reason we didn't hit the invader squarely enough to kill him, the job was still basically done. We sent him off bruised and battered with a PhD in the consequences of stealing our corn. We were sorry to hurt him but hoped he would tell his friends about the fierce warriors on the stand in the field.

Sometimes when we thought we had killed the baboon, we would approach it cautiously only to have it jump up, teeth bared, and launch its own revenge. We learned to get a long stick and first reach out to touch its eyeball. Even the nastiest baboon couldn't resist blinking if he was just playing possum.

As in everything we hunted, we always aimed as accurately as possible, then ran to the fallen beast to kneel at its side to speak to it before it died. We would apologize if we had caused it pain and promise that it would not go to waste. In reverent tones and often in tears, we promised to use it to feed our people.

And so the harvest was brought in each year. The older we got, the more accurate we became with our slings. Basically by age ten, if we could see something and our slings could go that far, we could hit it.

If you watch the evening news and see the Palestinian kids attacking the Israeli military with slings, you may think they are hopelessly mismatched. But look carefully: you never see the Israelis in open Jeeps, with windshields and mirrors to break. All you see are tanks and armored personnel carriers. That is for a good reason.

Now maybe you will understand why, when my mother told us boys in a Sunday school class under a mango tree about the Bible epic of David killing Goliath with a sling, we merely shrugged. Instead of getting the point of what an amazing thing God could do with just a little boy and a lot of faith, I remember thinking, *That was one stupid giant. I could have done that myself! Great big forehead, stationary giant just a few feet away— no problem!*

The bit about David choosing five smooth stones from the stream (1 Samuel 17:40) made perfect sense to my little band of marksmen. No, not because of the elaborate conjecture I've since heard from Bible expositors about Goliath having four fierce relatives to be killed, and so this was some great symbolism for the future. When you live and die by the sling as we did, you're always walking around with one eye on the ground looking for the next perfect stone. Round rocks are hard to come by and can make all the difference in the world. If one has a little bump on a side, the rock can veer off in flight. Flat rocks? Forget about it. You're not going to hit anything.

I'm pretty sure David picked up five smooth stones simply because there they were right in front of him. All us boys knew he should need only one to take care of Goliath, but why pass up the other four?

TWO ENDS OF THE BRIDGE

Fast-forward about forty-five years, and here I am again, all grown-up now. I've lost a bit of my slingshot accuracy, although I keep my original weapon close by in my third-floor office in Colorado Springs. There's just not as much stuff to shoot at now. I haven't seen a lizard or baboon around here in years. How sad!

I also hang on to my knowledge of poverty and its effect on little children. After all, I was there. I watched as preventable diseases stole my childhood friends in the village, one by one, and it broke my heart. I travel back and forth these days between two worlds. I jokingly tell people that my job is pretty tough. On one side of this international bridge, my role is to minister to the poor, to "comfort the afflicted." And then I cross the bridge, coming back to the Western, more affluent world, where my role is to speak and write to "afflict the comfortable." To do that with the same love can be a challenge.

Jesus did it very well, of course. He honored the poor woman who gave her last coins, the widow's mites. But he also cared about the rich young ruler who wanted to give but just couldn't; he was owned by his stuff. The Bible goes out of its way to highlight that "Jesus looked at him and *loved* him" (Mark 10:21). He knew, understood, and valued people at both ends of the economic spectrum.

I take seriously the verse that says, "From everyone who has been given much, much will be demanded; and from the one who has been entrusted with much, much more will be asked" (Luke 12:48). I have been given much in terms of experience and insight. I know deep in my soul that when it comes to children, we must stop thinking *someday* and start thinking of their worth and needs *today.* Our churches and missions have to go beyond their usual three-year corporate plans and start making thirty-year plans that include the discipleship of children and their role in the future. These plans must begin not someday but today.

Childhood in most non-Western societies, like the village where I grew up, is a constant, gentle flow that moves from infant to toddler to child to youth and on to adulthood in a steady, integrated progression. In each phase of childhood, the child is allowed to be as much a part of the ebb and flow of daily life as his or her capabilities allow. The fun and games we experienced as children in Nielle were mostly a child's lighthearted spirit being applied to the duties and chores of daily life in the village. We didn't have rooms full of toys where we would go to play; we didn't have an hour or two where the schedule called for "play time." No, "play" just happened as we lived our lives in the village. We laughed and teased each other sitting in the shade of mango trees or around the cooking fire in the courtyard as we shelled peas or stirred the pot over the fire for supper. The little girls didn't play with Barbie dolls, pretending to care for them as if they were grownups. Instead, they actually took care of younger brothers and sisters who needed them—and had fun in the process.

The babies spent the rest of the day at their mother's feet or lovingly strapped to her back. They felt every laugh, heard every conversation, saw every tear drop, smelled every flower, and watched from a safe distance every pot of cooking rice. They swayed with the movement of their mothers as they worked in the fields, and in the evening they swayed again in perfect unison as Mom danced around the campfire.

The little ones were not excluded, either, from worship services in the mud hut with thatched roof that we called First Baptist Church of Nielle. Talk about a valid name; it was the first church of *any* kind for a day's drive in almost any direction. Church services were rarely the quiet, reflective, child-free sessions we seem to crave in the United States. They were punctuated with the natural sounds of everyday life as the generations mixed to sing, pray, laugh, cry, and worship—together as always.

Every morning the little boys scattered outside the village to gather firewood. The littlest toddler couldn't carry a big bundle of sticks, but he could at least pick up kindling while the older boys swung a machete to cut and split wood for the evening fire. We all enjoyed life as only children can, while contributing to the needs of our families and village.

The same was true in fetching water, cooking, hunting, and harvesting peanuts. The path to adulthood started in early childhood. As a child grew, he or she did more and more of what adults did. We were taught, challenged, praised, teased, and loved, all on a steady path toward becoming adults.

By the time my buddies were around fifteen years old, they knew almost everything they needed to know to be productive, contributing members of the Senufo tribe. (By the way, ask your grandparents or great-grandparents whether this was also true of America seventy years ago. How did we lose this precious aspect of growing up?)

I learned quickly after my first day at Coney Island that life for children in Western society was much different. Children were rarely viewed as useful and not often allowed to participate in the normal flow of life's duties and activities. I found teenagers my age who were frustrated, bored, and bitter at always being excluded, as if they had been placed on a shelf to wait out the adolescent years. They were just looking in on life, muttering to themselves, "I can do more than they think I can. I want meaning in my life. I can't wait to actually do something for somebody, to make a difference."

For littler children, it was the same or worse. In parents' great love for them, they lavished toys on their children that would allow them to pretend they were grownups. Sometimes adults would get down on the floor and play along as if they were baking cookies in the toy ovens but would then stand up and return to the "adult" world, feeling pretty good about themselves and their little excursion.

Without a doubt, it takes more time, effort, and perhaps patience to bring a child up to "our" world and actually make cookies in our kitchens. Oh yes, there will be more flour on the floor and more eggshells in the batter, but there will also be a treasure of giggles and compliments that build spirits and memories. My dad liked to tell my sister and me about coming home in the evening to a kitchen in full disarray, with a smiling but seriously disheveled wife plus two bubbly, delighted young children who proudly announced, "We helped Mommy make snickerdoodle cookies today!" Inviting a child to participate actively in the real life of our homes beats an hour of isolated make-believe in the most lavish toy room.

Allowing children into the mainstream of our lives lets them learn and understand their worth, not someday, but today. The most precious thing we can give our children as parents is warm, positive memories. More important than making cookies, getting the shopping done, or cleaning the house is what happens along the way. Childhood happens!

Likewise, children are not tomorrow's church in waiting or in training. They are an important part of today's church. In today's selfish, "it's all about me" mentality, we may have passed the point of no return in our ability to welcome children back into our sanctuaries to worship with us. Or to let them actually lead us in worship.

The wife of my collaborator on this book, Grace Merrill, is an accomplished piano teacher. A few years ago she said to one promising student, "You're doing so very well on this hymn arrangement! Why don't you see if you could play it some Sunday at your church?"

The student's eyes dropped. "No, in my church," she quietly replied, "you have to be eighteen before you're allowed to do anything on the platform."

The real integration of children into our lives is happening all across the world—just not very much in Western society. Here we have forgotten that there really is no higher calling than to raise a child. We tend to do a lot *for* our children but not nearly enough *with* our children. In many of today's dual-income households, parents hire others to do most of the privilege of child raising.

Providing for our children is important, but it isn't nearly as crucial as many American couples seem to think. Enough *really* is enough. Trust me on this: there actually is a type of poverty on the far side of "enough"; wealth and possessions often bring a misery and emptiness all their own. Beyond "enough" can be lost opportunity to impact and enjoy our children.

When I came to work at Compassion International back in 1977 with a passion to help children in poverty, I solemnly promised my wife, Donna, and challenged myself that I would not do so at the expense of the well-being of any children God might entrust to us. Well, he did—Jenny and Katie. And I haven't! I work far more diligently at my role of papa than I do at being president of the corporation. My daughters are now twenty-two and eighteen years old, but not once have they been able to honestly say, "Daddy, you cared about the other children of the world, but you forgot me."

When all is said and done and I stand before my Lord, I am sure he will value more what I have done in faithfulness to my two children than the ministry to millions of children in poverty. I don't know what you are doing in the workplace or what impact on the world you are making, but if you have children entrusted to you, I am dead certain the same is true of you. They are precious, deserving of our time, attention, and serious commitment—not someday, but today.

2

BUILDING CASTLES
IN THE CLOUDS

For children, today is all about tomorrow. By nature, they look to the future, since so very little of life lies behind them. Everything worthwhile is "in front." The future is waiting to happen for them.

How a child feels about his or her future has everything to do with what is going on in life *today.* In their mysterious and wonderful minds, children observe, absorb, and apply a tremendous amount of information from their earliest moments. They are busy discovering their world, finding their place in it, figuring out what they might do. It is a delicate and formative span of time.

I love Dorothy Law Nolte's well-known poem "Children Learn What They Live":

If children live with criticism, they learn to condemn.
If children live with hostility, they learn to fight.
If children live with fear, they learn to be apprehensive.
If children live with pity, they learn to feel sorry for themselves.
If children live with ridicule, they learn to feel shy.
If children live with jealousy, they learn to feel envy.
If children live with shame, they learn to feel guilty.
If children live with encouragement, they learn confidence.
If children live with tolerance, they learn patience.
If children live with praise, they learn appreciation.
If children live with acceptance, they learn to love.
If children live with approval, they learn to like themselves.

If children live with recognition, they learn it is good to have a goal.
If children live with sharing, they learn generosity.
If children live with honesty, they learn truthfulness.
If children live with fairness, they learn justice.
If children live with kindness and consideration, they learn respect.
If children live with security, they learn to have faith in themselves
   and in those about them.
If children live with friendliness, they learn the world is a nice place
   in which to live.[1]

Nurturing a child's sense of personal worth and therefore hope and dreams for a wonderful future is perhaps the most important responsibility of every grownup in a child's life. God has certainly done his part. At the moment of each child's birth, I believe he looks at the tiny newborn, smiles, and says, as he did on Creation day, "That's good. That's perfect!" Formed in the image of almighty God, this child is already equipped with gifts to bring to the world. What happens in the next moments, hours, days, and years determines whether that God-given potential will be realized or lost to us all.

I learned in my childhood in Africa that a child may be born in poverty, but poverty is never born in a child. The worst aspects of poverty are not the deplorable outward conditions but rather the erosion and eventual destruction of hope and therefore dreams. When a child gives up hope, dreams are forever shattered. With lost dreams goes the potential and ultimate impact that a child might have had.

If we nurture the dreams of children, the world will be blessed. If we destroy them, the world is doomed!

In Nielle, poor as it was, the little village banded together to keep poverty out of the spirits of its children. Our dreams were treasured by all the adults around us. They wanted to hear them, nurture them, and help launch them as best they could. We spoke boldly of our aspirations for the future, no matter how grandiose or far-fetched they must have seemed. The village grownups joined our childlike world and included us in their world. We didn't feel we had to wait until we were grown to be useful.

Along the way, dreams were born and expanded in the ebb and flow of village life.

When things were slow for us boys on the lookout stand as we guarded the cornfields from monkeys, or as the sun was sinking low in a dazzling tropical array of color, we would dangle our feet over the side and share our thoughts. Padubeh, the best shot among us, wanted nothing more than to be a mighty hunter. "It's a lot more exciting than farming. I'm going to bring in enough meat for the whole village!" he boasted. In reality, however, we all knew you had to do both jobs in order to survive in the harsh environment. Even schoolteachers had to double as agriculturists.

"I'm going to grow up to be the next blacksmith," announced Alezana. We all admired Nielle's brawny metalworker. He was currently hammering out a rusty, hollow tie rod from an abandoned Jeep to transform it into a flintlock musket. Sometimes he would let us slip into his sweltering hut to work the handmade cowhide bellows and get his fire white-hot. Always to some rhythm in our heads, we would pump until our skinny little arms were about to fall off.

Another boy wanted to be the village carpenter. With no power tools, the carpenter worked the wood by hand and clearly had the most manly physique in town. Seeing him used to make me wonder if Jesus really was that slender, pale, fragile guy in the Bible pictures. I figured he must have looked more like our brawny woodworker.

"Maybe if I study hard, I can grow up to be a pastor," said Alezye. With silent nods we all acknowledged that he certainly was the smartest among us, smart enough to achieve such a lofty position.

If Alezye wanted to be a pastor, I wanted nothing more than to assist him somehow. So I volunteered, "I just want to help my dad get the Bible translation done in Senari so Alezye will have something to preach out of."

Everyone laughed. They knew how I looked up to my best friend. Dad had by now finished the gospels of Mark and John in that miserable tin shed where he worked. I had peeked around the corner one day to see my father kneeling at his folding chair, surrounded by French and English versions of the Bible, tears streaming down his weathered face. He felt so inadequate to the task, but it was desperately needed. Day after day he poured himself into God's Word for the souls of the people in Nielle and the surrounding region. I was so proud of him. The finished Bible would someday be our crowning achievement.

It would also lead the Senufo people out of the fear and worry that haunted their daily lives. The witch doctor had them convinced that any misfortune—a family sickness, for example, or the loss of an animal—was the work of evil spirits that only he could help them appease. Outside the village was his special domain, the sacred forest—off limits to all but adult men. You would be told to go there and sacrifice a chicken in order to cure your child or reverse your bad luck. And, by the way, you needed to bring the carcass back to the witch doctor afterward (this was how he kept food on his own table). In all of this, village life was under his thumb.

We boys talked about these things, of course. On a few occasions we even dared to check out the sacred forest to try to see what was so ominous about it. The medicines my mother gave out were obviously a faster road back to health, we noted.

Little boys with big ideas, big dreams, we gazed across the savanna and wondered what life would bring. Then a rustle in the grass snagged our attention. We grabbed our slings and went back on guard duty.

The Sharpshooters

Our contribution to the village food supply also took the form of harvesting a delicacy, the huge and relatively stupid fruit doves. They were as big as a chicken and just as tasty. Down in the swamp, we could easily stalk them. They were real suckers for la gum.

There was no real honor in nailing one of these with a rock unless you decapitated it cleanly. We never aimed for the body. Why damage the meat? When French hunters would occasionally come through and pride themselves on blasting these delicacies to smithereens with their fancy, Paris-made 12-gauge shotguns, we would laugh ourselves silly thinking of the shrapnel-laced kabobs they would wash down with cheap wine. Our mothers would shake their heads in disgust.

When it came to herding cattle, of course, we weren't trying to hurt them with our slingshots. We only wanted to keep them from wandering off by landing a well-aimed rock along their flanks from time to time. To these leathery behemoths, it probably felt like a tsetse fly sting. We laughed at the thought that they probably said to one another, "Did you ever notice how nasty the flies bite when those little boys come around?"

By the way, these were more than young calves; these were huge Brahman cattle like you see rodeo cowboys try to ride. Yet a herd of fifty such cattle could be managed by no more than two or three little boys, sometimes as young as seven, with slingshots.

When we weren't firing at animals, we used our weaponry for other useful things, like picking mangoes. There's nothing as sweet and juicy as a golden tropical mango. For several months of each year's rainy season, these tall, leafy shade trees gave us the life-sustaining gift of their fruit.

The problem is that the fruit grows far out on high branches. You can wait for mangoes to ripen and fall, but then they are damaged and beyond their peak flavor. Nothing was funnier to us kids than when a mango would cut loose from a tree while a meeting was going on underneath. You could hear it careening from branch to branch, like a runaway pinball. Grown men would cover their heads with their arms, and the meeting would stop in suspended, anxious silence until with a heavy plop the mango would crash—hopefully to the ground. But in our opinion, it was even better if it ricocheted off the head of a teacher or a visiting dignitary. With peals of giggling and laughter and all dignity cast aside, a mad scramble would ensue to retrieve the prize.

The proper method, of course, was to harvest the mango from the tree at the correct ripeness. However, mango trees tend to be infested with swarms of nasty, stinging red ants, making them virtually impossible to climb. To try to shinny up a mango tree was to announce to the entire world, "I am a complete idiot and don't know any better." Only monkeys with their thick fir had passports to the limbs of ant-infested mango trees.

So we boys would shoot mangos down with a rock. Not by hitting the mango itself, of course, which would bruise the fruit. Instead, we targeted the long slender stem by which each fruit hung. We would crane our necks, spot the ripe ones (yellow, orange, or red), ignore the unripe, green ones, and then proceed to zing a rock up there and cleanly clip the stem. Our buddies would catch the falling mango—or get hit by it, which was even better.

Truth is, even this wasn't enough for our finely honed slingshot skills. After all, the target was just hanging right there in plain view. So we took the challenge up a notch by aiming at the mango stem *while jogging* past the tree.

RIGHT-HAND BOY

My father's view of all this was benevolent enough, possibly because he was an outdoors type himself. A practical man who had been a civil engineer in Colorado before coming to mission work, he was perfect for the rigors of surviving in the outback of West Africa.

Dad built our little cement block and tin-roofed home with his own hands. On a scrap of paper, he designed an L-shaped house that was ideal for moderating the harsh, oppressive heat of the Ivory Coast. Like a sailing ship in a sea of grass, it caught even the tiniest hint of a breeze. Ken Stafford was a jack-of-all-trades: minister, linguist, doctor, hunter, electrician, plumber, mechanic, farmer, carpenter, and wonderful father to his little daughter and son. He had the amazing ability to allow a six-year-old boy to tag along for whatever he was doing and to make me feel he couldn't possibly do his work without me. I used to announce proudly to our rare outside visitors that "me and my dad" built that house. It wasn't until years later that I understood their chuckles and smiles.

Our partnership found its way into actual mission work…well, sort of. Whenever he would drive off in our old pickup truck to visit other villages across the Département de Ferkessédougou, as the French government called our little corner of the Ivory Coast, I got to go along. The trip itself was an adventure, of course. Huge boa constrictors stretched lazily across the road and disappeared into the elephant grass on both sides so that you couldn't tell which end was the head and which was the tail. Talk about a "speed bump"!

Troops of baboons literally blocked our progress at times, with huge warriors standing defiantly in the ruts of the road like military guards, while mothers scampered across with babies clutching their sides. We would roll up our windows and hold our ever-present gun as the fanged males would sometimes climb onto our truck's hood to stare menacingly at us, faces pressed against our windshield. Switching on the wipers at precisely the right moment could launch them three feet into the air, much to our delight.

On the return at night, we could see glowing eyes and shadowy shapes of big leopards, panthers, hyenas, and other night terrors slinking back into the elephant grass as we bounced along. We prayed for the truck not to break down "in the valley of the shadow of death."

We bolted huge planks to the top of our truck, because inevitably at a stream or swamp, the rickety bridge of sticks and mud would need to be fixed before we could drive our truck across. Once the bridge was ready, only Dad would risk his life by driving over the void. The rest of us would walk gingerly across and pray.

The roads were unbelievably rough. Women with babies strapped to their backs and huge loads of firewood sticks on their heads would sometimes pass us, making better time on foot. So would the odd bicycle loaded with chickens hanging by their feet from its handlebars.

We would typically arrive at the village by midafternoon. Dad would join the men hoeing rhythmically in the fields surrounding the mud-hut enclosures of the village. I would go hunting with the village boys. My sister, Carol, would help the girls care for the little babies and toddlers. Mom would join the women in pounding corn using a mortar and pestle, getting ready for the evening meal.

In honor of our visit, the village would gather to eat under the largest tree, usually in the chief's courtyard. Whether dipping rice from the community bowl or off a large banana leaf with only the fingertips, they would deftly roll the sticky rice into a ball and dip it into the large gourd of hot, spicy peanut gravy. Then with a flick of the wrist, they would pop it into their mouths.

It was important to remember to use only my right hand, never the left. Even eating with one's fingers while squatting on the dusty ground in the heart of Africa had its strict rules of etiquette. Left hands were used only to wipe one's nose and do other disgusting things. Otherwise, someone was likely to comment, "What?! Were you raised by hyenas?"

Then as the sun would edge toward the horizon, painting a beautiful sunset because of the dust and smoke from the village fires, Dad would lean back against the tree and begin to tell a story from the Bible. This was entirely natural. There was no bell, no announcement; the gathering just seemed to flow from supper into "church." Storytelling was a beloved part of village life, and anyone with a good story got center stage. With the Bible as his script, Dad had an unlimited supply of unknown tales, a valued commodity in a culture where the same weathered but beloved fables could be told night after night without complaints.

This was a land with few radios and no television, movies, or even books; hence, people always listened intently as a story was told. Soon a singsong response began to rise up. At the end of each of my father's sentences, it was the duty of the oldest man in the group to give a resonant "Mmbaa," which meant "Go on, tell us more; we're with you." The most senior woman had the duty of adding a counterpoint "Mmmm, mmmm." The stories came alive; the group was mesmerized, at times laughing or even crying unabashedly. The longer the story went on, the more engaged the audience became. At the end a peaceful calm would fall over the group, and nobody would speak for a few meditative minutes.

Only one distraction presented itself: noisy birds. First it was the cackling of the guinea hens as they assembled in the trees for the night. Their cry sounds very much like fingernails dragged across a blackboard. It can be ignored at first, but as more and more gather, the cacophony can become deafening. Then the village weaverbirds would come flying to roost in the trees. These little birds are amazing. They have black heads and wings but orange bodies, and they delicately weave the most elaborate nests that dot the trees of the savanna. The nests are little, enclosed, upside-down baskets with clever entries from the bottom instead of the top to confuse snakes. The weaverbirds' distinguishing feature is their deafening chirp. They warble and chatter as they gather in their roosting trees.

The noise of the first twenty or so weaverbirds and guinea hens was distracting but tolerable. However, when it got to be hundreds of them, people had to strain to hear Dad's gospel story. From the edge of the gathering, I could sense him struggling to speak louder and louder.

And then, without missing a beat, he would turn my direction and give an ever-so-slight nod. I knew my duty. I would immediately take my trusty slingshot from around my neck and zing a rock into the tree. As it fell from branch to branch, the weaverbirds and guinea fowl would fly away—thus giving the missionary another fifteen minutes or so of relative quiet to finish his talk. I would repeat my "ministry" as often as needed.

I took great care not to actually hit one of the birds. Had I done so, everything would have stopped, and the whole mood would have been shattered. As it was, I did my job in obscurity. Dad rarely said anything, but on the way home, he would reach his big hand over in the truck and give my knee a squeeze. Words weren't necessary; we had done it together. I felt tremendously affirmed. Without someone to control the guinea hens and the weaverbirds, how was Africa going to hear the gospel?

OUTSIDE THE BOXES

You may be amused that eight-year-old Wesley, armed only with his slingshot, could think he had a strategic role in world evangelism. Did I honestly think I had helped my father dig our well, plant our garden, or build our house? Was this just the fantasy of a self-confident, even arrogant, child? Or was it the result of a village and a father who knew how to nurture the dreams of the young?

Tougher still, is this kind of child discipleship still possible on the other side of the ocean, decades later, in a complex and fast-paced society?

I'm convinced that although the values and conditions in a remote African village were conducive to such child-focused development, the same is still within reach of today's Western society. I would go so far as to say it is imperative. We simply must learn to engage our children and walk with them day by day to foster their dreams and make them come true.

Africa had several advantages to make this happen naturally in the flow of life. This was a culture, for example, that knew very little of age segregation. Adults in a relatively primitive society could more easily keep a childlike spirit that allowed them to laugh, dance, and play lightheartedly in the midst of their work. Children, at the same time, were engaged in real work to the extent they were able at each stage of their development.

There was no artificial category of life called adolescence. We never felt the frustration of being physically and mentally ready for life's challenges but not legally allowed to take our place in society. Instead, we slipped gently into adulthood, fully trained since our earliest steps in infancy. In Nielle, I never heard an adult growl in exasperation, "Would you just grow up!" Nobody ever told us to wait until later, when we finally might be worth something.

My heart goes out to youth pastors I've met in the United States who are completely frustrated with their work because they think they are expected to entertain teenagers. Laser tag, paintball, bowling, trips to amusement parks—they are running out of ways to keep kids tied to the church so that someday they might play a role.

Thankfully, some in youth ministry are now discovering that kids can do important things *today.* Kids want more than entertainment; they want the chance to make a difference. They are itching to get out of the pigeonhole into which we have shoved them. They hate being marginalized.

In America, when a child is small, we don't even let him butter his bread, because it means handling a table knife. In the village where I grew up, children that age were out gathering wood with a machete. We blow on kids' cereal so they won't burn their little lips. In Nielle, kids were lighting the cooking fires.

I am not saying we should expose anyone, young or old, to needless danger. But I do believe we have constrained our views of children to an unhealthy degree.

So how do we discover and nurture the dreams of children in our complex, fast-paced, whirlwind society? It requires a deliberate, go-against-the-flow effort. I see several paths open to us as adults who understand the importance of helping children's dreams come true as we nurture hope and expectation in their spirits.

1. Go to them. Enter their world.

When children live in a nurturing, safe environment surrounded by family, friends, and a supportive community of people who love them, believe in them, and affirm their lives, they dare to dream of what they might become.

If you want to have some fun, eavesdrop on a child who is playing, engulfed in his or her own world of make-believe. You will glimpse what is really going on in the child's mind. One of the tragedies in Western society is that as we grow up, we tend to redefine what is "play."

Men especially tend to leave the heart of a child behind. Many find it awkward to genuinely play with their children. Playtime with sons tends to be built around what grown-up men do: sports, bulldozers, war. To sit and play in a little girl's world can be even tougher. That's probably why Jesus admonished a group of men in Matthew 18:3, "Unless you change and become like little children, you will never enter the kingdom of heaven." He knew how tough a challenge that was!

The good news here is that modern-day fathers, in spite of the pressures of life all around, are spending more time with their children than their fathers spent with them. A little over a decade ago, research reported that dads spent only twelve minutes per day in direct interaction with their children. Today it's a little closer to two hours.

However, with each additional ten thousand dollars a dad earns, the kid time decreases five minutes per day! Apparently, while quality time with our children is more valued, the wage chase works against it.[2]

If you are invited (okay, begged) by your children to join in their imaginary world, you have indeed been honored and should jump at the chance. Mothers and fathers who are willing to sit on little stools and have a tea party with their tiny daughters might feel a bit silly at first, but it is worth it. They are giving you a precious opportunity to affirm them and even teach them how to be gracious. As their guest, you can show how to put others first, to share. You can model how to carry on a polite conversation. You can tease and be teased.

My little daughters always offered me tea with "sugar and creamy." Donna and I sipped from our little teacups, pinky fingers raised properly, and demonstrated how to listen, tell stories, and be grateful. A child can learn a lot about life, at least the really important stuff, in a playroom tea party with Mom and Dad. And in the process, Mom and Dad can learn a lot about their children.

Once you have been accepted into their world, you will be amazed at what all goes on in their precious little heads. Questions will be raised in that context; dreams will be revealed. Fears and joys will be shared in ways that the "real world" of your everyday home will never allow. The openness and sincerity of a child is amazing when you find ways to tear down the social barriers of parent/child, big/little, old/young, strong/weak, and right/wrong that usually dominate the relationship.

When I first began working at Compassion International nearly three decades ago, my ministry required a great deal of international travel. My little daughters knew it was those big metal birds that regularly stole their daddy from them for days and even weeks at a time. Imagine how it broke my heart to learn after one such trip that my daughter Jenny, just a toddler, had seen the contrails of a jet way up in the sky, pointed to them, and uttered one of her very first words: "Daddy!"

As sad as that was, I did my best to make up for it when I returned. My daughters came to know that I would always rather be home with them than anywhere else in the world. One of their clever ways to bring our worlds together was to play "airplane." I would come home jet-lagged to death and sick of flying, but there in our basement, my little girls would have arranged their chairs and beanbag cushions into the configuration of an airplane. Coach, business, and first-class seats were filled with Snow Whites, Seven Dwarfs, Muppets, puppets, Barbie dolls, Ken dolls, and an assortment of stuffed dogs and cats. The flight attendants were in "uniform" and poised to welcome Donna and me aboard.

I would try every trick in the book to get a seat in first class, but I usually wound up in the "cattle car," seat 6D. Those little girls were tougher to con than real flight attendants! What followed was a time of giggles and squeals of laughter as the guy in 6D kept ringing his "call button" and drove the flight attendants crazy. He could never seem to get things just right. He spilled his coffee ("sugar and creamy" and all). He begged to switch seats with Sleeping Beauty so he could sit by the window. After all, she was just sleeping anyway. He requested pillows, blankies, and more pretzels. He kept up an endless stream of questions and demands.

My seat partner in 6E was a monkey puppet named George that had his lanky arms and legs Velcroed around my waist and neck. He would say and do the most outrageous things, much to my chagrin. My girls considered him the most obnoxious monkey on earth. His biggest tormentor was Dusty, our family cat, in 6F (or wherever else his heart desired). Dusty would stare incredulously at the monkey, then attack him like a saber-toothed tiger throughout the "flight."

Meanwhile, Donna was always the picture-perfect passenger who commiserated with the flight attendants and apologized for the demands of 6D and the craziness of 6E. Between George the monkey, my wife, and me, we could engage our precious daughters in every conversation imaginable. It was such fun for everyone, and the lessons learned (in both directions) were memories for a lifetime.

Eventually the flight would have to "land," and the passengers, no matter how obnoxious or demanding, had to hug the flight attendants before hurrying off. I think back on those precious times of play with my family, and even today, as my girls are wonderfully grown up, our dinners can be reduced to tears of laughter as we remember those wonderful times when our worlds came together in the basement "airplane."

I don't know what kind of games your children play, but with a little imagination and willingness to play along, you can earn your way into their world. Once there, you will reap the great joy of listening, learning, and lovingly shaping values and dreams that will last a lifetime. It's about as much fun as you'll ever have, and the impact on nurturing hopes and dreams in your little ones will never be forgotten.

2. Bring them into your world.

It's not as much fun, mind you, but another wonderful way to connect with the children in your life is to bring them along as you go about your world. I can hear the weary mother of toddlers sighing, "You mean there is still a world out there that's mine?" Yes, occasionally—okay, rarely—but when you're there, your children are at your side, watching and learning.

I know it would have been much easier for my father to leave his little boy behind in the house. He didn't need my help in digging the well, but he converted a little shovel to just my size and let me get down in the muck—a boy's heaven. I now realize my digging time was usually when the men were resting anyway, but as far as I was concerned, I was doing my part, just like a grownup.

I remember being lowered on a sling by rope and pulley to what I thought was the bottom of the earth. Looking up, I could see the sky and my father's face in a small disc of light high above the murky darkness of the well. I loved that man and would do anything for him. There was precious little going on in my life that I wouldn't gladly share with him. We were friends!

Likewise, there had to be other ways to get rid of noisy village weaver-birds than letting your little boy fire stones from his slingshot. And I'm pretty sure now that my millions of questions and suggestions didn't really advance the pace or quality of our house as we built it. But along the way, the spirit and confidence of a boy was nurtured. Being befriended by the greatest man I knew shaped my character, made me feel valued, and let me dream big dreams.

Years later with my own daughters, I tried to do the same. It's not easy or even safe to take young girls overseas into the midst of the kind of poverty in which our organization serves, but I took them with me as early in their lives as I could. They have served with me in the desperate slums of Haiti, the dangerous streets of Brazil, and the jungles of Ecuador. In fact, both of them were baptized, along with fifteen sponsored children, by an Ecuadorian pastor in the same river where five missionary martyrs perished back in 1956—an emotional moment for us all.

Along the way, they have developed compassionate hearts, sponsoring children with their very own money from the time they were nine. Donna and I tried to connect our ministry world with theirs by spending quality time with them at bedtime. Every night I would tell them a story of Africa. It would always begin the same way: "When I was a little boy in Africa…"

But I had to say it just right, with a thick French accent and drawn out dramatically, amid giggles and cheers.

We prayed for our sponsored children by name: Emmanuel, Diego, Rene, Laura, Alba, Mercedes, Yolanda, Vanessa, Sisay. This brought my world into their lives. We knew that at the same time, those children in faraway places were praying for us. Especially Mercedes, who grew up in one of the ugliest environments I have ever seen. Her family's tiny home sat on stilts over the harbor sludge and raw sewage of Guayaquil, Ecuador. Yet she cared about us—and we knew it.

When our younger daughter was born ten weeks early and weighed only three pounds, doctors did not think she would live. Donna and I were heartbroken; for a time we hovered over her crib twenty-four hours a day (trading off four-hour shifts) to make sure, along with a monitor to which she was attached, that she kept breathing and her heart kept beating. We asked everyone to pray for her, including Mercedes, to whom Donna wrote, "Our little baby has been born much too early, but we believe God can spare her life. Will you pray for her? Her name is Katie."

After almost eighteen months, we were finally able to discontinue the use of the monitor, and Katie began to sleep through the night at last. Sometime later, I went on a trip to Ecuador. When I arrived at one of our projects, a little girl jumped up from the back corner of the room and ran toward me. It was Mercedes. She recognized me from the pictures we had sent. Wrapping her arms around my legs, she blurted out, "How is Katie? I pray for her every day."

I stood there in amazement, wondering if the prayers of this Ecuadoran girl had saved my daughter's life. A picture flashed through my mind of this girl dropping to her knees on a bamboo mat in her wretched little house, believing with her whole heart that God would hear her prayers for a baby in America. What an incredible gift.

I came back home and sat on the edge of my two-year-old's bed one night to say, "Sweetheart, you may owe your life to a little girl I met in Ecuador. Her name is Mercedes." I told her the wonderful story of our meeting. In the months and years that followed, from the time Katie could lisp a bedtime prayer, she never failed to mention Mercedes. She eventually grew old enough and strong enough to make the trip to Guayaquil and meet her friend in person. They ran into each other's arms, burst into tears, and exclaimed, each in her own language, "Thank you for praying for me!" It was the ultimate moment of drama.

Mercedes is now in her twenties and pursuing a career in architecture. She knows, as we know, that God responds to the prayers of children, regardless of nationality or socioeconomic status.

Psalm 78:4 speaks about adults who "will not hide [the lessons of the past] from their children; we will tell the next generation the praiseworthy deeds of the LORD, his power, and the wonders he has done." This dialogue brings God into the very center of our lives, both young and adult, which is where he truly should be.

3. Merge the two worlds.

When the pathways of our lives and our children's lives blend together, when we get into their world and bring them into ours, the result is something called friendship. We go far beyond the responsibility and role of guardian; in fact, we are no longer aware when we "playfully" enter their world or "deliberately" include them in ours. Instead, we genuinely like being with each other. This is child discipleship at its best.

It was actually God's original discipleship idea for the family. Long ago with his newly articulated Ten Commandments, he instructed parents on what to do:

> These commandments that I give you today are to be upon your hearts. Impress them on your children. Talk about them when you sit at home and when you walk along the road, when you lie down and when you get up. Tie them as symbols on your hands and bind them on your foreheads. Write them on the doorframes of your houses and on your gates. (Deuteronomy 6:6–9)

To put it in motto form, "Along the way, and day by day." What is needed is a genuine friendship with our children in which we really enjoy their company and they ours. How does this look in the realities of a Thursday morning trip to the grocery store, for example? It goes beyond mere containment of the young child, making sure he or she doesn't break anything. It puts enjoyment of the time together above preoccupation with the task. I have seen some moms do this so well that I wanted to give them a medal for heroism.

I have also seen scenes so horrible that I cringed and breathed a prayer for the poor mother and miserable child. I've actually stepped in once or twice between a frustrated, dangerously irate mother and her terrified child in the shopping cart—to protect both of them! That is pretty risky child advocacy, but sometimes it has to happen.

We are all probably better at one part of the two-part strategy than the other. In my father's generation, men rarely entered the make-believe world of their children. He grew up in a home where the children sat ramrod straight and didn't even speak at the table if Grandpa was present. So it was rare indeed for him to deliberately enter my world of play; I can't actually remember it ever happening. I never saw him, for example, touch my slingshot, much less shoot it. His specialty was the other part of the equation: bringing me into the ebb and flow of his world.

Each of us does well to reach out to children in the style that fits us best. We can then work deliberately at the part that doesn't come as naturally. Along the way, the dreams of our children are nurtured.

Children are more than we think they are; they can do more than we think they can do. All they need is a vote of confidence from grownups, whom they will ultimately replace anyway. Their dreams today will become the realities of tomorrow.

Trust me, the day is coming when the generational tables will be turned. It may be hard to imagine now as you wipe their tiny noses or help them with their homework yet again. But the day will come when that tiny daughter who now begs to snuggle in your lap at an inconvenient time will hold your welfare in her hands. That small son who needs one more drink of water before sleeping will be the one who controls your destiny.

Someday when you are the one yearning for time with them, those energetic toddlers will be grownups in the corridors of power, with busy calendars and guardian secretaries. By then you may find that *you* are the marginalized element of society, without voice or power.

It cannot wait until tomorrow. Today is the moment to shape children's spirits, character, and values, to help them build castles in the clouds.

3

IT REALLY DOES
TAKE A VILLAGE

You may not be aware of it, but an American marketing-information giant named Claritas already has your household figured out. You belong in one of forty-eight scientifically analyzed pigeonholes with colorful names ranging from "Upper Crust" to "Hard Years" so that business planners know what to pitch your way.

For example, their address list entitled "Lap of Luxury" includes "families with teens, very high income and education, homeowners who are managers/professionals." On the other hand, "White Picket Fence" stands for "young families, low to medium education, medium income, laborers." If you are dubbed part of the "Struggling Metro Mix," you are said to be "young, single, urban, cultural mix, renter…in older multi-unit housing."

In this way we slice and dice ourselves into a multitude of segments based on money, education, marital status, race, region, and, most of all, age. I have a question: is this a good thing? I don't know about you, but I don't like being pigeonholed into predictable little boxes. I also don't think it is right to allow children to be viewed as a separate label group, as "them" rather than part of "us." How does this affect our sense of caring and responsibility? Where did our sense of community go?

It wasn't always so in America. Homesteaders once headed west in covered wagons, six or eight or ten families in a cluster, each supporting one another, looking out for one another, defending one another against outside threats. In time they settled into towns, and the spirit of community that had helped them survive the perils of the wagon trail carried on as the backbone of society…for a while. But somewhere along the way in the last century, our village concept died. We gave up sitting on the front steps or porch swing in the evenings as our neighbors would stroll by and pause for a pleasant conversation. Rare are the gentle pockets of society who sit still and relax with neighbors to sip lemonade as the sun slowly sets. For that matter, we rarely pause even to watch a sunset.

As wonderful as air conditioning is (and believe me, after the heat of Nielle, I would nominate its inventor for a Nobel Prize), it has made us go inside and close our doors and windows. There we sit, basking in the cool-ness—but alone, isolated, cut off from our neighbors.

Our games for children have moved from the neighborhood summer evenings of hide-and-seek or capture-the-flag to isolated video games (and the accompanying carpal tunnel syndrome as well as boredom). Those children who want to join a park district sports team or become a Scout or 4-H Club member often can't, because there are too few adults to coach or teach them. Every town pleads for such volunteers. What a tragically missed opportunity for God's people across the nation!

Meanwhile, elderly people can't quite keep up with the brisk pace of modern life, so they are left behind—secluded, alone, sad. The value of love, instruction, and role modeling that should flow from generation to generation is lost. It can't be bought with money; it requires time and rela-tionships, which are two things now in very short supply. Both the very old and the very young are the losers. The whole village slowly withers and dies. The more wealth and comfort we gain, the more we lose our sense of community. A poverty of spirit is slowly and imperceptibly suffocating us.

Ask any American man to name his really close friends. Sadly, few will need more than the fingers of one hand to count them. In Nielle, where I grew up, the poorest of the poor would need both hands and the toes of both feet and still wouldn't be done. How poor our wealth has rendered us!

We are disconnected, accountable to no one, bereft of counsel and love and shared wisdom. No wonder the U.S. suicide rate exceeds the murder rate by 50 percent. Our children grow up equally isolated. We need com-munity far more than we are willing to admit.

In the absence of human contact, we are now trying to substitute vir-tual relationships on the Internet. People spend hours in chat rooms, writing witty comments back and forth to strangers in Charlotte or Anchorage or London. Don't get me wrong—some of the Internet is useful, and it isn't going away. But other parts can be downright dangerous from a moral or even physical perspective.

I've noticed that people in the individualistic West sometimes have trouble appreciating the Old Testament because its worldview is so keyed to *the group*. God promises to bless the obedient to the third and fourth generation and to punish the disobedient similarly. Achan sinned against the Lord (see Joshua 7), and not only he but his whole clan paid the ultimate price. Modern readers are quick to say, "Wait a minute—that's not fair!" We are fiercely independent, and nothing riles us faster than getting lumped into a group of some kind.

I have become convinced that the more wealth a country accumulates, the more isolated and lonely its people become. The loneliest are usually the children and the elderly. Children learn what they live, and isolation in the "village" is one of the most destructive messages we daily write on the tablets of their hearts.

In contrast…

All Together

Evening in Nielle was the reward for a long, hot day of toil. As the sun edged lower in the western sky, painting brilliant sunsets, villagers who had spread out to the surrounding fields to cultivate or to hunt began heading back to their round mud huts. Nielle in those days had only two rectangular buildings, both built by missionaries; all the rest were circular, made of posts interlaced with mud brick mixed with cow dung. Every roof was made of thatch. Each year the owner and his friends would add another layer of grass to compensate for the bottom layer that had disintegrated.

The village had no right-angle streets or corners, either. It was instead a meandering honeycomb of courtyards surrounded by three or four huts each, enough for one extended family. To walk through the village was simply to wind from one family's courtyard to another until you got to the big one in the center—the chief's.

There were no fences, since ownership of property was not a big concept. Everybody just knew who owned what. You didn't have to verbalize, "That's my chicken," because everybody already knew that particular chicken was hatched in the little nest right outside your hut, so obviously it was yours. The same was true for cattle; nobody branded anything. They didn't need to.

If a person lacked something you happened to own, it was your obligation to share. If a woman's clay cooking pot broke, you readily loaned yours until she could make a new one. More than once I saw women at events wearing just one sandal instead of two. Why? Because they had loaned the other one to a nearby friend whose sandal had broken. If I saw someone with just a left sandal, I usually didn't have to look far to find a matching right one on another woman's foot.

The evening meal preparation was a community affair. The women who weren't tending the fire would gather in groups of four to pound corn or millet in a large mortar, using poles four or five inches in diameter and up to five feet long. They plunged their poles into the corn, one after another, and after each stroke they tapped the pole against the vessel's side to shed any excess.

As they did this, a wonderful rhythm would emerge. *Boom-tap-boom-tap-boom-tap-boom-tap.* Slowly the whole village would begin rocking to the cadence. The women had to thrust their poles into the mortar at precisely the right instant so as not to block the next person. It all sounded like the Enchanted Tiki Room at Disneyland after a while, with multiple rhythms interlacing and creating a warm and inviting pulsation that meant the evening meal would soon be ready.

Those who had been working in the fields, meanwhile, had stopped at the *marigot* (French for "marsh") to clean up. This body of spring-fed water, maybe a quarter mile across and three-quarters of a mile long, was home to snowy egrets, golden-crested cranes with their long legs, and all manner of other wildlife. Men discarded their baggy cotton pants, women their long skirts, and all plunged together into the cool water to splash off the dust. Nobody stared at a member of the opposite sex; nobody gawked.

An unwritten rule of the tribe said it was not a person's responsibility to hide his or her nakedness; it was everyone else's responsibility to preserve the other person's dignity. Thus, people bathed innocently, secure in the confidence that nobody was thinking lustful thoughts. Cleaning up was an open, unshielded activity of life.

So was bodily elimination. The village had no designated latrine; everyone simply took care of their needs in plain view, often at the outer edge of a field where the tall grass began. The rest of us were expected not to watch. You had to have enough dignity not to shame the other person by staring.

The same was true for the nursing of infants. This happened constantly in the open, of course, and no one thought anything about it.

I did get a lecture once, however, for not realizing that white mothers played by a different set of rules than African mothers. We were on a trip with other missionaries and had stopped along the road. I was about seven years old and came around the back of the Jeep, where a missionary wife was nursing her baby.

"Wesley!" she screamed. "You naughty little boy! Can't you see I'm nursing? Go away!" I beat a hasty retreat, mumbling to myself, "What's the big deal? Moms nurse their babies all the time. I don't get it!"

When I was nine years old, we came back to America for a year of furlough so my parents could visit their sponsoring donors and also help my sister and me reconnect with our grandparents, aunts, and uncles who had been mere photos on the wall for the past four years. It was during that year that I discovered American boys were, for some inexplicable reason, fascinated with breasts. What an odd obsession, I thought. The next year, back in the presence of Nielle's mothers, I felt not the slightest twinge of curiosity or arousal. It was all part of the rhythm of life.

In the Lap of Community

While the adults cleaned up and cooked, we little boys had the job of using our machetes to chop grass for the chief's horse, cattle, and goats. We would bring it back to the village in big round bundles carried on our heads.

A layer of smoke from the cooking fires would be building up over the rooftops. It smelled so good. *All is well,* we sensed; another day was done, and we were heading home.

The cooking fires were built on a base of three rocks in a cluster, with sticks fed toward the center like spokes of a wheel. As the fire would consume the sticks at the center, someone would simply tap the outer end to push more fuel into the middle. My father, when he showed slides back in American churches, jokingly referred to this as a "Tappan range"—just a little tap now and then kept the fire going. The cooking pot in the middle held the water that was heated to the boiling point in order to cook the porridge or meat or whatever we had to eat that evening.

Anyone who happened to be in a courtyard when the food was ready got to stay and eat. You ate from whatever pot was in front of you. There was lots of talking and laughing, and when the main meal was finished, people migrated from their own courtyards to that of the village chief, where the evening would be spent. After all, there was no electricity in Nielle, so why stay home alone by your own little fire when you could go to the big gathering?

Even the elderly and infirm were included. If a little widow lady couldn't walk anymore, we kids would go and carry her to the campfire. In fact, while most of us just squatted on the ground, these honored guests would be given a little stool with four legs about six inches long, carved out of a single piece of tree trunk. Everybody mattered. Nobody got left behind.

The chief reclined on a chaise lounge made of bamboo slats. His hair was now white, and he was taller than most other men in the village. He wore a coarse robe, and he always had a sword—not that he ever used it, but it served as a symbol of his power.

He also had a hat woven of grass that came to a point at the top, with a little knob and leather adornment to cap it off. He had undisputed authority, and none of my friends could remember anyone else being chief before him. I honestly don't know if he came to his office by election or inheritance—that was never clear to me. But his dignified bearing was regal, so no one questioned his authority.

Little conversations would bubble here and there, punctuated by outbursts of laughter. The mood was easygoing. We'd throw half a dozen yams into the coals to steam. Once they were nicely cooked, we'd pull them out and carve off the burnt shell with a machete. The inside was delicious, like a baked sweet potato.

Sooner or later the group talk would congeal into one main discussion, often reporting on what had happened during the day. Somebody had fallen off his bicycle in the marketplace and landed on a chicken. Everybody howled at this news. Someone else had stumbled into the path of army ants on his way home from the field. As he described his torment, he jumped up and down, dancing and swatting at himself. We children squealed with laughter. He would then make us solemnly swear to step on every ant we saw the next day, just to get even.

"Well, have you noticed that the goats are a little thinner?" one of the elders would comment. "The boys were chasing them again, and they're losing weight." Murmurs of disapproval would rise up, and my friends and I would cringe. Chasing goats or chickens was so much fun that we couldn't restrain ourselves, but now we were being held accountable.

The worst part was when the elder would continue, "In the swirling dust I couldn't see who all the culprits were, but the little white boy was certainly right in the middle of it." Why did he always single me out? He couldn't name the other boys, but he had no trouble fingering me. Once again, it sure would have helped if God had answered my prayers for black skin. I definitely needed the camouflage!

Yet the scolding was tempered by maturity; it never became mean or sarcastic. This was a warm and generous community. Every child belonged to every adult in the village, it seemed. If you did something bad, they took you to task. But if you needed love and assurance, they gave it in full measure. I never remember falling down as a boy and skinning my knee without some African woman immediately sweeping me up into her arms, wiping my tears, and comforting me until I felt better once again.

Perhaps it sounds as though I think my village was utopia. You may think I'm being overly nostalgic, looking at the past through rose-colored glasses. Well, in contrast to some other parts of my childhood that I will tell you about later, Nielle *was* a perfect paradise for me. I can only describe it to you as I experienced it.

When darkness fell, people would supplement the light of the main fire with little kerosene lanterns scattered throughout the crowd. The market truck brought a fifty-five-gallon drum of kerosene every week, and the local merchant would sell it by the liter in small bottles with corn cobs stuffed in the neck.

Songs would rise up here and there, first soft humming, then with words. The tunes were haunting, built on the distinctive five notes of what musicians call the pentatonic scale. (To get the idea, play just the black keys of a piano, not the white ones.) Soon the entire crowd would join in the song for multiple verses, until it faded away. The songs were often based on proverbs that held timeless value for the tribe. As Christian music came to be written, these songs of praise were added and loved. Songwriters and storytellers sometimes made up songs spontaneously, the drummers picking up a tempo to suit.

I remember the emotional catch in my throat when I realized many years later that the tune of "Amazing Grace" uses only the notes of the pentatonic scale. One has to wonder where the ex–slave trader John Newton got his melody when he wrote his famous hymn in the 1770s. Could it be a fragment of something that wafted up from the wretched hold of his slave ship in earlier years as he hauled his human cargo from the West African coast?

To hum that song today still transports me back to the quiet evenings in Nielle. I am overcome by tears of distant loneliness but also gratitude to God for both the message and melody. No hymn can so powerfully move my soul.

Around our campfire, whoever had a story to tell was welcome to do so—even the elderly who might be growing a bit senile. Usually their minds worked quite well, and kids would cluster on the grandmother's lap to listen and sometimes stroke her hand. If occasionally the story ran too long or started not to make sense, we would gently move the conversation to a different topic. But generally speaking, the older you were in Nielle, the higher your prestige.

I remember one little lady named Nyokoon. She was just skin and bones; most of her teeth were gone. But when she felt like telling a story, we all listened intently. When she felt like dancing, the rest danced with her. She was one of the first villagers to become a Christian.

Some of the stories recounted the olden days, the heritage of the Senufo people, the sources of their proverbs, and the roots of their values. Others were lighthearted and funny. Everyone made jokes about the French, whom they referred to as *blancs* ("white people"). My dad and I would sit there, the only two white faces in the whole courtyard, and we'd laugh as hard as anyone. *Man, I'm glad I'm not blanc,* I would think.

One of the common jokes had to do with how the French spot inspections never really worked. The French liked to roar into a town or village unannounced and check on tax collections or other government requirements. They were always mystified at how everything was in good order for their inspections. They never seemed to figure out that the minute they hit the first village on their route, the drums would crank up with coded messages, like a Teletype machine in the Old West, to pass the warning along: "Frenchman was here. He's coming your way next." People as far as five kilometers away would get the message and smile. By the time the convoy of Jeeps arrived, all was in tiptop shape.

The drums around our campfire were made of goat skin stretched across the top of hollowed-out tree trunks or big gourds. The drummers brought them near the fire so the heat would warm up the skins and make them taut. On the skin's surface, they rubbed in various kinds of tree sap and pitch, which created a variety of tones as the different sections were struck with the hands or an L-shaped stick.

There were also little kettledrums to add a staccato accent, almost like machine-gun fire. The intricacy of the African rhythms never ceased to amaze me. The minute the drums would begin in midevening, people would get up and begin to dance. I mainly watched, because I couldn't seem to hear or feel half of the rhythms everybody else did. People teased our family by saying that white folks couldn't dance, and they were basically right!

Once my father realized how important drums were to the culture, however, he took the somewhat progressive step of incorporating them into our Christian services. Other conservative missionaries had long debates with him about this. But he asserted that the drums were not just beating out a rhythm; they were passing on the Christian message to everyone listening throughout the village, many of whom would never dare to actually attend a church gathering.

A similar debate arose about dancing to the drumbeats, especially by young children. Senufo babies don't learn to walk nearly as early as Western children; they ride on their mothers' backs for as long as two and a half years. It's a way of staying out of danger, such as falling into cook fires. Once the children come down to ground level, however, their fathers put little bracelets with bells on their ankles. The tinkling sound encourages the child to take steps.

The question arose, Is this merely a harmless encouragement for the child to walk, or is this also a fetish to keep the evil spirits away? Most Christians said it was all benign, but elderly non-Christians would say, "Well, but have you noticed that the evil spirits never come around when the children are dancing?" Evil spirits were very much a part of African life, and we could frequently see evidence of satanic activity around us. I doubt, however, that the tinkling of children's bells did much to deter the forces of hell.

As the evening wore on, we kids would grow tired and lean onto an adult's lap to fall asleep. Dad and I usually left early, not wanting to intrude or overstay our welcome. Meanwhile, the rhythm and music played on. The sounds of the drums were always the last thing I heard as I drifted off to sleep at night.

In fact, they kept going into the wee hours or even all night. Why did they play so late? Part of the reason, it seemed, was for the village's security, because the noise kept the wild animals at bay. While my buddies and I roamed the area freely during daylight, the tropical night was a different matter altogether. The snakes came out. The hyenas scavenged, not only for animals already dead, but for live prey they killed amid screams of violence. Their haunting laugh could send chills up your spine.

Leopards crawled out to rule the night. Owls and other night birds would shriek. Rabbits would scream when caught; so would the small deer. Occasionally you would hear a lion roar or grunt deeply. Outside the perimeter of the village and its fields, all kinds of danger lurked. No one ventured out alone.

Ivory Coast got its name from the elephant, of course. By the time of my childhood, the herds had been overhunted, so there were far fewer elephants than before. But if a drought reduced their normal food supply, they would tromp through a cornfield at night, ripping it to pieces within minutes. Needless to say, none of our slingshot stones would deter them. The drums, however, helped scare them away. If necessary, we would run out with lighted torches, pounding on metal pots and pans to add to the clamor.

Our chickens knew better than to venture out at night. They roosted high in the trees, out of harm's way. Goats as well knew that the leopards or panthers would get them in a minute. The dogs of the village were furnished with thick collars made of dried vines to protect them from leopards that would otherwise pounce and snap their necks.

If for some reason the drums stopped during the night, I immediately sat up in my cot, wondering what was wrong. When the music resumed, I knew all was well and drifted back to sleep.

Breaking Down Walls

When children are part of a close-knit group, they feel safe and know they are not abandoned. They enjoy life in the shadows of taller people who genuinely care about what happens to them. The poor, the weak, the small, and the young receive the benefit of common concern. Adults, they sense, are less interested in the Darwinian survival of the fittest than in the improvement of the whole. The mature do not pull away into their individual cocoons; they participate instead in the flowering of the community, however large or small it may be.

This point of view may force us to reassess some of our everyday assumptions. For example, let's consider the church, which we fondly refer to as "the family of God." It is a place meant for inclusion and nurture, we tell ourselves.

Then why do the various ages scatter in opposite directions the minute we pull into the parking lot? We may even enter the building through separate doors, regrouping only when it is time to go home two or three hours later. Our Sunday schools and activity clubs are tightly stratified by age and interest. Three-year-olds go here, ten-year-olds go there, senior high teens go to another place, and adults breathe a sigh of relief at the thought of being free from kids for a while.

As an educator, I am aware of the value of age-graded curriculum for cognitive learning. I just fear that the pendulum may have swung too far in that direction. Attitudes and behavior are more powerful outcomes than mere cognitive knowledge.

Even adults don't seem to want to associate with people more than ten or fifteen years older or younger than they are—hence the proliferation of groupings for young adults, those in the midlife years, seniors, and so forth.

Is this what the apostle Paul meant by "you are all one in Christ Jesus" (Galatians 3:28)? Is this the hope he extended when he wrote that we could be "no longer foreigners and aliens, but fellow citizens with God's people and members of God's household" (Ephesians 2:19)?

Some churches have taken the bold and revolutionary stance that learning does *not* need to be segregated. As one pastor of a thriving Seattle church told *Christianity Today,* "We pay as little attention to age as possible. If you come to our church on a Wednesday night, you'll see 60 young people, ages 2–17, all in one group! Working with them will be 30 adults—a 1:2 ratio—guiding a wide range of learning experiences.

"The other night I stopped by, and there was this wonderful Kodak moment: a cluster of four or five energetic little kids gathered around two adult workers: a lady who's in a wheelchair—she's probably in her early seventies—and a 24-year-old single guy."

This church has had to dig hard for usable curriculum or has been forced to write its own. But the rewards have been worth the effort. Sharing between the generations happens on Sundays as well and even on short-term mission trips. Says the senior pastor, "The Bible doesn't even have a word for *teenager.* So when visiting parents come up to me or call the office and ask, 'What programs do you have for teenagers?' I smile and say, 'We have church!'"[1]

This pastor and his congregation would have felt right at home in our church in Nielle. We met all together, adults and kids, in a mud hut with just one row—a mud bench about a foot high that went all around the circle. The bench would fill up with dads and moms and children and anyone else, and if it looked full, it really wasn't. A new arrival would walk in, pick out two people who appeared movable, then squeeze between them and start wiggling until seated! We could always accommodate one more person, it seemed. We were a unified, close-together, skin-to-skin community.

(The Americans would have been surprised, however, by having to step up and over the mud sill—some eighteen inches high—at the church's doorway. Its purpose? To keep the snakes out. Snakes would not usually climb over a barrier that tall; they would instead keep slithering around the outside bottom of the wall, leaving us to worship in peace.)

In most of today's Western churches, I know the thought of having children present in the worship service is anathema. God forbid that the holy atmosphere should ever be pierced by a baby's cry. Everyone under the age of ten must be packed off to a soundproof nursery or other activity, it seems.

But in so doing, we forfeit the chance for children to see their dads and moms engaged in earnest prayer. They miss the classic hymns of the faith. They fail to catch the rhythms of a well-delivered sermon, which carry a message of their own even if the child cannot yet grasp the theological specifics. They are excluded from the spiritual family gathering in the presence of God.

A friend of mine was a keyboard player for a church that, in its Sunday evening service, provided no childcare for children older than two. This man's three children are now grown. But some of their fondest recollections are of the end of the service when their father would play quietly during a time for extended prayer. One or more of his children would edge up the side aisle and sit beside him on the bench just to watch his hands and listen to the music he made. When the evening finally ended, the child got the special joy of flipping the switch to turn off the instrument for the night. More than two decades later they still cherish that memory and talk about it.

Whatever the methods, the need remains for adults to surround children—their own and other people's children as well—with love and attention and support. We are all in this together. None of us is meant to be an island. The word *community* is more than just a gray sociological descriptor. It is a God term, designed by the Creator of children to water their souls and enhance their spirits as they grow. To ignore this is to sow seeds of dysfunction and future trauma. To welcome the young into the center of our lives is to enrich not only them but ourselves as well.

4

GETTING THE FULL
PICTURE — BODY AND SOUL

I f we lead integrated lives, as described in the last chapter, we will find it easier to do integrated work, attending to the full range of needs in the lives of children—and, for that matter, anyone else we serve. People are not a bank of pigeonholes. Their physical health is not walled off from their emotions, their finances, their social relationships, their sexuality, their skills and talents, or their spiritual beings. To treat one while ignoring the others is shortsighted and often unproductive.

If we are to meet the needs of children, who are the weakest and in some ways most precious members of society, we have to pay attention to a wide variety of issues. We are not raising a crop of potatoes here. We are not assembling a bunk bed. We are shaping *human lives,* with all their wondrous complexity. If ever there was a project that required a multifaceted, holistic view, this is it.

Bringing children to stable adulthood is not a simple task, as every conscientious parent knows. Formulas don't cover it. What else in life do we attempt that requires multiplied thousands of hours, day and night, over nearly two decades? And time is merely part of the story. Fulfilling our mission with children requires intense thought, observation, and prayer. We may focus on one slice of the task—nutrition, let's say, or child discipline or education—and meanwhile neglect three or four other slices.

I am so grateful that I had the great privilege of being raised by big-picture parents. They didn't specialize in one or two things and ignore others. In their private parenting of my sister and me and in their public ministry to others, they kept the whole task in view. And that leads me to another story...

INTO THE BUSH

All I had seen for hours from the backseat of my father's bicycle were the tall green stalks of elephant grass on either side that brushed against me, glimpses of the blue African sky overhead, and my father's sweaty back as he pedaled along the narrow path. I felt the powerful strokes of his legs as we snaked our way through the savanna. I took a measure of pride in swaying along with his movements so as not to add to his effort. The greatest compliment I could receive at the end of a long, hot bike trek was "I almost forgot you were back there, Son."

The two-rut road where we had parked our pickup truck now seemed like an interstate highway. It simply didn't penetrate into the remote settings where we felt compelled to travel to open new villages to the gospel. The path was just a foot wide, a ribbon of dust through the tunnel of green.

The occasional squishy bump in the path could be a puff adder, a dangerous viper whose venomous strike could kill a grown man in a matter of minutes. With any luck, it would be just a spitting cobra. We never stopped to find out, but I would lift my bare little legs high and shudder involuntarily at the sound of angry thrashing in the grass behind us.

Some of the peasants in these parts had never seen a truck or even a bicycle. In some places my father and I were the first white-skinned people to show up in nearly two centuries. The French colonial officials never ventured this far from "civilization." Thus there was a good chance that the last white men to stop here had come to snatch slaves! The Ivory Coast is part of West Africa, from which more than two million sons and daughters were taken in shackles. It was the ancestors of these people we were visiting whose anguished songs had wafted up into the night on slave ships plowing the Atlantic, taking them farther and farther from home.

The horror of the slave trade had been kept alive by word of mouth for numerous generations. So terrified were these remote people that in some villages remnants of high mud walls to ward off invaders could still be seen.

Alezye and a local villager who had ventured out to meet us would serve as our guides, interpreters, and, if necessary, "protectors." They would help dampen the age-old rumor that white people ate black children.

We made a number of forays such as this to various villages—all part of the mission mandate to bring the gospel "to the ends of the earth" (Acts 1:8). Eventually our bicycle would emerge from the dense elephant grass into the clearing of fields that surrounded the village. Although the village drums had announced our approach, and we were accompanied by a trusted village member, the actual sight of two pith-helmeted whites riding a wire contraption into the clearing would still trigger fear and panic among the people. With shrieks and shouts of warning, young and old would flee the fields to the security of their huts in the village. Peering around my father's body, I was always deeply moved. We were anything but slave traders; we loved these people. If only they knew!

By the time we had dismounted our bike at the village edge, not a soul would be in sight. All were huddled in the dark of their huts. No doubt they were thinking, *The legends are true! At long last the white men have found us!* My father would hold my hand reassuringly, and our little band would start walking slowly, deeper and deeper into the seemingly abandoned village. Through courtyard after courtyard, we'd wind our way along the empty maze, each step making us more and more vulnerable to attack. Seeing no one along the way, we would eventually arrive at the chief's courtyard in the center.

My father would then raise his voice. Speaking in Senari, he would call out, "Please don't be afraid! We have not come to take slaves. We come as friends. We have come to tell you of a God who loves you and cares about you!" If necessary, the local villager who had invited us would then add his translation as well as his reassurances to the unseen listeners.

Standing there in that moment, I knew it helped that I was present. The presence of a child, even though white, helped put fears to rest. The slave traders hadn't arrived with kids in tow.

After a few moments of silence, the first to show themselves would be the little children. Unable to contain their curiosity, they'd peek tentatively from behind the doorsteps. African huts, like our church building mentioned earlier, had a foot-high mud wall designed to discourage snakes from entering. Gazing at these barriers, we would spot not much more than white eyes and occasionally some teeth, if I could get them to smile.

Seeing no harm coming to their children, the next strata of society to venture out would be the women. They would come cautiously to me first, stretching out timid hands to touch my straight, brown hair. They would giggle with wonder at such a strange thing. Next they would touch my arms, rubbing gently to see if the white would rub off. I would join in the fun, rubbing my skin hard and acting disappointed that the white would simply not wipe off. *If you only knew,* I would think. *Believe me, if I could get rid of the white by rubbing it off, I would have done it long ago.*

"Does your black rub off?" I would ask. The audience would shriek with laughter. Child to child, the ice was broken, and the next thing you knew, the youths and men had also joined us. The final person to emerge and add his blessing to this meeting of two different worlds would be the village chief.

A New Kind of Love

The day we arrived in a remote place called Kashongo, however, things went a bit differently. It was the mothers who ventured out of the huts first. Tied to their backs or resting in their arms were not smiling, bubbly children but very, very sick ones. There was no laughter in Kashongo that day. People's hearts were frightened and heavy with grief at the sickness and even deaths of the village children.

The comforting words "We have come to tell you of a God who loves you and cares for you" fell on deaf ears. We could see the hopelessness in their eyes. The drums we had heard at our arrival bore a double message: not only the news of our approach but also the news of their tragic losses. They were funeral drums.

When the chief of Kashongo stepped out of his hut, he tried to be a gracious host, but his anxiety and grief were obvious. We sat down to talk. As the conversation unfolded, my father took a little boy, maybe six years old, onto his lap. The child was listless and had a huge, tight, distended belly. His mother described his diarrhea, fever, and lack of appetite. "He is my *zye*," she added mournfully—her firstborn son. Her voice trembled and her eyes filled with tears as she explained that her littler ones, her *"zana* and *beh,"* were no more. They had both died in the previous two weeks.

It was one of the few times I ever saw my brave father cry. His chin trembled, and his eyes welled up with tears. I was sitting at his feet, and as a tear trickled down his dusty, sweaty cheek, our eyes met in one blurry moment of sorrow. In that instant I got a glimpse of my father's heart and what it means to be moved with compassion.

I should pause a moment and tell you part of what made that moment so precious and even strategic. My father and the other Conservative Baptist missionaries of his era who first took on the monumental task of putting the Senari language into writing and then translating the Bible ran into a perplexing problem. After months of discussion and research, they discovered Senari had no actual word for full-orbed love. As loving as these people could be toward one another, the concept of true love, unmerited and unconditional—God's love—did not seem to exist. The closest they could come to the concept was *dene,* which meant "to be pleased" by something. There were ways to say, "My wife pleases me. My children please me. My goats please me." But it was an inward, self-focusing concept that fell far short as a descriptor of God's amazing love for humanity.

So what were the translators to do with that pivotal Bible verse so central to understanding God's love and his plan of salvation, John 3:16? How could they get across the true and full meaning of "For God so loved the world that he gave his one and only Son, that whoever believes in him shall not perish but have eternal life"? The whole concept of redemption was at risk.

To simply translate it "God was so pleased with the world…" would not suffice. After much discussion and prayer, they found that if the word *keele* was added to *dene,* the combination would mean an affection that flows freely. That was the phrase my father had used when he had said, "We've come to tell you about a God who loves you."

Now with a dying child in his arms, this was the love that overcame my father that afternoon.

What could be done? He drew on his rural roots as a farm kid in Colorado and quickly recognized the effects of polluted water on the human body. Sitting under that tree, Dad asked the chief quietly, "Where do you get your water?"

The chief looked surprised. He pointed to the edge of the village toward the setting sun.

"May I visit it?" Dad asked. With that, the whole assembly got up and walked slowly toward the village water hole.

We arrived at a typical opening some four feet across that had been dug into the ground. Its sides were caving in from the rubbing of sisal ropes as homemade buckets were lowered and brought back up again. Animals roamed all around the mouth of the well, and signs of their waste were everywhere. Most seriously, the ground around the hole sloped so that any spilled water tended to run back into the well. It was a health hazard of gigantic proportions.

"I think I can help you with the problem of your sick children," Dad said to the chief, "but I will need some men to work with me."

The chief suddenly straightened up, looked around at the village men, and started pointing. "You, you, you, and you and your sons, help the white man."

We stayed that night in a guest hut, and the next day my father got to work. We knew this project would take awhile, but the villagers were more than willing to feed us. Their hopes were high.

Soon the well was cleaned out. A thornbush barricade was raised to keep the animals from roaming nearby and fouling the water. The mouth of the well was raised so that spilled water ran away from it, not back into it. On a return trip we brought in a pulley so buckets could be raised without banging the fragile sides of the well. A wooden cover was fashioned to protect the well at night.

Meanwhile, we sent a messenger to the mission hospital in Ferkessé-dougou to get medicine for all the sick children with Guinea worms. This is a disease contracted by drinking water that has fleas in it, which carry worm larvae. The worms eventually come out of the body through painful skin blisters, causing long-term suffering and sometimes crippling aftereffects.

I never saw my father so muddy, so sweaty, or so happy as he was those days. It was a labor of love, filled with laughter, hugs, and pats on the back for a job well done. The village chief eventually plunged right in with his men, and the work progressed quickly. As the children's health steadily improved, my father's credibility grew. When he spoke at the village meetings, people leaned forward to hear his words.

Within weeks the well was completely refurbished, the children were again healthy, and at one of the village gatherings, the chief rose and spoke to my father. "What was it about us, sir, that so pleased you that you did for us this great kindness?"

I watched the words register in my father's mind. *What about you pleased me?* Suddenly I saw his eyes brighten. He looked the chief in the eye and said, "There is much about you that pleases me now that we are friends and have done this great work together. But I didn't even know you when my son and I arrived in Kashongo a few weeks ago. All I saw was your need, the suffering of your children—and I loved you. I wanted to…I had to…help. That's what keele love does. That is how my God feels about you."

That moment was a breakthrough in introducing the gospel to that remote village. Deeds had spoken louder than words ever could. Physical needs had opened the door to spiritual ones. Suffering had been the precursor of blessing.

It wasn't long before many in that village chose the "Jesus road." They understood love and wanted it in their lives. A village church was launched.

THE FATEFUL LETTER

One evening a few months later, back home in Nielle, our family was sitting around our folding card table, which doubled as dining-room table, desk, and ironing board. By the light of the hissing Coleman lantern, we were discussing what should be the topic of our next "prayer letter," which we and almost every missionary family sent home to keep donors informed. What would stir people's hearts, motivate them to pray, and spur them to support us financially? As usual, the Staffords were way behind in their support level, and the mission headquarters was gently prodding us about having to "carry" our account.

There is perhaps no greater blight on the life of a missionary than the prayer letter. It has been my observation after a lifetime in all corners of the earth that the better the missionary, the worse the missionary letter seems to be! The quality of the missionaries' work seems to be in direct disproportion to the attractiveness of their reports. This also holds true in the pulpit when they do their rounds back in America on "deputation," as it is called. Marginal field workers who don't really accomplish much overseas can somehow come up with the most intriguing stories and pictures of their exploits that hold pew-bound supporters in awe and send them digging for their wallets when the offering plate comes by. Meanwhile, truly great, cross-cultural, courageous, sacrificial missionary pioneers seem so out of place in air-conditioned sanctuaries that they stammer and falter as they attempt to speak, and their modesty belies their amazing accomplishments. Parishioners who are accustomed to far better oratory doze off.

Perhaps I exaggerate, but only slightly…

My father was definitely in the second class: a great cross-cultural ministry giant who would shrivel up and die in the pulpit. In his really low, discouraged moments on deputation, as the car headlights would pierce the night on yet another lonely highway heading home from yet another Wednesday night missionary service in Podunk, he would moan, "Wesley, there are only two kinds of people who make a living doing what we do: us and circus performers."

On this evening around the card table in Nielle, I offered to help my father with something exhilarating for the next prayer letter. "I have an idea," I spoke up excitedly. "Tell them about the opening of Kashongo! Tell them about the well we fixed, about their figuring out *love* by our helping their children, and about the new little church that started!"

Dad sat up at that idea, a gleam in his eye. Grabbing a piece of paper and a pencil, he set about writing furiously. We sat back and smiled. Another month taken care of.

He wrote joyfully all that evening. I could see him reliving the great emotions and process of that remote village church. But he continued to labor over his papers several evenings and way into the night. More often he was staring off into space, erasing, rewriting…

Finally Mom typed it on onionskin paper and stuck it into an airmail envelope, and I delivered it to the market-truck driver to mail once he returned to the city.

As usual, months went by before the market truck brought a copy of the finished product back to us from headquarters in Chicago. The letter had long been in the hands of our constituents before we saw it again.

In stunned silence I read my father's words. "Praise the Lord for the mighty moving of his Spirit in the village of Kashongo. By God's grace, a little group of believers has been established. Pray that God's love will penetrate that place and a mighty work will be established for the kingdom of God. Thank you for your great generosity and prayerful support. Faithfully yours, the Staffords in Ivory Coast."

I couldn't believe my eyes. Talk about sucking the life out of a story!

"Dad!" I protested the minute I ran through the door of our house. "You missed the whole point. Why didn't you tell them about the sick children? What about the well? Remember how grateful they all were? What's all this spiritual mumbo jumbo?"

I will never forget the dejected look on that great man's face. "I know, Wesley," he said, "but the more I wrote and thought about it, the more of the story I had to erase. You see, Son, those people sent me to Africa to do spiritual things, like preach the gospel and translate Scripture. I don't think they would understand my spending three weeks deep in the mud digging a well in Kashongo."

I stared at him in disbelief as tears welled up in my eyes. I could see his heart was broken. Mine was outraged. I slammed my little fist down on the table and wailed, "Daddy, if that is not what missionaries are supposed to do, I don't want to be one!" I ran sobbing to my cot.

I could not have spoken stronger words to my father. We were part-
ners. We did everything together. In my mind I was already a missionary.
This was all terribly, terribly wrong, and in my childlike spirit I knew it.

No Either-Or

Little did I know that this was the first of many such battles I would experience, and I would spend the rest of my life teetering on that razor's edge
of physical versus spiritual ministry.

Granted, some headway has been made in the Christian world since
that day in the late 1950s. Many leaders have stepped forward to declare
that Christ came to rescue the whole person—body, soul, and spirit. Formal declarations have been drafted by the Lausanne Committee for World
Evangelization (LCWE) and others, emphasizing the worth of holistic
ministry.

But even today, the work of relief and development is still suspect in a
number of mission organizations. They either leave it to groups such as
ours at Compassion, as if it were an odd specialty, or else they commission
a small staff of their own that is highly segregated from the mainstream.
Integration still eludes them, it seems.

Meanwhile, other groups seem to have swung the opposite direction.
They are quite willing to feed the hungry and bind up the wounded, but
they get skittish about using the "J word": *Jesus*. They are afraid to clarify
their motive for humanitarian assistance.

In contrast, our official tag line at Compassion International is this:
"Releasing children from poverty in Jesus' name." It is plastered everywhere
on our literature. E. Stanley Jones, the notable Methodist missionary to
India in the first half of the twentieth century, had it right when he compared spiritual and physical forms of ministry in a 1970 speech just a
couple of years before he died. The first, he said, is "a soul without a body,"
while the second is "a body without a soul. One's a ghost and the other's a
corpse; you can take your choice. I don't want either one. I want both."[1]

Ministry to children does not have to be either-or. In fact, their minds are rather straightforward; they don't do well at guessing why we do what we do. They need to sense that we love them, care for them, believe in them, and stand beside them—all in the name of the greatest Friend a child ever had: Jesus Christ.

TIME: A RIVER RUNS THROUGH IT

C hildren get the short end of the stick in nearly all areas of life—except one.

They obviously don't measure up when it comes to physical stature. In fact, we take note in the maternity ward that the newborn is just "twenty inches long." This statistic goes on every pink or blue birth announcement sent out to family and friends. As the years go by, the child rises slowly into the adult forest of giants, but the process takes at least a decade and a half.

Kids obviously don't have much money. In the early years they get excited over their few nickels, dimes, and quarters, while their parents are managing thousands of dollars. Children are almost totally dependent upon adults to buy for them the necessities of life.

Children likewise are woefully short on life skills of all kinds. It takes them months to learn to tie a shoelace, spell *cat,* or balance on a bicycle. Their days and nights are filled with challenges they don't know how to handle.

But on one scale, they are fully equipped from birth and are on par with every proud adult. What is this scale? They have as much *time* as anyone else. Twenty-four hours each day, 168 hours each week—children enjoy the full allotment given to us all.

Of course, they don't know it as such. Their gift of time is subconscious. They certainly do not know how to measure time and thus how to allocate it scientifically. They keep no datebooks or Palm Pilots to tell them what should happen next.

Early in children's lives big people endeavor to teach them how to tell time. This task has become easier now in the age of digital clocks, although any child who can count must still wonder why the minute called fifty-nine is not naturally followed by sixty, then sixty-one, then sixty-two, and sixty-three. But while the science of telling time is difficult, the daily *enjoyment of time* by children proceeds unhindered. Only gradually do time constraints start to make an impact.

Personally, I didn't have to cope with such difficulties while growing up in Nielle. There was no such thing as a firm schedule. I did not wear a watch until age fourteen, when we came back to America, and I belatedly learned that you couldn't live without one. I was more accustomed to life in a village where everyone just knew that church started when the sun was, oh, up above the tree line about so far, and it continued until the sun was, oh, about halfway to the opposite horizon. That was precise enough.

America was much the same, by the way, as recently as the nineteenth century. Even towns that had clocks set them locally so that 8:15 in one village might be a quite different time in the village five miles away. Now, only 130 years later, we in the developed world are absolutely obsessed with time management. We pack our lives to the last nanosecond. We have electronic reminders to tell us what to do next. We jam appointments back to back, arriving at day's end exhausted from the intensity.

Having packed their own lives full, many parents proceed to do the same with their children. The week becomes a blur of school, sports practices, music lessons, and—soon enough—part-time jobs. Kids have scarce opportunity to lean back and stare at the sky or notice a flower; they have to get to the next activity.

U.S. News & World Report recently ran an eight-page cover story on what's gone wrong with kids' sports. It described how, on top of normal Little League baseball and Pop Warner football teams, a whole second level of turbocharged sports called travel teams are now demanding even more of kids. As a result, a disturbing percentage of talented young athletes burn out and stop playing their sport altogether. Nobody seems willing to admit the statistics, but anecdotal evidence is everywhere.

Young people simply were not made to be the fulfillment machines of adult wishes. They need time to breathe, to imagine, to wonder, and simply to relax. This is not to condone laziness or inactivity in front of a television for hours on end. But a key part of growing up needs to be living at a reasonable pace.

TRIAL BY CLARINET

Children can be pressured in ways other than athletic. In some homes, music or academics take the place of sports as an obsession. I remember a fabulously wealthy home in France where I worked as an *au pair* during my master's degree studies. The father, a fiercely intimidating man, owned a worldwide chain of hotels; the mother ran a catering service. I was responsible to care for their two sons and teach them English.

One night at the end of dinner, the older boy playfully said to his father, "Would you like to hear me play 'Frère Jacques'?" He tooted out the melody on his plastic toy horn.

"Very well!" said his father at the end. "Do you like that horn?"

"Yes, father," said the young Pascal.

"All right," the executive declared, "we'll get you started on learning to play the clarinet." With that, his course was set. By the next day he had brought home for his son a professional-quality instrument worth more than a thousand dollars. He had also lined up the first-chair clarinetist of the Paris symphony to come to the mansion and give weekly private lessons.

Pascal was speechless at all this flurry of activity. I told him I could help him because I, too, played the clarinet.

Well, the teacher turned out to be equally as domineering and impatient as Pascal's father. All week long I tried to get the boy ready for his fate down in the first-floor salon. I would then listen through the walls to the squeaks and squawks of a novice's playing, followed by the screaming tirades of the exasperated teacher. At the end of the hour, the door would burst open, and little Pascal would run up the stairs to flop on his bed, sobbing. "I hate this! I can't do anything right!" he would cry in anguish.

My task then was to try to patch back together his shattered ego and get him somewhat ready for next week's lesson. This went on for months.

Of course, it is easy for me to criticize some other parent's drivenness without admitting how prone I am to the same kind of behavior. At the Stafford house on Sunday nights, we don't actually have an organized meal; we simply graze through leftovers in the kitchen, seeing and fixing what looks appetizing. One night my daughter Jenny plucked a burrito out of the freezer. The rest of us were milling around in similar search of sustenance.

She popped her burrito into the microwave and punched four, zero, zero. The machine began to hum.

Before I could stop myself, I was snapping at her. "Jenny! Now the rest of us all have to stand around and wait four minutes!"

My precious daughter stared at me with a deer-in-the-headlights look on her face as the seconds ticked down. Almost instantly I was hit by a wave of remorse: *What are you saying, Wess! It's only four minutes. She didn't do anything wrong.*

"I'm so sorry. I can't believe what I just said," I volunteered, reaching out to her. With that, everyone relaxed and began laughing. It's now a family joke.

The saintly Dutch survivor of World War II concentration camps, Corrie ten Boom, once said, with marvelous insight, "If the devil cannot make us bad, he will make us busy." *Busy* is in some ways a four-letter word. It is also a mandatory word in our society; you have to say it. One modern mom meets another: "Hi. How have you been?" "Oh, really busy!" If you're *not* busy every day, every week, all year long, what's the matter with you?

The pace at which we run our lives, usually by default, has the capacity to poison both us and our children. We know better, but we can't seem to stop ourselves. We're too busy running to the next event.

INVASION OF THE BUREAUCRATS

I will never forget a certain Wednesday in Nielle when I was about ten. It was a market day; the big truck from Ferkessédougou had made its treacherous trip and was disgorging bundles and boxes. Meanwhile, hunters, fishermen, farmers, and weavers from several villages had spread out their wares under the mango trees. The village air was filled with jokes, stories, and laughter as the banter and barter of the day unfolded. Of course, there was very little money to go around, so from a business point of view, when all was said and done, a lot more was being said than getting done.

In the midst of this convivial atmosphere, suddenly a convoy of French colonial officials roared into town in their Jeeps, stirring up an extraordinary cloud of red dust. We had received no advance warning from the drums of the neighboring village, or perhaps we were making too much noise to hear them. Suddenly here were the bureaucrats in their khaki shorts, tailored shirts, and pith helmets, imperiously gathering the village leaders into a small circle at the edge of the marketplace. Out came their clipboards and pens. They were bent on conducting a government survey that day.

The French officials were hot and sweaty and wanted nothing more than to get this over with and then escape the miserable, dusty place. They began firing questions regarding their theme, which was "expectations of the future."

"What do you think the population here will be in ten years?"

"How big will the school be?"

"When will you expand it into a high school?"

"Will you have a hospital here by that time?"

"How many kilos of millet will you harvest by that time?"

The chief and his tribal elders tried to explain to their exasperated visitors that they really didn't know the answers to those kinds of questions, because the future had not yet arrived. When the time came to pass, then the results would be apparent.

This was totally unacceptable. This conversation was putting everyone in a foul mood. The government officials said that if there truly were no answers, they would have no choice but to report this village to the capital city, Abidjan, as being resistant and uncooperative. That would not bode well for our "future development" opportunities.

Finally, with everyone in ill humor, the French packed up their stuff, piled into their still-overheated vehicles, and stormed off down the road. They were presumably in quest of a more cooperative and progressive village. Meanwhile, our chief gave a nod, and the drummers ran off to alert those down the road that a convoy of government folk, mad as wet hens, was headed their way.

The festive mood of the marketplace was dampened, and the chief stormed off to his courtyard. We kids had never seen him this upset, and we followed him to see if we could cheer him up. He just smiled weakly and waved us off. "Tonight at the fire we will have a serious talk," he announced.

At dusk the village gathered quietly and respectfully in the chief's courtyard. He still hadn't calmed down. At the appropriate time he rose from his bamboo chair, cane in hand, his sword of authority hanging in its sheath from one shoulder. He had an air of burden about him. His strong hands trembled, and he looked older and more tired than usual. The villagers sat in complete silence, waiting to see what their leader would express.

He sighed a deep sigh and began. "I want to talk to the children tonight," he began, looking from child to child. "The day is coming when I will be gone. One of you will be chief then. It's a time they call *la venir*— the coming, the future. There is much we do not and cannot know about that time. We are all curious about it, but it really cannot be known.

"The Frenchmen who came to Nielle today do not understand that. They asked me many questions about the future—as if it could be known! When I told them we don't know what will be in the future, they became very angry. And so did I. I am sorry you saw me like that. It is not how we should be. It bothered and saddened me to be angry.

"They went away angry too, but I think they are often like that. Worrying about the future can do that to you."

He took another deep breath and then continued. "We are not like them. To them, time is everything. Did you see those silver circles on their wrists? Those things measure the day into very little pieces. I have seen such things on the walls in Abidjan, too.

"Frenchmen think that counting time is very important. A day can be divided into twenty-four parts, and each of those parts can be divided into sixty smaller parts." He didn't tell us that those smaller parts could be divided into sixty even smaller parts. Either he didn't want to confuse us, or perhaps he didn't know about seconds that tick away all the time.

Then came a profound statement. "The smaller that men can measure the day, the more angry they seem to be," he said with a shake of his head.

"For the Senufo, the movement of the sun is as much measurement of the passage of time as we need. We know when to get up. We know when to work the fields and when to hunt. We know when to rest in the shade. We know when to go home. We know when to sleep. Children, it is enough!

"Time is like a river," he continued. "It flows along like water, from the future to the present and into the past. But there is a bend in the river. We know the water is coming, but we can't see it or know very much about it. All we know is that it is coming.

"The present is now—the days we live today. This is God's gift to us. It is meant to be enjoyed and lived to the fullest. The present will flow by us, of course, and become the past. That is the way of a river, and that is the way of time.

"The Frenchmen cannot wait for the future to arrive. They crane their necks to see around the bend in the river. They cannot see it any better than we can, but they try and try. For some reason, it is very important for them to know what is coming toward them.

"They want to know it so badly that they have no respect for the river itself. They thrash their way out into the present in order to see more around the bend." At this the chief began to pantomime, hiking up his long robe to do a high-step dance around the fire. Everyone laughed as his robe flapped with each exaggerated step.

"They stand in the middle of the river, facing upstream," he continued, "and though the river swirls dangerously around their knees and nearly topples them, they don't care. To them, it seems that the present is only a vantage point to better see around the bend to the future.

"They miss so much of the joy of today all around them. Did you notice that as they stormed into our village, they didn't notice it is the best of the mango season? Though we offered them peanuts, they did not even taste them. They did not hear the birds in the trees or the laughter in the marketplace. We touched them with our hands, but they did not really see us. They miss much of the present time, because all they care about is the unknowable, the future.

"Because they strain to see around the bend in the river, the present nearly knocks them down as it swirls around their knees. It slips behind them and keeps flowing. It becomes the past without their even noticing. The past, for them, is forgotten. The memories fade, and they make the same mistakes all over again. That is why their questions made no sense today.

"Children, we are not like them!"

An excitement seemed to quicken his countenance as he looked around the fire ring. "We also see the passage of time like a river, but we respect the river! We cannot see around the bend into the future any better than they can, but that is all right. We know it is coming, and although we don't know all about it, God does. We can trust him with the future.

"We would never disrespect the river by crashing into its powerful flow. We sit quietly and respectfully on the banks of the river and watch. The future comes when it is ready. It will arrive in its own time and in its own way. Soon it will be in front of us. Oh, what a gift that is!

"The present is all we can fully know and experience, so we must. We must love each other. We must smell the hibiscus flowers. We must hear the singing of the weaverbirds and the grunts of the lions. We must taste with joy the honey and the peanut sauce on the rice. We must laugh and cry and live."

Suddenly he grew sober again, the twinkle gone from his eyes. We knew from his cadence that something very important was about to be said. "Children," he continued, with tears glistening in his eyes, "do not forget the past! It is just as much a part of the river as the future and the present. I will be there one day…and someday, a long time from now, so will you. You must remember what you have seen and heard and learned. You must tell the stories of today to the younger ones, your sons and daughters, when it becomes yesterday, the past.

"Although the future is not known to us, it is known to God and only to God. He holds it in his hands. You don't need to worry about it; it will come. God will take care of it. All we can see and feel is the present. All we can remember and honor is the past. It is enough, my children."

In the gathering darkness, there were nods of agreement all across the courtyard. We knew the chief had spoken wisdom that night.

He was not meaning to say that forecasting and planning are bad. He himself looked ahead to the growing season and directed that crops be planted on time so there would be a future harvest. But when it came to questions about unknowable things, he refused to be anxious about them. He emphasized two main points to us all, young and old:

One, live *today* completely. It is important in its own right.

Two, tomorrow lies in the good hands of God. Therefore, we do not need to be restless about it.

As a child in Nielle, I found his perspective reassuring. It explained why our village life was so vibrant and full. The underlying philosophy said that today was really all we had, so we should relish it to the full. People matter. Food matters. Smells matter. Stories matter. Dancing matters. Hard work matters. *Now* matters.

That night, even though I was just a boy, I saw the big picture more fully than at any previous time. *So that's why we are the way we are,* I told myself as I walked home beside my father in the darkness.

IN THE FULLNESS OF TIME

Time must be our servant, not our master. It cannot be allowed to dictate to us. We must use it wisely and keep it under our control.

When news came to Jesus that his friend Lazarus was seriously ill, he did not scurry around packing his suitcase for a quick trip to Bethany. He took his time—two days, in fact. He refused to be stampeded into action.

Both Martha and Mary chastised him for this when he finally arrived: "Lord, if you had been here, my brother would not have died" (John 11:21, 32). The Son of God did not even bother to defend himself. He kept his focus on the real purpose, which was to raise Lazarus from the tomb and thereby demonstrate his resurrection power. He moved at a deliberate pace.

His entire life on earth was that way. Although he accomplished a great deal, there's no report he was ever frantic or in a rush. His whole arrival in this world had been arranged to occur "when the fulness of the time was come," says Galatians 4:4 (KJV).

Bible scholars write about this fullness in geopolitical terms, pointing out that Jesus was born during the Pax Romana, when Caesar's rule had brought a measure of stability to the Mediterranean sphere. Two languages (Greek and Latin) were dominant across the empire, improved roads allowed for efficient travel, and old religions were crumbling. At a deeper level, the yearning for a Messiah had fully ripened in the Jewish nation. The entire advent of Jesus carried with it a sense of "Finally...at last!"

I believe there can be moments in your life and mine that echo this dimension—not in a messianic sense, of course, but with regard to fulfilling God's purposes for us. One happened to me a few years back when I was visiting a Compassion International project in Ethiopia. We were standing that day in a semitrailer that had been pulled onto the site of a little church to serve as our office. The pastor and local project staff members—more than a dozen altogether—were enthusiastically showing me wall charts that tracked each sponsored child in that project: their school attendance, their growth in height and weight, their Scripture memorization, the last time they had written to their sponsor, the last time the sponsor had written back, and so forth.

Clearly this church was passionate about the growth and development of its children. All of a sudden I began to weep. *This is what it's all about!* I told myself. My hands went down on my knees, and I dropped my head as the tears flowed. This is why my staff and I write reports and raise money and get on airplanes and endure jet lag and all the rest: so that little children can have a chance in life to know Jesus and serve him productively.

The Africans waited silently and respectfully for the white president from America to regain his composure. But I couldn't. A second thought hit me: *If only something like this had been organized back in Nielle...* So many children back in that village, though loved and appreciated by the adults, had no overarching plan to develop their potential and help them become all that God no doubt meant for them to be. I began to see the bigger picture afresh. I could not speak for a few moments as I pondered the "fullness of time" for this generation of youth.

Finally I looked up and said, "I'm sorry. I was just overwhelmed. Sadness and joy collided in my heart. Sorrow that this wasn't available when I was growing up, and great joy that it is happening now. I am so, so proud of you folks. What you're doing in these children's lives will transform this community—I promise you!"

If we are not attuned to the divine rhythm as we move through our lives, we will miss the richness of *today* as well as the potential of tomorrow. If hurry dominates our lives today, we and our children will simply flail along in the whirlwind. We will arrive at *tomorrow* all out of breath, frightened and disoriented, anxious and fearful of what's coming around the bend. God will be saying, "Just trust me with your future," but we will lack ears to hear his words.

The familiar proverb says:

Trust in the LORD with all your heart
    and lean not on your own understanding;
in all your ways acknowledge him,
    and he will make your paths straight. (Proverbs 3:5–6)

I happen to think this four-line proverb is almost a contract, spelling out three things for us to do in order for God to respond with the fourth. *If* we trust in the Lord, and *if* we don't lean on our own understanding, and *if* we acknowledge him in all our ways, *then* God will be more than willing to take care of our future.

To trust is to relax, to take a deep breath and let go of the inner tightness. It is like a child jumping off a diving board into the arms of a waiting parent in the water. It is to say, "I don't know everything about how this is going to work out, but the other person does, and that's enough for me."

I remember taking my young daughter to a supermarket where they were selling helium-filled balloons—something she absolutely adored. I bought one for her, and we began our shopping. But soon a tragedy occurred: she let go of the string, and the balloon floated up to the store ceiling.

"Daddy!" she cried, the tears gushing down her face. "I lost it!"

"That's okay, honey," I replied. "We'll go back and get another one for you."

This time I took the precaution of tying the balloon to the grocery cart handle, then letting her hold the middle of the string once again. We resumed our shopping. After a while I looked down and saw that her knuckles were white with tension as she held that balloon string in a death grip.

"Jenny, you don't have to hold on so tightly," I said.

"But I don't want to lose the balloon, Daddy!"

"You won't lose it. It's tied to the cart," I explained with a smile.

"I know, Daddy, but I still don't want to lose it!" She refused to let go.

Those of us who are obsessed with our time, and who build that obsession into our children, are people who refuse to acknowledge that our heavenly Father has our future tied to his sturdy cart. It's not going anywhere that he himself doesn't go. He makes sure we are safe.

This means we would do ourselves a great favor to "lean not on [our] own understanding," as the proverb says. Intellect and knowledge are fine, but they won't secure us over the long haul. God's ways, in fact, do not always "make sense." The values of the kingdom of God are frequently upside-down.

What the Bible asks of us is simply this: "In all your ways acknowledge him." Not just on Sunday mornings, not just in formal rituals, but throughout the ordinary days and nights of our lives, month after month, year after year. When the passing of time for us and our children is centered on God, he removes the strain. We know that he is directing us, he is in charge, and that is enough. We can breathe deeply and enjoy the journey.

Children will not learn this pace or perspective from uptight, driven adults. They will only gain its benefits as we show them how to be still and know that he is God. He knows what lies around the bend.

6

WHEN IS ENOUGH... ENOUGH?

It's a prosperous time to be a child in America. Parents work hard, often putting in more hours than they wish, and assuage their misgivings by spending money on their kids. As a result, fully one-third of all thirteen-year-olds in this country now own a cell phone. So do 4 percent of their kid brothers and sisters who are only ten. Whenever and wherever they want to talk to their buddies or their girlfriends, the technology on their belt clips is ready and waiting.

Three out of five American teen bedrooms now have their own television. Studies show that these kids watch five and a half *more* hours of television per week than if they had to use the set in the family room. Food to munch along the way is available in abundance, of course, which is part of the reason we have an explosion of youth obesity in the United States.

When it comes to direct spending by young people, 70 percent get allowances. According to one survey, the average weekly amount for a five-year-old is $3.15; for a ten-year-old, $7.18; and for a fifteen-year-old, $15.57.[1] No wonder kids are obsessed with going to the mall, and no wonder the American landscape has twice as many shopping malls as high schools.

Of course, the stuff on sale in all those shops isn't quite so thrilling a month or two later, and rooms get filled up. Eventually Mom comes along and declares a clean-out crusade, filling bags with things to give away or throw away. It is a bit outrageous to learn that Americans spend more for garbage bags each year than 90 of the world's 210 countries spend for *everything*.[2]

I've been to some of those countries, by the way. I've watched how carefully they conserve what little they have. It's often hard to find a wastebasket, and when you do, it is so *tiny*! Our ubiquitous forty-five-gallon garbage cans on wheels are nowhere to be seen.

Most kids in the Western world know, however, that if they really want something new, their parents can be persuaded to get it. Moms and dads, it seems, are even willing to borrow for the child's comfort. Credit cards make this easy to arrange. That is part of the reason debt levels have soared in recent years, along with personal bankruptcies. It is claimed that the average American household is now carrying more than $7,000 of credit-card debt. Well, not really, because 40 percent of those households pay off their balances each month, thus carrying no debt at all. That means the other 60 percent who let things ride are carrying *more like $12,000 in credit-card debt per household per month*. (The 40 percent who do pay promptly and thus avoid interest charges are privately scorned by the credit-card industry as "freeloaders" and "deadbeats." So much for the virtue of frugality.)

Shopping remains an all-time favorite activity. To accommodate our many acquisitions, homes keep getting larger and larger. In 1950, the average American single-family home was 983 square feet. By 1970, that figure had grown to 1,500 square feet. By 2004, it had ballooned to 2,329 square feet.[3]

And still, it's not big enough for all our stuff. That is why we patronize more than 35,000 self-storage facilities across the nation. We have to have a place for all the extra bikes, books, and barbecues we're not using right now...but might someday soon.

WHAT DOES A CHILD TRULY NEED?

Such statistics might lead us to pause a minute and ask, "What does a child truly need? How much stuff is enough? What makes for a healthy, well-balanced, contented person? What, in fact, works in the opposite direction?" We ask ourselves these questions a lot where I work since our calling is to nurture the poor children of the world. After all, we can throw money at problems and, if we're not careful, end up creating more trouble than solutions.

I have always appreciated this definition of failure: "to succeed at something that doesn't really matter." If you exert all your might to climb a tall ladder but it's leaning against the wrong wall, you have failed. How many of us have lavished toys and clothes and entertainment on our kids to the point of extreme, only to produce selfish, bored, demanding, irritable teenagers? This can happen in any country of the world.

Many readers will be familiar with psychologist Abraham Maslow's hierarchy of needs, made popular in the middle of the last century. He proposed five levels of human need, starting at the most basic: *survival* (air, water, food, rest, the avoidance of pain, etc.). If we lack these, we are obsessed with getting them; we can think of nothing else. But if these needs are satisfied, then our attention migrates to the next levels:

2. *Safety* needs—to be secure, protected from danger
3. *Belonging* needs—to be loved, to be part of a group that holds you close
4. *Esteem* needs—to be respected and recognized, to have someone's attention, to be treated with dignity, to be self-confident, to achieve
5. Finally, said Maslow, a very few people rise to *self-actualization,* which means to fully realize one's potential. If you are in this category, you have managed, in the words of the army recruitment slogan, to "be all you can be."

Now here is a question: does the gathering of more and more material goods help a child rise to the higher levels or not? I think we all know the answer if we stop to think for a minute. While certain purchases indeed bolster the bottom layer of the pyramid (food, for example), and others can increase safety and security, the marketplace products are not very good at making any of us feel more loved, respected, or self-actualized. In fact, they tend to distract us from what is truly important.

By contrast, God is the one who loves us when no one else seems to care. He is the one who gave us inherent dignity. He has plans for each life that are greater than we would dare to dream. As long as we seek these things on our own, without him, we are sure to get off track.

Read the histories of civilizations. You can tell a society is nearing its ultimate collapse when it is consumed with comfort, pleasure, and entertainment, when it no longer feels it needs anything from God, the Creator. For the Greeks, Romans, Incas, Aztecs, and soon perhaps Western civilization, the path has been the same.

By the way, the path doesn't have to take centuries. Remember the story of Robinson Crusoe? In a moment's terrifying shipwreck, he went from the heights of civilized society—the comfort of the captain's quarters on a state-of-the-art ship under the flag of the greatest civilization on earth—to a waterlogged, desperate scramble for mere survival. His story captivated my imagination as a young boy. I can still hear my mother's voice as she, day after day, read me Daniel Defoe's exciting novel. Crusoe's first quest was simply for water to drink. Then came food. After that, he achieved fire and shelter—a fort, no less, which was the next logical need as he progressed up the pyramid.

When finally secure from threat and attack, he began to sense an aching loneliness. Remember his great joy at discovering footprints on the sandy beach? The company of another human being he called Friday took him to a whole new level of socialization. The roles of boss and servant took shape—a semblance of social hierarchy.

All seemed to be going well until a white sail appeared on Crusoe's horizon. In spite of having all his needs met, he could not shake the lure to return to the "real" world. It broke my boyhood heart, but he couldn't help himself; he climbed aboard a ship and resumed his life back in England. He had plummeted from the top and clawed his way back up through the entire range of needs in a few short months.

In our society, when a guy who flips a basketball through a ten-foot-high hoop can make as much money in three hours as a schoolteacher, who is shaping the lives of the next generation, does in a year, something is horribly wrong with our values. When we pay exorbitant amounts of money to actors, many of whom would fail miserably if they had to perform on a live stage and seem great only because of the magic of studio editing, something is seriously out of whack. At Compassion International, we've decided that some of the most important things we can give a needy child are (starting at the bottom and working upward):

- Food every school day (which they sometimes take home to share with their families, we find)
- Inoculation against major diseases
- Health screening and treatment
- Education
- An introduction to Jesus, who will love them for a lifetime
- An exposure to possible vocations—in other words, a route to becoming productive

Yes, this requires money. But it's about much, much more. And in fact, money used unwisely can disrupt the whole relationship. Sometimes a well-meaning child sponsor here in America will write to say, "I just love this child in Uganda so much that I want to send her five hundred dollars as a special gift."

At that point we intervene. One of our staff will respond, "We hear your generous heart. That is a wonderful thought, but we can't let you do that. It would be more than that child's father earns in an entire year. The gift would absolutely destroy his dignity and throw the family structure into chaos.

"We believe this little girl is making good, steady progress toward a better life, thanks to your monthly gift of thirty-two dollars. If you have extra to give, how about sponsoring a second or third child in the same way? This would be truly appreciated—and effective."

The village where I grew up in Ivory Coast spent most of its attention and energy on physiological needs—the bottom level. People were just trying to survive. They also dealt with security issues and even made time in the evenings for love and community, as I have described.

But any disruption of nature—a flood, a brush fire, a plague of locusts, an epidemic of measles—could plunge us back down to survival mode overnight. We never left our extreme vulnerability for very long.

The nearest hospital was a full day's drive away. When a deadly viper bit someone, missionary nurses would heroically try to save the person's life, sometimes succeeding, sometimes not. I remember more than once sitting on the ground and holding little friends who had been bitten, knowing they would be gone in thirty minutes. We just rocked them and loved them until they slipped away from us.

But on less traumatic days, we picked ourselves up and kept going. We managed to endure and even rejoice in the simple rhythms of life. We didn't know anything about "lifestyles of the rich and famous" in faraway lands. We had no idea what we were missing.

The richest person in Nielle was, of course, the chief. He even owned a horse! Aside from that, however, I now realize that his net worth was probably no more than a few hundred dollars—hut and all.

The house my father built (with my help, of course!) at the edge of the village was larger. But the village people found it strange. It wasn't round at all. People would cluck their tongues and shake their heads at the pains we took with plumb lines, levels, and trisquares to get the foundation, walls, and window frames perfectly rectangular.

New believers who had begun to "walk the Jesus road" would chide my father by saying that if he really wanted to be like Jesus, he should build a house "God's way. Look around you, monsieur, at what God has built!" they would say with a smile. "Look at the rocks, the flowers, or even the hills. Look at the sun, the full moon, the orange, the grapefruit, or the coconut. None of them are straight up and down. Nothing is perfectly flat. Is anything perfectly square? They are all round—like our houses!"

My father, a civil engineer by training and the son of a carpenter, could not bring himself to compromise on this one, even though he was otherwise very culturally sensitive. "I guess you're right," he would reply with a grin, wiping the sweat from his brow. "But God is very forgiving. I hope he will love me anyway!"

GLIMPSES OF THE WEST

Our only exposure to Western products was what we would see in a rare magazine that a fellow missionary brought back from furlough or something we heard listening to the shortwave radio. We could pick up ELWA, the Christian station in nearby Liberia, and once in a while the BBC.

As for our neighbors, they knew only what the market truck happened to bring each Wednesday. This rusted-out, belching, hissing vehicle came gasping into town by midmorning. The load of bundles and baskets usually far exceeded the height of its cab or the rails of its cargo area. With no overpasses to worry about on the road from Ferkessédougou and with few tree branches to rip off its cargo, the back of the truck rose easily twice as high as the cab. The behemoth rocked and swayed over the ruts and threatened to career onto its side with each curve in the road.

There was a certain protocol to stacking the load on the market truck. Heavy items such as wood, grain, barrels, and boxes went on the very bottom. Inside some of them might be the latest tools and merchandise that the outside world seemed to find indispensable but the villagers had somehow managed to live without for centuries.

Live cattle and goats made up the next level. On their backs came cotton, bolts of cloth, and cages with various little critters such as chickens and ducks.

On top of it all rode the crown of God's creation: people. They would cover the back, poking their legs down through the load to stand on anything that would hold their weight without biting them, pecking them, breaking, or just plain dying.

As the truck belched its way toward Nielle, would-be sellers stood along the route with their merchandise, waving their arms wildly to attract the driver's attention so he would stop and let them on. The basic understanding was that there was always room for one more person and his or her bundle of stuff to sell.

Behind the roaring truck billowed a huge cloud of red dust. All loading and unloading of passengers was done in virtually zero visibility, as the dust engulfed everything like a blanket. The truly lucky ones got to ride in the cab—but with windows rolled up and no air conditioning, of course. When you peered into the cab through the windshield, it usually looked like bleachers at a football game, with heads squeezed together and piled several layers deep. The driver would be plastered against his side window with no more room than any of the six to eight others who shared his bench.

I should stop to say that by the time the truck arrived, the rest of the Nielle marketplace was already set up. Peasants and merchants had come from all around, either on foot or (as civilization slowly found us) by bicycle. The bikes were piled impossibly high with merchandise.

The best market stalls were taken early, at the crack of dawn. (Even in Nielle, business was all about location, location, location.) As the scorching tropical temperatures rose, the heat waves shimmered off the dusty ground like dancing vapors. The shade of the big mango tree proved increasingly attractive so that no matter what was for sale under its leafy branches, the crowd eventually congregated there.

Off to one side were the wicker cages filled with cattle, goats, pigs, and anything else alive. It was my favorite part of the market—a symphony of squeals, grunts, quacks, clucks, and the never-ceasing crowing of roosters. Next to it was the vegetables and fruits section. These were always beautifully displayed—perfect stacks of tomatoes, mangoes, and coconuts, all set out in front of the vendor.

Hardware had its section, as did cloth, baskets, and containers. One guy always sold strips of inner tube for tying bundles together and, more important, for making slingshots. We boys always converged on him first, as the best strips of rubber were taken by the early customers of the day.

A cow was always slaughtered first thing in the morning, to be sold in little bits and pieces throughout the day. It had to be gone by sunset since there was no way to refrigerate it overnight. The cow chosen for market wasn't always the best animal in the prime of life, so the wise shopper got to market early enough to see the cow while it was still on its feet. That helped you decide whether to buy and, if so, how much.

What really amused my mother was that the cuts of meat were sold strictly by weight, so much per kilo. It didn't matter if you selected filet mignon, T-bone steak, or the guts or tail—it all sold for the same price in the midst of the same swarm of flies. Actually there were no real bargains to be had here in any case, since all the cattle were of Brahma descent and were basically as tough as leather. Even the best cuts of meat had to be beaten to a pulp with a spiked metal hammer just to make them chewable. When beef was served in my house, there was very little conversation—just a lot of serious chewing!

The Dyoula tribe down the road would always show up to sell their arts and crafts. Wooden carvings, voodoo masks, and little stools were their specialty.

In the various stands, prices were marked on nothing; negotiation was the order of the day. This was done with a great deal of teasing and laughter. The fair price was usually about a third down from the original asking price. The fun was to act astonished at the asking price. You would try to find anything wrong with the product, meanwhile pleading your poverty compared to the seller's affluence. The jokes and laughter rolled on and on.

Visitors often didn't know this unspoken rule. If they paid the original asking price, the vendor could easily be insulted, as if to say, "What, you didn't want to talk with me?" But normally, purchasing was done in such good spirits that it ended with a handshake, a hug, or a compliment. I loved every minute of it.

One desperately hot day in the dry season the truck dropped off something new: a wooden case of bottled Coca-Cola. Of course, it had been bouncing and jostling its way along the rutted roads for a long time. Apparently, back in the big city some marketing genius with a soft-drink firm must have figured that in this scorching climate Coke would be so good and irresistible it would sell itself if people would just taste it. So he instructed the market-truck driver to deliver a free case of twenty-four bottles to the "gas station" in Nielle.

(Yes, believe it or not, Nielle actually had a gas station. It was basically a mud hut with a fifty-five-gallon drum sitting out front in the sun with a crank on top. The barrel groaned and banged as its contents expanded by day and cooled by night, waiting for a client. We kids were scared of it. Some claimed a demon lived inside, which accounted for its scary noises. Its sole mission in life was to dispense gas into the rickety old truck that had delivered it the week before, the missionary's pickup, or any stray vehicle that might find its way to this remote outpost.)

I didn't see the arrival of the first Coke samples. Several weeks went by.

The gas station attendant, not having a clue what they were, kept stacking the additional cases in his hut, awaiting instructions. Finally one market day he stopped my father as we were deep in negotiations for a small pile of mangoes.

"Monsieur, please come with me," he requested. "I need your wise counsel at my gas station." My dad followed him toward the hut. "I have been receiving glass bottles of something for several weeks on the market truck," the man explained as they walked. "It comes with no instructions. I don't know what it is, how to open it, what to do with it. I don't even know what hole in the truck engine I am supposed to pour it into!"

Now he really had Dad's curiosity piqued. They arrived at the station and pushed the rickety wood door open. There in the dark interior sat a dusty stack of wooden crates with bottles of dark liquid in them. Dad blew the dust off one and burst out laughing. By now a crowd of curious people had gathered.

"This is a drink from America," my father explained. "It's called Coca-Cola. You will probably like it. It is made from the very cola nuts your old men and women chew all day long—those nuts that make your teeth yellow." At least this was a familiar connection they could comprehend.

"Let's give it a try," Dad continued, reaching for his pocketknife with a bottle opener blade that had not seen the light of day for nearly four years. He deftly flipped off the cap.

You must remember that these bottles had been sitting in a very hot hut for weeks. They were even hot to the touch. They were basically Molotov cocktails in thick glass bottles marked Coke.

An eruption of white foam spewed into the air and onto everyone nearby. The fizzing and sputtering sent dignified men shrieking and scattering in all directions, fearing for their very lives. My father nearly collapsed with laughter.

One by one they timidly returned after the explosion died down without apparent fatalities. "This is delicious, you guys," my father coaxed. "Here, have a taste! Come on—it won't hurt you!"

The gas station attendant was thrust forward to serve as the guinea pig for all. Fear filled his eyes as though he was about to drink something very much alive. After a good deal of ribbing for being a coward, peer pressure made him bring the bottle to his lips. There was a hush of anticipation.

Ça pique, ça pique—comme un serpant! he screamed, dancing around and fanning his burning mouth with his hand. ("It stings, it stings—like a snake!") Nobody doubted him. After all, the strange dark stuff had certainly hissed. Why not assume it also would bite you? There were peals of laughter as the man offered the bottle to others. He got no takers.

"Well, Monsieur Stafford," he announced for all to hear, "if you like this and are willing to risk your life with it, it's all yours!"

Dad insisted the stuff actually did have worth and paid him what he guessed it would cost in the outside world. From that day forward, our lives took a big step upward. This Coca-Cola sample system went on for several years, much to our delight. Each day we would come in from the scorching heat at noontime, ceremonially open a single bottle of Coke, pour it over precious ice from our kerosene-driven refrigerator, and listen to the fizz. We split each bottle four ways.

But otherwise, the marketing ploy was a miserable failure. Neither boys and girls nor dads and moms in Nielle ever came to think that they *needed* Coca-Cola to live the good life. They remained quite content drinking lukewarm water from the village well. They weren't convinced that the beverage known round the world was all that essential for them.

FASHION SHOW

The village people did warm up a bit more easily, however, to another mystery package that the market truck brought their way. The driver had finished unloading his usual bundles of merchandise one Wednesday, and just before he slammed shut the tailgate, he rolled off one last huge bundle into the dust. Taped to its side was a piece of cardboard.

Nobody recognized from the shape of the bundle what was inside. Several of the children courageously stepped forward, pulled the tape from the cardboard sign, and scampered off to take it to the village chief. By now, the marketplace had come to a standstill; all eyes were riveted on the mysterious parcel.

The chief turned the sign over and over in his hands to determine which side was up. He couldn't read at all—not his mother tongue, Senari, nor French. The former, in fact, had only recently been put into writing by my father and other missionaries. Neither language would have helped, however, because as I read over his shoulder, I saw the words were in English! I was the only one standing there who knew what they said. Even I had to sound them out syllable by syllable. "A Gift…from…the…People… of…the…United…States." It took me a moment in my head to translate this back into French and then Senari. The people of the United States? Suddenly all eyes were on me. "It is a gift from my *other* people far away… to you!" I explained.

Eyes shifted back and forth from me to the bundle on the ground and back again. I shrugged, having nothing more to say.

At last the chief got up slowly from his stool in the shade and walked cautiously over to the bundle as if it were something dangerous. He drew his machete from its sheath and, with one sweep of his arm, cut the cord that held the package together. The tightly wrapped bale burst apart. The chief took his cane and pushed things around. Clothing! The people I came from, whom I could scarcely remember, had somehow sent a gift of used clothing to my village.

It is worth a moment to pause here and point out that clothing, as nice as the intent was, was not really a "felt need" in Nielle. Nobody wore much in the 110-degree heat. Men wore cotton drawstring shorts for everyday work. They also had one billowy robe for important ceremonial events. Women wore a bit of cloth wrapped around their waists and generally nothing from there on up. Children younger than ten or eleven wore only the birthday suit God gave them as they entered the world.

I was of course an exception to this; I generally wore a pair of shorts and some plastic sandals that my mother insisted upon, much to my chagrin. The sandals weren't even practical, I tried to tell her; they provided hiding places for scorpions in the night, which you had better remember to knock out before you pushed your foot in the next morning. If you didn't, the bite would strike like a hot iron and put you in agony for the next eight hours. My barefoot friends didn't have to worry about such hazards.

My father wore the same kind of shorts and sandals as I did, except he added a shirt to his fashion ensemble. My mom and sister wore loose-fitting sundresses.

The village stood in silence now as the chief surveyed the scattered clothing. Poking here and there with his cane, he was working to take it all in. Of one thing there was no doubt in anyone's mind. The chief would decide the fate of this bundle. He had the power to reject it or to allow it into his village. Furthermore, whatever he wanted out of that pile, if anything, was his right. He had first choice of anything lying there.

After giving it serious thought and holding up one item and then another, this big dignified African chief settled on his choice: a large-size, frilly, pink negligee! He must have thought it was as close to an official ceremonial robe as the people of the United States had to offer. It took some doing, but he finally managed to slither that thing over his muscular frame, then looked up proudly for the response of his people.

It was the funniest sight I had ever seen, and standing beside my best friend, Alezye, I bit my lip in a desperate attempt to keep from bursting out in laughter. But this was no laughing matter. Instead, like everyone around me, I clapped politely. "Nice choice, Chief!"

He smiled broadly and then gestured for others to choose their "gift." African society is nothing if not structured, so everyone knew the protocol. The next to choose were the men of the village, starting with the oldest. Wanting to be like the chief, the elders of my village selected similar nightgowns, bathrobes, ladies' slips... I watched in horror.

When the men were done, it was the women's turn. By now, only overalls, blue jeans, and heavy flannel work shirts were left. Once the women finished, the children were allowed to pick from the leftovers in the dust. Most wound up with baggy underwear, woolen gloves, and socks. Alezye and I got a lone pair of white socks between us. We each took one. "Twins!" we said smiling.

That evening at the family dinner table, we had a lively discussion about what had transpired in the marketplace that day. The gift from our country had turned into a fiasco. What was to be done? In the end we realized there was no way to salvage this cultural blunder and still preserve the dignity of the chief, or the whole village for that matter. My sister and I were told never to laugh, at least not out loud and never in front of anyone from the village. Whenever the people of our beloved Nielle expressed their gratitude to us for the gift from "our" people in the United States, we forced ourselves to smile sweetly and say, "You are welcome."

It was my mother's daily prayer for the next eighteen months that those clothes would prematurely fall apart as they were beaten on the rocks at the village's riverside "Laundromat." She reasoned that if God could keep the Israelites' clothing from falling apart for forty years in the wilderness, he could certainly use the same divine power in reverse to cause ours to fall apart fast! That is, in fact, what happened. The negligee and other articles mercifully faded, frayed, ripped, and ultimately disintegrated.

We never did learn the origin of that mysterious bale of used clothing. It was about the time of the launch of the Peace Corps and a great American awakening to poverty and suffering in the world. I figure that somewhere today in the United States a pair of wonderful old ladies must be quietly rocking on a country porch. "Mildred," one is saying to the other, "I wonder whatever became of that huge bundle of clothing our town gathered and shipped off to darkest Africa? Wasn't that a wonderful thing we did? I hope they liked everything! I still can't believe you threw in that big ol' pink negligee."

A GENEROUS SPIRIT

Silly though it was, this was my first real moment of pride at being, in some distant way, an American. So that was why my parents insisted we speak English in our home. They wanted us to identify with a place of compassion and generosity. What kind of people cared enough about others all the way across the world to actually "give the shirt off their back"? Now I knew.

At the same time, I was seeing an openhanded spirit every Wednesday among the village people. To wander through the stalls and displays spread out on the ground was to get straight into the heart of the Senufo culture. Generosity was the rule of the day. Poor as everyone was, they weren't about to be accused of being unfair or selfish.

If you bought a pile of anything, it always came with a *cadeau,* a "gift," which meant an extra one thrown in—a baker's dozen. Foodstuffs such as ground cornmeal, millet, and other grains were sold in containers, piled as high as absolutely possible. People seemed to practice the New Testament advice to give "a good measure, pressed down, shaken together and running over" (Luke 6:38). Anything sold by the length was measured precisely with a meter stick—until the last meter. Then the stick was put down, and the merchant stretched out his goods an extra twenty or thirty centimeters beyond what the stick would have required. Buyer and seller looked each other in the eye and nodded with mutual appreciation for each other.

I realize today that in the competitive world of modern business, some would call that foolish. Jesus, on the other hand, would approve any gesture that implies things are not the highest goal in life. He saw right through the barriers that possessions tend to create, putting us into categories of "haves" and "have-nots." He saw straight into the hearts of people in both camps.

His heart broke for those who didn't have enough but also for those who had too much. He understood the poor, their place in God's priorities, and spent a good bit of his ministry efforts in meeting their needs, feeding them, healing them, and comforting them. But he also was comfortable with the rich. He ate in their homes, stayed with them, and even was buried (temporarily) in the tomb of a wealthy man who respected Jesus a great deal.

His message to the poor was comfort. His message to the wealthy was caution.

He defined his primary mandate, his "job description," in his first public opportunity to preach in his hometown synagogue in Nazareth. Of all the scriptures he could have chosen as his text, he selected the surprising passage of Isaiah 61:1–2.

> The Spirit of the Sovereign LORD is on me,
> because the LORD has anointed me
> to preach good news to the poor.

He has sent me to bind up the brokenhearted,
    to proclaim freedom for the captives
    and release from darkness for the prisoners,
to proclaim the year of the LORD's favor.

Then he dropped his bombshell: "Today this scripture is fulfilled in your hearing" (Luke 4:21). Having thus declared his mission and identity, he immediately made clear his heart for the poor, the neglected, the marginalized.

Of course, Jesus also healed the child of a powerful Roman centurion (an enemy of the Jewish people) without batting an eye. He even complimented the man's great faith. On another occasion, however, he spoke very straightforwardly about how the love of money and possessions can enslave one's soul. "It is easier for a camel to go through the eye of a needle than for a rich man to enter the kingdom of God" (Matthew 19:24).

The same point surfaced in the home of another wealthy man named Zacchaeus, a tax collector. After Jesus invited himself to the man's sumptuous abode, Zacchaeus felt confronted with his ill-gotten wealth and that very night vowed to give away half of it to the poor (Luke 19:8).

Yes, it's tough, but the rich and privileged *can* enter the kingdom.

One of my great joys is to travel to the third world with powerful, successful, even wealthy people and to bring them face to face with the other side. Where these two worlds come together, it is often holy ground. It is a quantum leap for many to confront poverty and what it means to their own lives. I hold my breath to see what will happen. They are usually amazed at the warmth, generosity, joy, and even contentment they see in the lives of the poor, especially those who have placed their trust in Jesus.

One of my dear friends, Ken Davis, is a very successful, funny, enthusiastic public speaker. He has often spoken to North American audiences on behalf of Compassion. But he found every excuse in the book to avoid actually going overseas with me to witness poverty firsthand. Finally he reluctantly gave in and traveled with me to Ecuador.

One day in a very poor village accessible only by dugout canoe, we found ourselves in a little mud church north of Guayaquil. In front of us were hundreds of children and their parents. At one point the jungle pastor asked his congregation to stretch out their hands and pray for these visitors who had come from so far.

I stood beside Ken, my arm around his shoulders, as the children rose enthusiastically to their feet and began to pray passionately for us. Their little voices beseeched heaven in unison on our behalf. Ken is a big, strong guy, a macho outdoorsman, a comedian, as American as they come. But as the children's voices rose up, entreating God on our behalf, I felt his shoulders begin to shake.

That night at supper, I said, "Ken, what happened back there? What did you experience at that moment with the children?"

He looked at me with tears welling up in his eyes and said, "Wess, I avoided coming to visit the poor with you for a long time. I was afraid my heart would be broken by their condition. Instead, today, I found my heart broken by *my* condition."

I have seen this kind of powerful impact time and again over the years. When the wealthy and the poor get together, each ends up meeting the desperate needs of the other. Too often Satan achieves his wicked agenda by keeping them apart—geographically and philosophically. The result is that one tends to die in need, the other in greed. But when Jesus brings us together, the genuine needs of both are mysteriously and wonderfully satisfied. In God's amazing economy, the rich and poor need each other, the common message being, "Enough really is...enough!"

WHEN TRIUMPH
IS DISASTER

Eight years before I was born, an American president went before Congress and cast a bold vision. "We look forward to a world founded upon four essential human freedoms," said Franklin D. Roosevelt, who then named them: freedom of speech, freedom of worship, freedom from want, and freedom from fear. Today I feel a similar passion as I issue a Rooseveltian call on behalf of the world's children, whether they be American or any other nationality. God gave us the awesome responsibility to protect them from harm and raise them up to mature and productive adulthood. They are an incredible treasure that must not be left to languish or deteriorate.

In this part of the book I am championing a set of four freedoms, if you will, that every child deserves:

- Freedom from drivenness, time pressure, and hurry (chapter 5)
- Freedom from materialism—the obsession with things (chapter 6)
- Freedom from corrosive competition (this chapter)
- Freedom from daily fear (chapters 8–9)

These are among the most vital gifts we can bestow upon the coming, vulnerable generation. Without them, they will be forever stunted, misshapen, and thrown off stride in attempting to reach their full potential.

WHY COMPETITION?

You may be thinking, *What's wrong with competition? That's the American way! I understand the problems with the other three things you listed, but why is this one included?*

Before you lay down the book in disgust, notice that I qualified the word with the adjective *corrosive*. While striving to do our best is indeed an admirable trait, certain aspects of competition have the ability to undermine and eat away at a child's well-being—a fact not always remembered by some parents, teachers, Little League coaches, and other youth workers. To fully explain what I mean, let me once again employ a global perspective.

In most of the developing world, the concept of winning at the expense of someone else is considered not only strange but unacceptable. You are free to achieve whatever you can—so long as you don't hurt, embarrass, or demean the other person.

I don't recall that our village even had a word in Senari, our tribal language, for *competition*. The concept of achieving personal victory at the expense of another's defeat was not only foreign but, when explained, repulsive. For us the lowest form of social behavior was to withhold from a brother or sister in time of need. To be selfish was among the worst crimes we as children could commit.

The elders lived this out all day long and then taught it to us around the village fires at night. If you were made strong, it was so you could help the weak. If you were courageous, it was so you could protect the frightened. If you had, you gave. The cruelest thing you could have done to me as a child in that village would have been to give me two pieces of candy. I would have looked at them in the palm of my hand and assumed that one piece was intended for me, but what about the other? Surely both were not mine. What would I have done with just one piece of candy to give and twenty friends standing all around me?!

This mind-set is what sustained us all when times were tough. Nobody was rich and far ahead of others, but neither was anyone left behind or forgotten. In the midst of the drought or after the locust plague, everyone had less—sometimes dangerously less—but everyone had something.

This value ran into a serious headwind in the local primary school that our French masters had set up. The colonial education scheme, imported straight from the cobbled streets of Paris, was what educators now call the banking system. The idea was to basically open our little African heads, dump in quantities of largely irrelevant facts (the flora and fauna of France, for example), and then require us each Friday to take exams to see if any of that knowledge had lasted the week. We memorized our lessons, chanting in unison at the top of our voices so all the village could hear. To us, the whole point of schooling seemed to be competition with one another, determining who was the smartest and who was the dumbest.

The teacher posted our class rankings prominently on the classroom door each Monday. But we refused to look at the charts. It just wasn't right! It felt evil to us to elevate some students and humiliate others, and we refused to play along, no matter the consequences. Though we complained to the village elders, they, having never attended school themselves, hesitated to criticize its system or protect us from it.

The teachers were either Frenchmen who for some reason had been banished to this faraway wasteland or Africans of another tribe taught by Frenchmen in the big cities. To impose their will, they took to stalking the aisles between our wooden benches with rawhide switches in hand.

One fateful day Alezana was singled out to stand up and answer a test question. "What is the capital of the United States of America?"

I watched him squirm, then tremble and scratch his head. I knew him well enough to know that next would come tears. My heart went out to him. And of course, I knew the answer. This was, after all, a question about my "home."

As the teacher grabbed his switch and headed for my friend, I leaned over and hissed, "Washington, D.C.!"

Greatly relieved, my little friend stammered, "*Oui*, Washington, D.C.!"

The teacher spun around in his tracks, marched down the aisle to the little white kid, and smacked me hard on the head. As my chin trembled and my eyes filled with tears, I sat up a little taller on my bench. I had done the noble thing, and everyone knew it. Anyone in the room would have done the same for me.

Now with a PhD in education, I realize teachers would call us world-class cheaters. But it felt entirely right to us. As I recall, there was a rapid turnover of teachers in our Nielle Primary School. We children didn't know anything about proper pedagogy, but we knew we would not be forced to compete, to win at the expense of another's loss or humiliation. We had been raised to share with those in distress—candy, food, time, and yes, even answers in the classroom.

Our village was not the only such culture on the planet. During my teenage years, my parents concluded their service in Africa and worked instead among the Navajos in Arizona. There I attended Mingus Union High School in the abandoned copper-mining town of Jerome. I learned that many of the Native American tribes still carry this amazing value in their hearts. Even today, children on the reservations refuse to compete in win-lose spelling bees, for example. They will not wear a gold star they may have earned. Of course, they pay the heavy price of being marginalized by the larger American society, which seems to thrive on competition and advancement of the individual.

WHAT ABOUT SPORTS?

Surely, you may say, the philosophy of sharing must be suspended when it comes to athletics. The very nature of a game is that somebody wins and somebody else loses.

Across the nations of the world, no sport is more competitive than soccer (or football, as it is usually called outside North America). We've all heard the horror stories of entire stadiums erupting in violence. Many world-class arenas are now ringed in concertina wire to keep irate fans from storming the field and attacking officials or members of the opposing team. Referees have been physically threatened for making a "wrong" call.

During a chaotic match of the 1994 World Cup, a twenty-seven-year-old Colombian defender named Andrés Escobar unintentionally made an embarrassing error; he kicked the ball into his own goal. As a result, the United States won that match 2–1, and Colombia was knocked out of the competition in the first round. A Scottish sportswriter said in his column that "the player ought to be shot for making a mistake like that."

Ten days later Escobar was coming out of a bar in a Medellín suburb when a gunman stepped up and murdered him in cold blood on the sidewalk. According to Escobar's girlfriend, the killer shouted *Gol!* ("Goal!")

for each of the twelve bullets fired. It was not clear whether the gunman acted out of his own rage or had been sent by one of the gambling syndicates that had bet large amounts on Colombia's advancing in the World Cup competition.

But all such extremism is not in distant, fanatical lands. Even in small-town America, soccer inflames competitive passions that amaze us. Parents and coaches have had to be physically restrained at times. Little children in shin guards have listened in shock to screaming tirades by their elders, whom they thought they were supposed to look up to.

As I've said, we played soccer in Nielle, too, but with a much different tone. We fully enjoyed the game in a gentle, noncompetitive way. It went like this...

First of all, everyone got to play. You didn't have to be one of the top twenty-two players in the village to get selected. You were free to jump in and play whenever the game found its way to you. Needless to say, no official uniforms or soccer boots were required.

Oh, and did I mention that we didn't really have a field? The whole village was the field. The game raced from courtyard to courtyard like a wild tornado. Women cooking at the evening fire would jump up, giggling and kicking when the game invaded their space, dropping out only if the action wandered far enough that they risked burning their meal. We were very adept at dribbling the ball, and the point of our game was not to defeat another team by scoring more goals than they did. The point rather was excellence and teamwork in ball handling. Thus the games were a cacophony of laughter, barking dogs, squeals of delight, dust, flashing feet, and a ball gone mad.

Actually, to be honest with you, we didn't have a ball. At least not one of those official black-and-white checkered ones. The leathery sphere we kicked around was...chicken guts! Yes, somewhere deep in the anatomy of the chicken are three intestinal tubes that come together in a central chamber. If you tie off two of these tubes and blow air into the third, you can inflate this chamber into a usable soccer-sized "ball."

Whenever a chicken was butchered for food, we children salvaged this prized bit of sporting equipment. Of course, we had to hang it from a branch for a couple of days so it could dry in the tropical sun. But the final product served us well.

Come to think of it, there *was* some pretty fierce competition in the midst of our soccer games—from the village dogs. They loved the smell and taste of our soccer balls and would dash in amid our thrashing feet, at great personal risk, to seize it for themselves. There would be a brown blur in the dust, followed by a muffled *pffft*. Suddenly the game would stop, and all of us would stare in dismay at a shamefaced dog with our limp, pathetic ball hanging from its mouth.

It may have been my imagination, but it seemed right then that every chicken in the village beat a hasty retreat, not eager to become our next Spalding. Of course, chicken was a common dish in the Senufo cuisine, so we always had a ready supply of replacement balls handy.

If in the midst of our scuffling, someone got hurt—stubbed a toe or twisted an ankle—the game stopped immediately. As the injured child cried, we would sit in the dust, hold the child close, and cry with him. I can still remember how badly I hurt when one of my friends was hurt. I felt his pain and wept for him as surely as I would have for myself. Nobody was glad that an "opponent" would have to leave the game. These weren't our opponents; they were our beloved friends.

Years later and far away from my village, I learned the name of the feeling that gripped our hearts when another suffered. It was *compassion*. This feeling swirled in the dust of our games, hung in the air of our classrooms, embodied our gifts to one another, and shaped our hearts.

The English word *compassion* is actually very similar to *competition*, isn't it? But they are miles apart in meaning. In the heart of my village, there was room for only one.

Long Afternoons at the Stone Wall

After winning reelection to a second term as president in November 1864, Abraham Lincoln said, "It is no pleasure to me to triumph over anyone."[1] While we have raised the value of success, we have intermingled a toxic habit of gloating over the inferiority of others, which has soured the whole mixture. We have taught children not to worry about how the other side feels. Just slam full speed ahead and keep your eye on the scoreboard. As famed Green Bay Packers coach Vince Lombardi taught us all, "Winning isn't the main thing. It's the only thing."

A few brave souls have dared to question this ethic and taken ridicule for it. One was American author (and World War II combat pilot) George B. Leonard, who wrote in an oft-reprinted essay:

> The final argument for hot competition all the way down to nursery
> school is that competition makes winners. The argument is, at best,
> half true. It makes nonwinners, too—generally more nonwinners
> than winners. And a number of studies indicate that losing can
> become a lifelong habit.[2]

I learned early what it felt like to be a nonwinner, because not all my soccer was played in Nielle. My parents thought, for good reason, that my schoolwork should be in English rather than French, so at the tender age of six I was packed off to a mission boarding school some 750 miles away. I will write more about this arena of my life in the next chapter. But for now, let me summarize by saying that my greatest childhood challenge was trying to figure out who I really was, what was right and what was wrong, while dividing my young life between these dramatically clashing cultures. The boarding school owned my soul for nine months of each year; the village nurtured me the remaining three.

I had a lot of time to think about that at boarding school as I sat on the stone wall beneath the nedebean tree afternoon after afternoon, watching the daily soccer matches. I say "watching," because it was very important there that only the best players got to play. There were as many as eighty missionary children from across West Africa attending that school, but on any given day, just twenty-two lucky and gifted ones (eleven on each team) were chosen to actually compete. The rest of us watched, wished, and waited for our day to come.

The selection process each day was a dagger to the spirit of all but the chosen few. Two of the oldest boys, team captains, would stand apart from the stone wall of hopeful children, scrutinizing their options. The best were selected first, the same individuals day after day. These then served as consultants to the captains on the remaining selections. *Wesley—do we want Wesley? Nah, he can't kick hard enough. Look at his canary legs! Stevie? No, he's a crybaby. Sally? Forget it. Let's take Jim.* Jim would grin and stride forward victoriously.

The hardest part was not to cry. Though my heart was breaking, I knew it would be the kiss of death to shed a tear. I would look away, roll my eyes, pretend to wipe my nose. Inside, my spirit was being shredded. Player by player, the teams were filled, and they would sprint away joyfully to play soccer as the rest of us climbed the stone wall to watch…again.

Besides the choice of players, there were other differences between this game and Nielle's. The game was strictly confined to a rectangular playing field about a hundred meters by fifty meters. For some reason I couldn't comprehend, it was very, very important that all playing happen within that space. It had whitewashed boundary lines, and if a ball was kicked one millimeter outside that line, no matter how well kicked, it was called out. Oh, the arguments and fistfights that broke out over millimeters in the dust! Apparently, it was so very important that honesty was temporarily pushed aside. We couldn't trust ourselves to tell the truth about such things, so referees and linesmen had to make such decisions for us.

I also learned that *time* was of utmost importance in boarding school soccer games. I don't mean the sun was about to set, making it too dark to play. No, I mean such questions as, was that goal scored one split second before the halftime whistle or just as the whistle sounded? The game was configured precisely into ninety minutes, and each of those into sixty seconds of immeasurable worth.

All this was so very important, I learned, because the whole point was to kick the ball through the other team's goalposts more often than they kicked it through yours. That calculation, after ninety minutes (or more importantly, fifty-four hundred seconds) made "winners" and "losers." The victory cheers and jeers of one team drowned out the tears of those who went down in defeat each afternoon. Being the guy who scored the most goals was the ultimate prize. It often got you carried off the field on your cheering teammates' shoulders like a conquering Roman hero. It surely got you picked early in the process for tomorrow's game.

Of course, not everything about this soccer was bad. One vastly superior aspect to village soccer was…the ball! It was actually round. It rolled in a straight line. It went far when kicked hard. Perhaps its greatest feature was that dogs were afraid of it! My, how they yelped when struck by a foul ball. Needless to say, chickens had no part in our games.

It didn't take me long to realize that something else was vastly different about this soccer. The point was to win at any cost. If you were dribbling the ball toward the goal, and the player guarding you stumbled and fell, that was not something to be concerned about. Hurt? Tough luck for him! That was your opportunity to be the hero. Don't stop! Go, dribble around him, and score the goal. Amid the wild celebration for your victorious moment, the fact that someone got hurt in the process meant nothing. Forget him; he was on the opposing team, anyway!

The memory of my village friends comforting a fallen opponent seemed far away. Though it never left my heart, I kept silent about it in this setting.

THE LITTLE ERASER

As you look at the life of Christ, can you find an instance when he competed with anybody for anything? I can't. His goal was faithfulness to his calling, his battle was strictly against Satan, and he refused to put ordinary humans in that category. The only exception might be his harsh words toward pretentious hypocrites; he did say once, "You belong to your father, the devil" (John 8:44).

But he certainly never trivialized the situation by labeling certain individuals his "opponents" for self-serving reasons. Instead, he viewed all of humanity as "sheep without a shepherd" (Matthew 9:36), those he had come "to seek and to save" (Luke 19:10). When his disciples showed a competitive spirit against someone else who was battling the powers of darkness, Jesus immediately rebuked them (Luke 9:50).

Our Western society is driven primarily by a sense of competition. We are bent on outperforming, outachieving, and outplaying the other person. Three theologians based in Washington, D.C., once worked together on a book on compassion and, as part of their research, went to visit the well-known Hubert H. Humphrey near the end of his life in 1978. They asked him about compassion in politics.

> We felt he was one of the most caring human beings in the political arena. The Senator…was visibly caught off guard…. Instinctively, he left his large mahogany desk, over which hung the emblem reminding visitors that they were speaking with the former Vice-President of the United States, and joined us around a small coffee table. But then, after having adapted himself to the somewhat unusual situation, Senator Humphrey walked back to his desk, picked up a long pencil with a small eraser at its end, and said in his famous high-pitched voice: "Gentlemen, look at this pencil. Just as the eraser is only a very small part of this pencil and is used only when you make a mistake, so compassion is only called upon when things get out of hand. The main part of life is competition; only the eraser is compassion. It is sad to say, gentlemen, but in politics compassion is just part of the competition."[3]

Jesus, on the other hand, held all kinds of upside-down viewpoints. He said, "Blessed are the poor in spirit, for theirs is the kingdom of heaven" (Matthew 5:3). He said the first would come in last, and the last come in first (Matthew 20:16). The weak are considered strong, and the strong considered vulnerable (1 Corinthians 1:27–29). The poor are rich, and the rich are poor (Revelation 3:17–18). The humble are exalted, and the proud are brought down (Luke 1:52–53).

And this is where our citizenship lies! This is our true culture, our home. This world is but a brief and temporary campsite. If the flow of our present society is to hurt each other, to beat each other, to vanquish each other, what's the solution? Do we just hurt each other as little as possible?

No, this is not enough, either for us or our children. We have to be compassionate as our heavenly Father is compassionate. This means being courageously and radically different in the midst of society. It means going against the win-at-any-cost mentality.

Again, let me be clear: I am not for mediocrity. God's kingdom deserves *excellence*. It just doesn't need the *conquest* of anyone except Satan. Competition has its place in society and even in sports. But its most noble, and perhaps only proper, role is to serve as a motivation for excellence. Striving to do anything we do to the very best of our ability is a worthy goal.

Competition turns corrosive when it includes the humiliation of one's rivals, who are also just trying to achieve their best performance. The very best athletes understand this distinction deep in their souls and often demonstrate it in postgame interviews. They don't gloat or denigrate their opponents. They usually talk about being satisfied with their own performance or disappointed that they didn't do as well as they had hoped and trained for. They don't make excuses, blame the officiating, or fault their teammates. The high-level competition has served primarily to enable them to compete against themselves, to measure their personal best.

Without a doubt, one of the epicenters of competition has to be Centre Court at Wimbledon. There every summer the top tennis players of the world compete for that sport's highest glory. Under the scrutiny of a global television audience that hears every grunt, analyzes every line call, and evaluates every stroke in slow-motion replay, the pressure of competition is intense. It's terribly lonely out there. Even the players' coaches are supposed to remain mute, distant, and removed. This is a temple to competitive agony and ecstasy.

The true heart of Wimbledon is etched in the archway over the door that leads to Centre Court. It is the very last thing the players see—if they look up—before they step onto that manicured grass to compete for the holy grail before a global cloud of witnesses. The powerful words come from the poem "If" by Rudyard Kipling:

> If you can meet with Triumph and Disaster
> And treat those two imposters just the same...
> Yours is the Earth and everything that's in it,
> And—which is more—you'll be a Man, my son!

That's a pretty high standard, and judging from some of the outrageous antics we've seen not thirty feet from that etching, some players didn't get it. But Kipling was quite in line with the much earlier words of the apostle Paul, who wrote in several letters about running the race and fighting the good fight. This man, though arguably the most qualified of the early church leaders in every way (heritage, education, position, leadership, eloquence, and writing skill), referred to himself as "the least of the apostles" (1 Corinthians 15:9). He began several of his epistles, "Paul, a servant of the Lord Jesus Christ." That doesn't really sound like a gold-medal kind of guy! Clearly, he understood the proper place of competition.

In the waning years of his life, Paul wrote to his young disciple, Timothy: "I have fought the good fight, I have finished the race, I have kept the faith" (2 Timothy 4:7). He looked forward to "the crown of righteousness, which the Lord, the righteous Judge, will award to me on that day," and ever the gracious competitor, he quickly added, "and not only to me, but also to *all* who have longed for his appearing" (verse 8). Again, competition was not for its own sake; it was to lead one toward faithfulness and excellence.

WHAT ABOUT HERE AND NOW?

I can hear you thinking, *Yes, but I live in twenty-first-century North America. Get real! How is this supposed to work in my cutthroat job, in my university, or on my child's baseball diamond? I can't just pick up the family and move to Nielle, you know.*

Yes, indeed. Let me tell you one more story. Sorry, it's about soccer again, but it could have been any sport.

When my daughter Jenny was in third grade, I volunteered to coach her Parks and Recreation Department team. There's nothing more Americana than a children's soccer game on a warm Saturday in a city park.

I had witnessed a good many disasters on our town's soccer fields over the years—angry coaches, frustrated parents, frightened children—all in pursuit of the big trophy at the end of the season. I determined that if I was going to invest the time to do this, I would do it differently—a kind of child-friendly soccer, if you can imagine.

Word had leaked out among the parents that the new soccer coach really knew his stuff. He had grown up in Africa playing soccer, played college ball, and even played on a German team while serving in the army. This was the year! Their kids were going to "kick some serious butt," they said.

I will never forget their faces at the first meeting as they went from delighted anticipation to bewildered shock. I told them that if this team's win-loss record really mattered to them, if winning the big trophy was their goal, they were going to be seriously frustrated with me as their kids' soccer coach. "I will consider myself and this team a success if they learn to love this game, play it well, and sign up to play again next year. Those are my goals. In fact, I won't know if I've been successful or not until this time next year!"

They sat in stone-cold silence. I suggested that if any felt inclined, it might not be too late to get their children switched to a different team. More silence. The meeting ended on an underwhelming note. After all, the kids had already decided to name themselves the "Mighty Hornets." " 'Cause we're gonna *sting 'em!*" was the boast.

At our first practice, I had the children scrimmage a bit so I could get a feel for what they knew and what they could do. It was not a pretty sight. I then announced to the kids that I didn't know how well we would do that weekend in the first game, but I was sure of one thing. We were going to do something *perfectly*! I decided to start with one of the most fundamental soccer skills, throwing the ball back into play when it rolls out of bounds. I had witnessed dozens of turnovers as teams lost possession of the ball just because the children lifted one foot or stepped over the line or didn't use both hands. We practiced other things that week, but we really focused on the one skill of throw-ins.

Saturday came. My little team appeared, eyes shining with anticipation above clean new uniforms. Moms had brought cameras, younger siblings, and enough orange slices for the after-game snack to feed the entire county. Dads assembled along the sideline, arms folded, full of expectation. I reminded my canary-legged little band, "No matter what, we are going to do one thing right. Right?"

My little Hornets got swarmed, and the score against them mounted quickly. But at halftime, I talked of nothing but how well we were throwing the ball in. The second half was much the same, and at the final whistle, the scoreboard read 9–0. A deflated bunch of pint-sized players walked slowly to the sideline. To their surprise, they were met by a wildly exuberant coach. He was cheering, giving high-fives, and practically dancing because he couldn't contain his joy. "You did it!" I shouted. "It was perfect! Not one! Not a single bad throw-in! I am so proud of you!" I was hoping that the silence of the parents gathered behind me wasn't the calm before the storm.

The next week we added another foundational skill—how to play and stay in one's position on the field. The supreme frustration of every children's soccer coach in the world is the same—"beehive soccer." No matter where the ball rolls, all the children pursue it like a swarm of hungry bees (in our case, hornets!). It's a fruitless spectacle of pushing and kicking (mostly shins, not the ball), producing mainly tears and bruises.

I made a plywood model of a soccer field and, using little toy players, taught my team all week exactly where each player should be under what game circumstances. We practiced it on the field, and we were ready for Saturday.

Again I reminded the children that success on this game day would be just one thing—playing our positions, no matter what! And, oh yes, doing perfect throw-ins, the same as last week. As you can imagine, this game's results were close to a déjà vu of the previous week. Playing our positions gave us a bit more of an advantage than before, and the score reflected it: 7–2.

The children didn't know what to expect as they shuffled off the field, shoulders slumped and heads down. "Wow, oh wow!" exclaimed the jubilant coach. "You did it! I am so proud of you! A perfect game! You played your positions and never missed a throw-in!" I turned to the astonished mothers and hollered, "Two candy bars for everyone! Your kids are winners!"

As the two-month season progressed, I doggedly stayed the course. Every week was a chance to master a new soccer skill—passing, heading, dribbling. I refused to let the kids talk about scores or winning. They began to relax and get the idea. Our practices became fun as we wildly cheered each other on and *learned* the game.

I always insisted that every child play in every game. Fathers went crazy when, despite a close score, I would send in a small, fragile girl to replace our biggest and best kicker, an Egyptian boy named Muutez. Going further, I also made sure every child had a chance to play every position before the season was over.

With all of my "innovative" ideas, I probably need not tell you that we arrived at the final game with a season win-loss record of 0–7. "Mighty Hornets?" I heard one father moan. "When are *we* going to do the stinging?"

The skill I preached that final week of practice was "Shoot the ball." If a player was in a position to kick the ball into the goal, I insisted he or she take the shot. Not one more pass, not a moment of hesitation—if you've got the shot, take it! And, of course, we needed to keep doing perfect throw-ins, staying in position, proper passes, headers, and all the other stuff they now knew so well.

Unfortunately, our final game was against the very best team in the league. The Warriors had never lost. We arrived at the field on game day and looked across at the opposition. We felt like the Israelites must have felt as they looked across the valley at the mammoth Philistines back in David's day. My intimidated little Hornets had already conceded defeat. I could see it in their eyes. "Forget about the score," I admonished them. "We've come here to do just one thing. What are we going to do perfectly today, no matter what?"

Resigned to their fate, they chanted in a meek monotone, "Shoot the ball; take the shot."

"Let's do it!" I cheered.

My little band of soccer stars went out and did all the stuff they had learned, including shooting the ball. At the halftime whistle, we were leading 3–2. The kids came off the field with a dazed look of "What have we done?" Parents' voices had long since gone hoarse in their wild glee, so they were champing down on the orange slices themselves.

Determined not to give in to temptation just because "victory" was staring us in the face, I disciplined myself not to talk about the score. I cheered them on in their superb job of taking every shot.

Back they ran to the field of play and executed the second half the same way. Across the field I could hear the other team's coach, beet-red angry, yelling at his kids and imploring the parents to "make 'em do something." The seconds ticked by in agonizing slow motion. I looked up just to make sure the sun hadn't actually stood still, as it did for Joshua. Finally the whistle blew. The scoreboard blinked out the verdict in indisputable certainty: Mighty Hornets 9, Warriors 8!

I walked to midfield to shake the Warrior coach's hand. He had a bewildered, dazed look on his face. "What the heck happened out there?" he stammered.

I shrugged as if I, too, couldn't figure it out. I wasn't sure he'd understand.

"Well, congratulations…I guess," he offered and stumbled off shaking his head, muttering something about voodoo. I just smiled. It kinda *was* magic!

Meanwhile, my team gathered on the sideline in wide-eyed wonder. "We won? We won!" For some it was an exclamation; for others, it seemed more a question. Doggedly sticking to my guns, I said nothing of the score victory but gushed with praise instead that my little team had played a perfect game. They had shot the ball, taken the shot!

The celebration party that evening was a thing to behold, a true Cinderella story. These sorts of things happen only in the movies, don't they? Before the season began, before I knew if we would win a single game, I had purchased individual trophies for every player on the team. I made sure they were of the same design as the big trophy the Parks and Recreation Department would award to the winning team. In my book every one of my little Hornets was a winner.

I finally admitted to them in my farewell speech that I loved to win just as much as anyone. "We knew it!" the children cheered. Fathers gave me silent, respectful nods, while mothers could not hug me hard enough.

My last questions that night for the little winners were these: "Do you love soccer? Are you going to play again next year?" The resounding cheer sent me home victorious.

I know this story sounds unreal, like something from Disney, but it is absolutely true. Remember my best kicker, Muutez? His family owned a sandwich shop in our local mall. For a decade afterward, I couldn't walk through the food court without their calling me over for a free roast-beef sandwich. They would tell anyone who happened to be standing there innocently buying a sandwich that I was "the best coach Muutez ever had." Muutez went on to become a high-school soccer star and then was awarded a college soccer scholarship. I like to think I had at least a little something to do with his developing not only a love for playing the game but a healthy respect for mastering the basics that evolved into his achieving excellence. If he has those, I won't mind if he focuses a little more intently on the scoreboard than I did.

What's my point? That there is victory beyond the victory on the scoreboard. We can all compete, but we shouldn't make it an end in itself. Realize it is a journey. Competition should be our servant, a mere tool to drive us toward excellence.

When your children, grandchildren, or the children around you experience success, acknowledge the victory with great joy and tell them how proud you are. But more important, in a quiet moment talk to them of the courage, determination, hard work, sacrifice, integrity, and character it took to achieve that victory. When you attend a school play, be the first one on your feet to lead the standing ovation even if lines have been forgotten or props have collapsed. Reward the effort, not the score. Whenever children do their best, cheer! Whenever they fail, pick them up.

Any failure includes some measure of success, and every failure can be turned into a success. Teach the children around you the delicate balance life requires between competition and compassion. Let them know that real victory lies in courageously treating Triumph and Disaster just the same.

8

THE SILENCE OF THE LAMBS

I have a confession to make.

What I have told you so far about my growing-up years in Africa has been entirely true—but not the whole story. Most of the previous chapters have been drawn from the periods I spent in the village with my parents. Unfortunately, those wonderful times were only three months of each year, from mid-December to mid-March. The other nine months of the year, my sister and I were 750 miles away at boarding school—a much different scene, to which now I turn your attention.

Until recent years even my wife and children knew very little about those dark days. For decades as an adult, I could not fit that painful piece of the puzzle into the mosaic of my life. So I simply tried to bury it in the grave of "The Past," and though it continued to haunt me, I spoke of it to almost nobody.

But there's a compelling reason for me to write about it here. It will take me some additional space to set the picture. I hope you will stick with me as I develop this theme.

We had come to Africa, like all missionary families, knowing that sacrifices would be required. We knew in advance that our particular mission had a policy for all school-age children to be dispatched to a boarding school operated by a sister denomination in order to receive "a good American education." The village school in Nielle was fine for me to visit with my friends, but the instruction was in French.

Some other mission groups, we heard, did allow their field families to do homeschooling, a novel and somewhat suspect concept at the time. But in our mission, there was no such alternative. The dads would load up the children into a convoy of pickup trucks each March and drive them for

days on rutted roads to a facility that I shall, in this book, call Bandulo
Christian Academy. There we would live and study for the next nine months
straight. We got a ten-day semester break in late July–early August, but it
was not feasible to go home, given the travel difficulties during the rainy
season.

I am sure this may sound extreme in the early twenty-first century, but
fifty years ago this separation was willingly accepted as necessary to the
cause. Taking the gospel to the far corners of the earth was the urgent need
of the hour, now that World War II had ended and peace prevailed. However, the winds of African nationalism were stirring, and the colonial he-
gemony might soon be overthrown. We had to work fast while conditions
permitted.

After all, hadn't Jesus promised, "Everyone who has left houses or
brothers or sisters or father or mother *or children* or fields for my sake will
receive a hundred times as much and will inherit eternal life" (Matthew
19:29)? Yes, it was a painful price to pay, but these missionary pioneers did
not flinch. They knew that *their* predecessors in the late eighteen hundreds
had faced even worse. The average tenure of a Western missionary to Africa
in those days, it was said, was less than one year, due to the ravages of
malaria, cholera, typhoid, and yellow fever. With clear-eyed realism some
of them packed their goods for the voyage not in crates or barrels but in
the steel confines of *their own caskets*. Odds were high that the caskets
would be needed.

My parents in the 1950s were not nearly so pessimistic, of course. But
both of them had experienced dramatic calls to missionary service, and
nothing would deter them from pursuing that work. They and their colleagues were passionate to do God's bidding. The worst thing they could
imagine would be to falter in their efforts.

The Bandulo campus to which my sister Carol and I were taken was
pleasant enough, situated in the jungle on a slope amid rolling green hills
with mango and guava trees that were home to monkeys and all manner of
interesting birds. Lizards scampered along the steps, but we didn't mind;
most of us loved the African outdoors already. There were teetertotters, a
merry-go-round, and a small swimming pool with a diving board for relief

from the tropical heat. A train chugged along through the nearby valley, and on the far horizon was Sugar Loaf Mountain to add drama to the landscape.

We students—thirty-five of us when I first arrived, and more as the years went on—were housed two to a room, the boys in one long wing of the dormitory, the girls in the other. I was only six years old when I came to Bandulo for first grade; Carol was two years ahead of me. At such tender ages, saying good-bye to our dad that day was excruciating; we cried and clung to his neck. The houseparents, a rather stern couple I shall refer to as Mr. and Mrs. Staber, waited nearby. To relieve the trauma, they told him, "It will be okay, Ken; don't worry. Once the parents leave, we find that the children settle in quickly and get along fine."

RULES AND RULERS

What none of us knew in the beginning was that Bandulo was a place of rigid control and fearsome consequences. To be fair, I must say that it had its happy moments—bike rides and picnics—but those were far outweighed by its repression. I quickly found this out as classes began. We had school in three rooms: one for the first through third grades, one for fourth through sixth grades, and a third for the "big kids" in seventh through ninth grades. The teachers rotated their attention—one hour teaching us first graders, the next the second graders, then the third graders. By the time I got to third grade, I had already heard the content of those lessons twice, which made third grade easy. But then, of course the next year would be a total surprise, with brand-new material and concepts.

Misbehavior was dealt with severely; we didn't just get our hands smacked with a ruler but with the *edge* of the ruler, which was far more painful. The privilege of going to the bathroom was dealt out judiciously. We had to raise our hands, forming a circle with our thumb and forefinger; I think it stood for *o* (outside) since the restroom was out at one end of the veranda. If the teacher was particularly unhappy with you for any reason, this privilege could be denied for a painfully long time. More than once I found myself debating, *Do I wait until my bladder explodes, or give up and wet my pants, which will bring a beating on my bare legs?* Sitting in a puddle of urine, waiting to be discovered and beaten, was a terrifying but common memory for many.

I quickly came to cherish any time, however brief, that I could be out of the classroom. I would gaze out the window across the little jungle valley toward a vine-covered hill with a flat-rock surface on its eastern side. By midmorning, the chimpanzees, baboons, red monkeys, and gray ones would gather there to sun themselves, which is why we students called it Monkey Rock. They would come quietly one by one, and in time they would begin to chirp and chatter.

Then a screech would cut the air. Some larger animal would want the space of a smaller one, and an outbreak of barks, howls, and squeals would crescendo into a clamor of fighting beasts. It would quickly get so loud that you couldn't hear what the teacher was saying just a few feet away.

Miss Long, my first-grade teacher, would stand up abruptly, walk out onto the porch, and scream at the top of her lungs. Word was that in the "good old days" teachers used to get a pistol out of their desk drawers, go out on the veranda, and fire a shot into the air. Either way, the sudden dominant sound of the angry member of the *Homo sapiens* species on the porch would outrank the biggest baboon and quiet the pack of monkeys— for a while, anyway. When the crescendo from the jungle built again, the whole scene was repeated as often as needed. I loved the whole ballet and was always rooting for the monkeys!

We learned to read from the old Dick and Jane books. These bubbly, nice, white, suburban children had wonderful parents, loved their little sister, Sally, their cat, Puff, and their dog, Spot. It fueled our dreams that America was the place to be. Actually, it gave me hope that at least somewhere in the world, little boys and girls got to stay with their parents, who were kind and cared for them. I knew this was going on in Nielle, but among white children? Nobody cried in these books; nobody got hit; teachers were kind as well as pretty; arguments were always resolved fairly... My, what a place.

As the weeks wore on, my spirit sank lower and lower. I developed a slurred speech pattern in the presence of adults; too frightened to speak, I began to talk without moving my lips. With children, I was fine, but otherwise I just looked down to the ground, murmured my words softly, and hoped the moment would pass without the infliction of pain. I also wrote that way. My penmanship was a flat line, a tiny squiggle of vague letters, with minimal peaks and valleys. Above the blackboard were placards of exactly how letters were to be formed and connected in cursive style. I could copy those letters on a paper, but when I had to use them to write a sentence or express a thought, I reverted to my vague, blurred penmanship.

I clearly remember hearing one of the first really big words I couldn't understand. It happened one morning when Miss Long must have reached her limit with my manner of both speaking and writing. I was in the dreaded situation of being singled out in front of the class to face her. I was trying to express myself when she grabbed the front of my shirt, picked me up off the ground, and screamed into my face, "*Enunciate,* you little idiot!"

I can still hear the screeching of her voice and feel her breath on my face and the stranglehold on my neck. My classmates sat petrified. She finally dropped me to the floor again. I stumbled back to my seat, choking back the tears, sat down, and wet my pants. What she didn't recognize was that my spirit had been so destroyed I didn't think anything I might have to say mattered to anyone. I didn't think anyone cared what I wrote with my trembling hand. Whenever I tried to be understood by an adult, it resulted only in pain and humiliation. I was a little animal, frightened and wanting only to survive.

I endured such treatment only by the grace of God and the care and kindness of the other children. Years later, after earning a master's degree in communications, developing a deep radio voice, and even creating a daily radio program, *Speak Up with Compassion,* which is now heard all across America, I couldn't help but think, *There you go, Miss Long. Are you happy now? Your "little idiot" makes his living* enunciating.

While my voice has recovered from the early intimidation, I must admit that my penmanship never did. To this day, my tiny scrawl is a challenge to everyone, from my wife to my administrative assistant to friends and colleagues. I'm sure a handwriting analyst would have a field day interpreting my neuroses from the constricted way I write.

The Bad News List

Within a year or two, I had concluded that school was something to escape as soon as possible. I knew I was doomed to stay there through the ninth grade—but after that, I would do my best to break free of this torment. Even along the way, I found various ways to disrupt the process.

With my love of animal life, I wasted no time learning about the rare but highly prized Saint Joe ant. These huge, black creatures, nearly an inch in length, have the unique characteristic of stinking to high heaven whenever they are killed. If one meandered into the room and came within reach of my outstretched foot, I would seize the opportunity to bless the whole class. I would smash the stinker, scrape him toward me so as to hide his carcass…and wait.

Within a minute the room would be filled with a terrible stench. The teacher would whirl around from the blackboard. "Okay, who killed the Saint Joe?" No one would volunteer, of course, so she would have to capitulate. "Everyone outside!"

Ah, my prayer was answered. We would dash outdoors, and the class would eventually resume with all of us sitting comfortably under the trees in my idea of paradise. Every one of my classmates knew I was the killer, of course, but they never told on me since what I did, at great personal risk, was a service to us all.

I was an energetic boy who loved being active. One day I ran and jumped off a stone wall maybe three feet high to catch a tree limb, and because it was wet from a rainstorm, my hand slipped. I fell to the ground, breaking my arm. In spite of the pain, my greater concern was that I knew I was in enormous trouble when I looked down at my muddy "school clothes." How would I ever explain this to Mrs. Staber?

I managed to hide that my arm was broken until my sister (future nurse that she was) saw my pain and insisted I report myself to the school nurse. That night a plaster cast was applied, and then I was spanked because I had done this acrobatic feat in my school clothes. I guess breaking my arm wasn't punishment enough for the crime.

The discipline system was actually quite elaborate, culminating each day after lunch with something entitled the Bad News List. While we were in class, Mr. and Mrs. Staber or some other designated adult would inspect all of the children's rooms. It didn't really matter that some of us were just six years old; the rooms had to be immaculate. The cubbyholes of our little dressers could have no hint of dust. We had to make our beds with absolutely no wrinkles, even if our short little arms could not reach the far side along the wall. Rugs had to be straight and all clothing put away either in the dirty-clothes bin or stacked, military style, in our cupboards.

With the end of lunch, a bell was rung. Mr. Staber would smirk and say with great satisfaction, "And now the Bad News List." I can still feel my stomach churn as I type these words. He would lean back in his chair and begin to read out the names of each little offender that morning, maybe ten to fifteen of us on an average day.

"Wesley Stafford! Pair of socks under the bed, a wrinkled rug, and a dusty top left cubbyhole." My heart would sink. I could do the awful math. A pair of socks was two items; therefore two swats awaited me. A wrinkled rug was mercifully just one, as was the huge infraction of a bit of dust in my dresser. Total for the day: four hits.

When he came to the end of the Bad News List, another bell rang, and there was the deafening scrape of metal chairs on the concrete floor as the escapees gratefully scampered away, dismissed for noon rest. We criminals, already in tears of terror, remained behind to line up outside the house-parents' central room. Mrs. Staber would open the door just as the previous child fled shrieking and crying out the door on the other side of the room. Stomach churning, I would enter. There stood this huge man with today's weapon of choice in his right hand. It could be the thick leather belt or else the ominous rubber slipper made from a truck-tire tread.

Like Judgment Day, my charges were read again to me. Then "Bend over," he would hiss.

"Please, no, Mr. Staber, no…pleeeease."

He would grab me and push me over the footboard of his bed or else make me grab my ankles so my shorts would be tight against my skin. Then…*wham!* The first blow hurt the most and sent a shock of sudden pain all the way through my little body.

Wham! The second took the pain to a threshold beyond bearable. Only the bravest could ward off an outburst of tears.

Wham! The third mysteriously went from physical to something akin to spiritual. I was already enduring more pain than my spirit could bear, and I felt a sob catch in my throat. What overwhelmed me at this point was the panic that I was totally helpless in the hands of a monster.

Wham! The fourth blow could usually reduce me to sobs that convulsed me so deeply I couldn't catch my breath. Now the hurt was deep within.

I felt violated, vulnerable, and overwhelmed by a grief I still cannot explain. Even now, I have to stop writing until my tears subside… What the Stabers couldn't or wouldn't understand was that such beatings were far more than mere physical torture. They destroyed our very souls. And it happened day after day, indeed, year after tragic year.

In telling this story, I do not mean to imply that judicious spanking is out of bounds; some strong-willed children may require this method. But never should an adult undertake this while angry. And there is absolutely no excuse for leaving welts or breaking the skin, as happened frequently at Bandulo. I don't even use the term *spanking* for what they did to us. It was straight-out vicious, vindictive beating.

Once released, I would struggle to stand upright again. My legs and feet could hardly muster the will to move. But in a short while I would propel myself through their curtain doorway into the hall and go sobbing to my room. I usually threw myself in despair onto my bed, there to stifle my screams with my pillow, a pathetic effort to extinguish the anguish of my spirit. *Oh, Jesus, have mercy!* I often cried out in a muffled voice.

In a few minutes I would hear the pleadings and screams of my friends who came after me on the list. The hall became a jumble of shrieks, pleas, cracks of the belt, and wailing children. Those who luckily hadn't made today's Bad News List wept for those who had.

The next phase of the macabre dance was equally dangerous for us all. Sleepy or not, for the next hour of noon rest you dared not make a sound or even be caught with your eyes open. To meet the gaze of a prowling adult meant only one thing: another beating. This one had no scientific limit on the number of blows. It depended on who you were, how much revenge the adult wanted to heap on you, and how long it took you to burst into tears or cry out for mercy.

Some of the older boys tried to withhold showing pain at the whippings. Blow after blow they held their cry in silent defiance at the cruelty. We little ones, on the other hand, shrieked with fear and cried out before the first blow was struck. "No, no, no, please, Mrs. Staber. Please, please!" we would sob. *Smack, smack, smack* would go the rubber slipper or belt.

Brothers and sisters knew the distinct cries of their siblings and, though in separate hallways, would sob aloud on each other's behalf. Carol knew my cry and shed many, many tears every week for her little brother.

Nothing angered the houseparents patrolling the hallways more than when some child, overwhelmed by the hurt of a friend, would slip out of his own doorway after the danger had passed and cross the hall to give comfort. This was a frequent offense for me and resulted in many of my beatings. The adults knew my tender heart and my inclination to go comfort a buddy. Mr. Staber delighted in doubling back on his hallway patrols, knowing he could catch me at this.

Little did he know that the little boy he was beating was the future president of an international ministry called—of all things—Compassion.

REIGN OF TERROR

Other infractions included arriving late at the dining room, arriving late after the shower bell had sounded, not eating all your food, eating your food too fast. The potential crimes were legion. By the time I got to third grade, I put my newly gained math skills to work quantifying how much beating was going on. We were being taught how to figure averages, so for several weeks I kept a secret chart that tallied my corporal punishment. *Shall I keep track of how many blows I receive,* I said to myself, *or just how many times it happens?* Trying to make the math easier, I decided to mark down just the occasions. After several weeks I did the sad calculation and found I had been beaten an average of seventeen times per week.

Was I just a really terrible little boy? What about the other children?

How did their math problems come out? I didn't know, but I was aware of others who were getting punished as frequently as I. Even if others got only half as many blows as I did, the total reckoning of child cruelty and abuse was still staggering.

One time a mason patched a piece of wall in the boys' bathroom, leaving a wet surface maybe a foot across. When supper ended that day, Mr. Staber solemnly marched all us boys down to the bathroom wall. Horror of horrors, there were three distinct fingerprints in the cement.

He lined us up and demanded to know which of us had touched that wall. We were all terrified; nobody would confess. We all shook our heads. "Not me. I didn't do it, Mr. Staber. Honest," we proclaimed.

"Okay," he announced, "nobody plays outside again until we find the culprit. Find out who did this." With that, he spun on his heel and walked away, leaving us stunned.

Soon the older boys began to run a kangaroo court. "All right, 'fess up!" became the cry. But nobody would admit to touching the cement, so nobody got to go outside to play that evening.

The next day, boy was pitted against boy in what became an ugly game of accusation, denial, hits, hair pulling, tears, and fear. That afternoon Mr. Staber stuck to his word and turned us loose again on ourselves to find the guilty party for him. All that day and the next, sure enough, nobody got to play. It looked like this would go on forever. The pressure grew and grew.

It was almost a scene out of *The Catcher in the Rye,* a child-directed but adult-sponsored torture chamber. " 'Fess up, Wesley. We all know you did it," screamed an eighth grader named Paul, the ranking kid among us. "None of us gets to play, all because of you!"

After three days that absolutely traumatized the school, Mr. Staber announced that the next day he was going to beat every little boy, that he no longer cared who actually did it. That tightened the screws all the more. I was the youngest and smallest of the pack. In a burst of masochism I got to thinking, *I am the littlest. I am always in trouble anyway. I get spanked more than anyone else. I can probably take the punishment better, being used to it and all.*

I finally announced to my friends that I hadn't done it but that I was going to say I had just to end this so we all could go outside and play again. "Before we grow too old," I added. The relief in the room was palpable. Nobody cared about justice anymore; they just wanted the quarantine to end, and here was little Wesley willing to be the scapegoat. Nobody said a word, not even "thank you." Nobody knew what to say.

Off I marched up the hall to my doom. Mr. Staber was as delighted as I had ever seen him. He picked me up by one arm, dragged me into his room, grabbed his truck-tire slipper, and spanked my little bottom and bare legs until he was breathless and tired. I withdrew deep within myself.

"More, Herman, spank him more!" It was the voice of Mrs. Staber from out of nowhere. She had silently witnessed the beating and was unsatisfied, even as her husband stopped to rest. *Herman*—that was the first I heard his name.

Mercifully, he quit. But his wife was not quite finished. I was given a piece of cardboard from the side of a carton. She put a crayon into my hand and hissed, "Write."

"Write what?" I asked through my sobs.

She spelled it out for me since I was too young to know the words.

P-E-O-P-L-E

C-A-N-T (At this point, she grabbed the crayon and made the apostrophe herself since I hadn't gotten that far in school.)

B-E-L-I-E-V-E

T-H-E (I knew that word.)

T-H-I-N-G-S

T-H-A-T

I

S-A-Y! (She also made the exclamation point. Somehow the words weren't powerful enough.)

"People Can't Believe the Things That I Say!" she read for me, recalling my earlier claims of innocence. "That's what you wrote with your own hand." Her husband then punched a couple of holes in the cardboard and tied a piece of string on it. She put the sign around my neck. "You'll wear this for a whole week," she spat and pushed me out into the hallway.

I picked myself up and walked, head down and sobbing, back to my friends. The beating hurt but not nearly as much as the words. I felt ashamed, humiliated, hurt, angry, and wounded. The little boys read my sign and stepped back from me as if I had leprosy. I was totally, totally alone.

Everyone was frightened and bewildered. The entire school had been traumatized by three little fingerprints in wet cement. I was sent straight to bed, where I screamed silently into my pillow.

The next day I learned about the power of the written word: If something is written down, it must be true. I knew my boyhood friends back in Nielle believed that concept as their language was first put into written form. But here was the same idea among us at Bandulo. Arriving at the schoolhouse, I took off my humiliating sign and tried to hide it under my pith helmet on the peg. The Stabers sent a note with someone that read, "Make sure Wesley wears his sign. Make the most of it!"

The teachers complied, and for the longest week of my life, I wore a badge of shame. My soul shriveled up and all but blew away. My sister, Carol, was my only real comfort. She believed me, held me close while I cried, and stood by me when all others were too afraid.

Such was the nature of the place. It wasn't just fingerprints that dried in cement that day; indelible marks were made in the wet cement of a little boy's spirit. They formed a lasting impression of injustice, cruelty, and the evil of which people are capable—even people of God.

CONSPIRACY OF SILENCE

By now you are probably asking, "How in the world did a mission school come to be run by such malevolent people?" Surely the sponsoring denomination did not intend for such horrors to be perpetrated day after day, year after year. As an adult, I have pondered this question more than once. What on earth caused a dozen adult missionaries to treat children so viciously?

I honestly don't know, but the most plausible scenario I can come up with is this: these people had no doubt gone to Africa, like all of our parents, to preach the gospel and save souls. I'm sure that's what they told their supporting churches and individuals back in the United States. But something must have gone wrong for at least some of them. They didn't make it in their original calling. Was it cross-cultural difficulty? Linguistic failure? Whatever it was, the mission executives eventually recognized the need to reassign them.

Of course, rarely are missionaries who have already raised their own "salaries" or support actually fired. If you can't fire them, you simply have to reassign them where they will do the least damage. That brings us back to "the end of the line" mentioned in the introduction—children. I am guessing that the harried field directors said, in essence, "We aren't sending you back home in disgrace, but, um, well, how about taking care of the missionary children over at Bandulo?"

Hurt and angry at this "demotion," these missionaries headed off to their fate. They brought no love, passion, or sense of calling to serve children. They simply had to save face and must have dutifully gone to their posts, taking out their resentment and frustration on their charges.

Little more was said thereafter. They were given unfettered authority and unmonitored reign over our lives. No governing board watched over the school or dropped by for visits. The campus was located in a remote jungle, on the road to basically nowhere. I never remember even any parents stopping in during the term to check on their children. Everyone assumed all was well.

I must say that I recall two staff members who were not cruel. The school principal was a kind man, but he simply could not control his faculty. I learned years later that one junior teacher during that era, a single woman, tried to report the abuses to the mission heads. She was essentially told to mind her own business.

The truth did not emerge into daylight until more than thirty years later, which is a story all in itself. (To read my role in this painful process with mission leaders, see the afterword, which starts on page 259.)

You might ask another question: "Why didn't you just tell your parents and get rescued from that awful place?"

All of us children wrote letters home every Sunday afternoon. The littlest ones were helped by the older ones. Before we had come to Bandulo for our nine-month stay, our mothers had lovingly addressed, stamped, and put wax paper inside the flaps of about thirty-six envelopes. The wax paper was to keep the envelopes from sealing themselves in the high humidity of the jungle. Every week we wrote home.

The tragedy was that we were strictly forbidden to tell our parents anything negative. The letters were gathered at the end of the day for the houseparents to read, ensuring that none of the awful nightmare got out. If we tried, we were summoned to their room and whipped. We then sat down in their presence and rewrote our letters.

My parents have shoeboxes full of my childhood letters with happy news. Here is a sample from my second grade year:

June 2, 1957

Dear Mother and Daddy

How are you? I am fine.

Friday night we played hidegoseek and sheep in the pen. Saturday Olen, Jimmy Stevin, David and I played cowboys.

Please ask grandmother to send some candy.

Love,

Wesley

XOXOXOXOXOXOXOXOXOXOXOXOXOXOXOXOXOXOXO

There's also a hand-drawn card for my father with a big yellow ocean liner on the front, smoke pouring from its smokestacks and seagulls in the air. The message inside, in multicolored crayon, reads:

Happy father's day.

I like Bandulo. I am fine at school.

I love you very very much much.

Love

from Wesley

The Stabers were clear: "If you tell your parents that you are unhappy here, you will be Satan's tool to destroy their ministry in Africa. They will become discouraged and may have to leave the field. If that happens, there will be Africans in hell because of you!" What a diabolical trap we were in. Our love for our parents and our love for God were used to conceal the horrors that were heaped upon us.

Believe it or not, this rationale was even strong enough to keep our lips sealed when we went home for the three-month vacation. Just before the truck convoy arrived to take us all to our mission stations scattered across West Africa, we were given one final, very stern warning: "Remember now—if you tell your parents things that will destroy their ministry, you condemn Africans to hell!" Talk about the "silence of the lambs." I never even told my own father, whom I loved dearly. His ministry in Africa for the Lord I knew he loved was too precious. I would be the willing sacrifice.

Child psychologists study this phenomenon with great amazement, as it has occurred throughout history. They have found that children can keep awful, awful secrets to protect the ones they love. And so it was with us, the children of Bandulo.

I should mention that this pre-vacation warning was couched in a cheerful context. The final week of each school year was dubbed "hobo week." In order for all of our clothes to be washed and ready to be packed in our suitcases, we got to wear old, castoff clothing gathered from previous years. The clothes never fit right, and we had great fun looking silly. The beatings also subsided that week, as I recall, perhaps to allow welts and bruises to fade before our parents would see them. It sent us off with a sense of goodwill about the place and served to ensure that nothing awkward leaked out each December.

But then, as Easter drew near and the dreaded truck convoy was again assembled, station by station, for the long trek back across West Africa, the heartache would begin anew. We children would plead to stay home with our parents. Our hearts were frightened, sad, desperate. I remember mothers hanging onto the sides of the pickup trucks as we drove slowly away, sobbing at the loss of their children. They assumed our grief and desperation was the same as theirs, that we simply didn't want to be apart from them. They had no inkling that we were suffering a far deeper anguish. We knew we were headed back to hell, but we loved them too much to say so.

9

BREAKING THE SILENCE

You would think that a bright spot in our otherwise dismal lives would be food. After all, what growing boy doesn't like to eat? The dining hall indeed could be a place of laughter and delight, depending on your table assignment. Get placed at a table with nine of your good friends, and your heart raced with joy. The eighth and ninth graders were usually placed at the head and foot of the table with eight of us younger ones on both sides. I loved to sit at either of the Torgesen twins' tables, because they used to spend the mealtime telling us stories they made up as they went along. Whenever the bell rang, Martha and Marilyn would smile and say, "To be continued!" We would all groan but wait excitedly for the next meal. We could always tell them exactly where they had left off.

Every Sunday noon our seating assignment would change. Our napkin rings, each one different from the others or at least labeled with our names, would show up at a new spot. My napkin ring was made of lime green plastic, I recall. When the bell gonged, all of us boys and girls would race in, giggling and excited, to see where we had been slotted for the coming week.

I would dash into the dining hall and start at the far corner with refreshed hope for a happy placement. Table by table, I would circle the room searching for my napkin ring. Not finding it right away, I would progress toward the center, which meant getting closer and closer to the Stabers' table, my heart heavier and heavier with each step.

Then at last I would see through tear-dimmed eyes that, sure enough, I had been placed once again either right beside Mr. Staber or, even worse, Mrs. Staber. This happened for months on end, it seemed. Every Sunday my hopes would soar...and then crash again.

My stomach churning, I would stand behind my chair, head down, resigned to my fate for another week. Mr. Staber would then begin the mealtime song, which we sang three times a day, seven days a week. It was the chorus of an old gospel tune about Jesus, the Bread of Life:

"Come and dine," the Master calleth, "come and dine;"
You may feast at Jesus' table anytime;
He who fed the multitudes, turned the water into wine,
To the hungry calleth now, "Come and dine."[1]

If this was indeed "Jesus' table," I thought more than once, couldn't the one who "turned the water into wine" perform the far more modest miracle of moving my napkin ring to a different table? I never figured out the answer to that one. With a thunderous roar, the chairs would scrape across the cement floor, and the meal would begin.

I spent my meals looking down at my plate to avoid the Stabers' glare. I had developed a nervous tic of rolling my eyes that they determined to stop at any cost. This usually meant a sudden backhand across my face or a hit on the top of my head after each occurrence. I was later diagnosed with an eye disease that, sure enough, caused them to be itchy and dry. Subconsciously I had been trying to moisten them by rolling them around. The symptoms were external, but the greater damage was going on inside me with each blow.

There was also the sudden jerking of my hand. Out of nowhere, my hand would spasm and cause me to jolt violently. If my fork happened to be loaded with beans, well, they flew into the air. This particular crime enraged the houseparents more than anything. I was threatened, yelled at, called names, and smacked with nearly every infraction—again, several times per meal. It was later discovered that I was having a muscular reaction to an antiparasite medication I was given. The dosage was apparently too strong.

The menu in our dining hall was generally nutritious, prepared by Ouseman, our wonderful African cook. But, of course, children will always find a distaste for certain foods. With me it was eggplant, a truly disgusting vegetable that is bad enough while warm, but if left until last on one's plate, it becomes slimy and stringy. I dreaded the stuff, and my tormentors knew it.

Our food was always served family style by the head of the table. Whenever eggplant was served, Mrs. Staber took great delight in looking at me first, cocking her head as if trying to decide what to do, then heaping my plate high with the slimy stuff and plopping it down in front of me with a flare. I had no choice but to get it down. My stomach would retch at times, and I would dash down the hallway to get to the toilets before I actually vomited. I remember so many times I didn't make it and threw up, midstride, splattering the hallway.

The result was always the same. Even at age six, I had to scrape the results together with my hands, scoop them into a bucket, and then mop the whole hallway. This took quite awhile, of course. Eventually I returned to the table, now seriously behind schedule, where the remaining eggplant waited more cold and slimy than ever. I gagged my way forward.

Regardless of the menu, the end of every lunchtime brought the dreaded Bad News List, with its promised pain and torment. I was skinny and always hungry. I gradually came to associate food with torment. To this day I cannot say that I truly enjoy eating.

BEWARE THE GREEN BEANS

Food, in a bizarre way, even got entangled in the question every little boy wonders about: where do babies come from? We knew this was a taboo subject even among our parents, so the secret was irresistible. Those who knew the truth were, I figured, sworn by some sacred pledge to absolute silence.

We boys had a million theories, but none of them made much sense to me. I knew a little from watching the village dogs and goats, but surely God wouldn't require people to do something that disgusting, would he?

Then one year my very good friend Stanley returned from furlough in the United States, the fount of all blessing and truth as far as we could tell. We were both about seven or eight years old at the time, and he told me that while away, he had found out what caused babies! I begged him to tell me. He made me swear an oath of secrecy. Then he led me down to the bathroom in the dead of night. We took the kerosene lantern into a shower stall and drew the curtain. I looked at him expectantly.

He leaned toward my ear and whispered, "Green beans. Babies come when you eat green beans!"

"Really!" I whispered. Then I added, "I kinda thought so," trying to seem equally worldly and well informed.

Green beans—who would have thought? Not even eggplant, which I might have suspected.

I was too young and innocent to notice that both men and women eat green beans but only women have babies. Anyway, I determined within my little soul (responsible boy that I was) that I would wait until I was old to have a child. Toward that end, I would not eat any green beans until I was old enough to actually care for a baby. The decision was very private, very personal—and very strong.

Well, that resolve opened up a whole new category of torment for me. Whenever green beans were served, I sought for ways to dispose of them. Initially I threw them one at a time under the table, as I often did bits of gristle meat that had been chewed to death. The dog, Pepe, always scarfed those up, usually undetected. But as it turned out, Pepe (the traitor) didn't like green beans!

My next maneuver was to try to hide them under my knife, fork, and spoon, all arranged in a sort of thicket at the top of my plate. Under the watchful eye of the Stabers, that, too, was discovered. The beatings began. Every time I saw green beans on my plate, I knew I was doomed to a whipping. This went on for several years.

What still amazes me is that no grownups, not a single one, ever bothered to ask me why I suddenly didn't eat green beans. If any of them had cared enough to ask, I would have been greatly relieved to explain. I was pretty sure they already knew the facts of life, so it couldn't hurt for me to mention it. But no, they just assumed I was a naughty little boy and applied the whip.

Today one of my primary messages to the Compassion International staff of more than a thousand people in twenty-four countries is this: *Lis-*

ten to the children! God gave us two ears and only one mouth for good reason: that we should do twice as much listening as talking.

I often worried if the Bandulo grownups talked about me behind my back. I assumed they did, especially when they would gather behind closed doors sometimes for hours on end. They called them staff meetings, but I wasn't stupid. I knew that was just code language for STAFFord meetings. My heart pounded with fear whenever I heard one being announced.

BACKRUBS IN THE NIGHT

Knowledge of our developing bodies took a far darker turn, however, in this climate of neglect and abuse. Beyond the physical and emotional cruelty, there was no protection against sexual exploitation. The very people to whom we should have been able to run for shelter were either the ones abusing us or were the last people we felt we could trust.

As with the other abuses, we all kept quiet. But it went on night after night for years. It was not just a one-time outrage wrought on a child by a wayward priest or a sexual encounter on a weekend campout. Let me tell about my situation. My tormentors were older boys who had figured out the abusive system and used the same terror tactics to victimize littler boys. These teenagers had no worry of being discovered as they forced us to masturbate them or even perform oral sex on them. Under the threat of making our miserable lives even more dangerous, their blackmail and perversion had an atmosphere in which to fester.

You would have thought that adult caretakers would have stopped such behavior. But actually, Mr. Staber had other matters to attend to…down the girls' hall. He used to prowl the hallway after the generator had been shut down for the night and lights were out. Room by room, he would shine his flashlight into the eyes of the little girls "to see if they were asleep."

My sister and others told me decades later that they learned to sleep with their faces to the wall. They would pretend to be sleeping even if they were not, steeling themselves not to flinch when his beam fell on their eyes in the darkness. Why? Because when he found one not sleeping, he would enter the room, sit down on the bed, and speak softly to her. "What, can't sleep? Here, let me give you a backrub." He would caress their frightened little bodies at will.

Then after a while he would murmur, "How's that? Better? Now turn over…"

I need not go into further detail.

All this was possible only because the evil conditions were present. Adults who should have been our protectors were instead among our destroyers. Spiritual guilt, shame, and manipulation only emboldened the predators and victimized the powerless. Budding teenagers learned to do as had been done unto them. Little children with no sense of personal worth, frightened by more powerful people, existed like wounded animals whose only goal was to please in order to survive.

The Bible admonishes in Proverbs 31:8, "Speak up for those who cannot speak for themselves, for the rights of all who are destitute." But at Bandulo, there were no child advocates, no one to protect us, and we suffered the worst.

No wonder so many of us were nearly destroyed. Many of my childhood friends fell to the ground and have never gotten up. Their adult lives continue down a sad trail of dysfunction, multiple marriages, addictions, and depression. I emerged with heavy damage but not beyond the reach of my heavenly Father's arms. To this day I am merely a product of God's grace.

I thank him that in those years, he let me return to my village and family each December after nine months of that cruel and abusive place. Those precious people in Nielle, who knew pain and suffering all too well due to their poverty, scooped up this damaged little white boy and for three wonderful months restored my soul. They embraced me as one of their own, comforted me, and rebuilt my sense of self-worth.

A GOD TO LOVE?

You may find it odd that in the midst of all this trauma, I did not turn against the God whose name everyone professed. After all, the very adults who abused us daily were also the ones charged with our spiritual development. We obediently followed their instruction to read our Bibles every day. We had a deep respect for God and his Word; we never put our Bibles under our chairs, for example. They had to be carried at least chest high, near or above our hearts.

What an amazing irony that, after a day of hitting us, screaming at us, and humiliating us, our tormentors would sit down at bedtime and read us Bible stories. Like little lambs, we sat at their very feet. We were so quick to forgive them.

Prayer times were interesting. The littlest kids would be in pajamas and bathrobes, meeting in the room where earlier we had been beaten. But when it came time to talk to God, there was a flurry of participation. The split second one child said, "Amen," twenty others would attempt to be next, rattling off the first few sentences like reporters at a presidential press conference, seeking to "get the floor." It could take three or four sentences spoken machine-gun style to outlast the other competitors.

Why did we strive so earnestly to talk to God? Because we sincerely loved him regardless of our circumstances and, to be honest, because we thought our show of piety might improve our standing with the adults who ruled our lives. Actually, I shouldn't say "we," because I rarely engaged in this nightly competition to be heard. I used to kneel on the floor with the others but would pull my bathrobe collar all the way up over my head, imagining myself in my own little cave. I could see no one, and I assumed nobody could see me. For one brief moment, I felt safe.

On the first Sunday evening of the month, we engaged in an even more strange ritual of taking Communion. We moved our dining-room chairs into the adjoining living room, transforming it into a holy sanctuary. We always sat by age—the littlest ones in the front row, the oldest in the back. Mr. Staber played the role of pastor.

He always read the 1 Corinthians 11 passage that most churches use to set up the ceremony. I remember only too well his strong voice as he emphasized that "he that eateth and drinketh unworthily, eateth and drinketh damnation to himself, not discerning the Lord's body" (verse 29, KJV). In other words, if you dared partake of the Lord's Supper, there had better be absolutely no sin in your life, or you would condemn yourself to hell. He would then pause, look sternly at us, and intone, "If anyone has anything to settle with anyone in the room, let him do it now."

Instantly we children would jump to our feet and scramble to the nearest friend or adult and ask a sweeping forgiveness for "anything I might have ever done to offend or sin against you." The adults all sat in their chairs around the edges of the room, almost like Santa Claus, as a dozen children lined up in front, waiting their turn to ask forgiveness from them. *From them!*

This confessional bedlam could go on for half an hour as anxious children tried desperately to conjure up any possible sin to confess. Gradually the conversation subsided. Children with tear-streaked faces found their chairs again, now pure of heart. But imagine the anguish of my young soul, having so many, many reasons to believe I was bad and deserved punishment. How could I possibly recount them all? Every Communion evening I was sure I once again condemned myself to hell.

Never once do I remember a single adult responding to my confession by saying, "And please forgive me too, little Wesley." This ritual was strictly one-way.

I truly wanted to please God. I had never felt otherwise in my whole life. In fact, in that same room during my first year of school, I had made a sincere and even desperate profession of faith. It happened during Bandulo's annual week of "special meetings," when a guest speaker would be brought in to address the student body.

I remember the night well. The speaker was a huge man with a beet-red face and hairy arms. I could see him well, of course, by virtue of my being only six years old and therefore sitting front and center in the first row. He wasn't more than three feet from me.

He began with a dramatic hush in the room. Then he opened his mouth. There was no friendly warmup. He got immediately to his point.

"All you little kids are sinners," he began, looking menacingly at each face for what seemed like an eternity. "You!" he yelled right at me. "You deserve the damnation of hell, the hot fires of Hades itself." I had no idea what the Greek word *Hades* meant, but it sounded pretty scary.

Suddenly from behind his back he produced an egg and placed it gently on a table. I stared at that pretty white oval for a long moment. Then just as suddenly, he raised a hammer in his hand. "You are this egg," he declared. "God is this hammer. You deserve to be judged and destroyed for your sins."

Well, he had me there. I had already come to believe that I was nothing but evil and deserved all the punishment that was heaped on me almost daily.

Next the speaker held up in his big, hairy hand a Nescafé tin can. He placed the can over the egg and raised his hammer. "But, children, hear this. Jesus came to take the punishment for your sins—punishment you richly deserve! When you cheat in school, you deserve hell." With that, he brought the hammer down on the can, denting its top. I sat wide eyed, remembering how I had used my good eyesight to check out Janice Mills's test paper the week before.

"When you tell a lie," he continued, pounding the hammer down again on the tin can, "you deserve to be destroyed. When you don't share your toys… When you complain…" By now I was shivering from this display of violence and power. I was also very worried for that egg. I thought there might be a chick inside. I was convinced this speaker knew my every sin. I fully agreed that I was awful and deserved to be smashed by God. Thank goodness for Jesus, the Nescafé can.

Suddenly his booming voice brought me back to reality. "But unless you invite Jesus into your heart, you don't have a Nescafé can." He paused a long moment, this time looking me straight in the eye. I still remember his flashing eyes, his bushy eyebrows, the spittle on his mustache, the silence of that moment. With a flare, he whisked away the can. "And this is what you'll get on Judgment Day!" With that, he brought the hammer down. The egg burst, flew slow motion into the air, and splattered across my face.

I dropped straight to my knees and in desperation shrieked, "O God! Don't smash my egg!"

I don't know if theologians would qualify that six-word exclamation as a valid "sinner's prayer" or not, extracted as it was under such extreme manipulation. What a horrible method to bring children to salvation. Let me say now as an adult that while this kind of visual aid is a highly effective tool for "child evangelism," please don't use it! Trust me, it takes decades to recover from the terror. To this day whenever I hear a loud clap of thunder, I instinctively cower, look upward, and whimper, "What? What did I do *this* time?" (Just kidding.)

Seriously, I must add that, despite the contradictions of the boarding-school experience, I wanted to be God's child. It never crossed my mind to blame *him* for my torturous existence at the hands of his misguided servants. Already at this young age, I was starting to figure out that God could be good even if people were not. I was drawn to his wise and loving character regardless. If any correction came directly from him, I figured he was only being fair.

The Unraveling

Such spirituality did not serve, however, to protect me from subsequent torment at Bandulo Christian Academy. I heard my name on the Bad News List as often as always. My spirit continued to crumble as the wrath of houseparents and teachers fell upon me. Alone with my tears, I kept asking if there was any way out of my misery.

The tragic pact of silence was finally broken when I was ten years old. We had been on furlough in America for a full year. I had attended fourth grade at a public school in Denver, where I found out that my boarding-school education, for all its other faults, was at least keeping me up to speed academically.

Now it was time to go back to Africa. A group of us missionary children gathered with our parents at New York's Idylwild Airport (the future JFK) to fly back. Our parents would follow by less expensive freighter ship. I knew I was now doomed to return to the grip of trauma.

At the gate I reached out to take my mother's face in my hands, looking at her very intently. I held on; I couldn't let go.

"What are you doing, Wesley?" she asked.

"Mommy, I just don't want to forget what you look like," I cried. For some reason none of us at Bandulo had photos of our parents. I suspect the administration discouraged this in a misguided effort to reduce homesickness.

We both began to weep. She held my arms in her hands, allowing me to keep looking at her beautiful face as she bit her lip.

Suddenly my own floodgates opened. I couldn't help myself. "Mommy, please don't make me go back to Bandulo. It's terrible! They beat us all the time for everything. They hate me. I just miss you and Daddy so much. I'm scared. Please, please…" By now I was sobbing so hard my words could hardly be understood.

My mother's countenance froze in shock as she pulled me into her arms, holding me tightly. "Oh, Wesley! I love you so much! I'm so sorry you're afraid… I don't know what to do.…" With that, her shoulders began to shake with sobbing.

And all too soon, within sixty seconds, it was time for Carol and me and the other children to board the aircraft. I sat down in my seat absolutely drained. Soon the flight was airborne over the Atlantic. I stared out the window at the evening sky, tears continuing to flow down my cheeks. I was relieved that I had finally said something. *At least now she knows,* I told myself. My fellow MKs (missionary kids) looked across the aisle at me as if I were doomed. I had done the unthinkable. I turned away from their glances and fell into a fitful sleep.

When our group arrived back at Bandulo, Mr. and Mrs. Staber were nowhere to be found. We felt greatly relieved—until within a day we realized that their replacements, Mr. and Mrs. Edwards, were cut out of basically the same cloth. The main tactics of control and abuse remained in place: the Bad News List, the patrols during noon rest, the incessant beatings.

Meanwhile, my parents' ocean crossing took a full month. Day after day they talked and worried about what I had blurted out. Could it really be true? Was there some gross misunderstanding? The weekly letters had sounded so positive, but apparently they hadn't told the whole story. So many questions, so many missing facts…

As soon as they disembarked on September 20, 1959, at the Port of

Abidjan, my father sent a letter to me seeking to verify the shocking comments I had made about Bandulo. He wasn't disputing my word, but this was a serious charge, and he wanted to make sure I wasn't complaining about punishment I actually deserved or parroting the complaints of older boys. He said, "I hope that you remember to pray for your mother every day… She still doesn't feel well all the time," and he asked me to write to her.

When his letter arrived at Bandulo, it was, like all incoming mail, read by the houseparents before it ever reached my hands. This was standard procedure. My father's paragraph of inquiry confirmed to the Edwardses what they had already heard from the missionary grapevine: that Marge Stafford was not doing well emotionally. Now they had the evidence of what was causing her distress.

At lunch one day, Mr. Edwards announced to the students, "Carol's and Wesley's mother is apparently having something like a nervous breakdown. This is a serious problem. We don't know what caused this, but we can all pray for her."

My heart began to pound in my chest. Oh no! What had happened to her? Now I was the one with a basket of questions. I had little time to think about them, however, because that evening at the end of supper, it was announced to all the children that a "special meeting" would be held in the dining room right then. No one could leave. Within minutes I was called to the front and told to stand on a chair above my friends.

"Let me introduce you to Satan's favorite tool," Mr. Edwards began. I looked up in shock. I felt my bowels begin to quiver. "Wesley has decided to serve Satan. He told his mother about what happens here, and now she is not able to do her important work here on the mission field."

The children, now about seventy in number, sat as if paralyzed. One or two coughed quietly; otherwise, it was still. "Satan has won," the man continued. "He used Wesley, and now there will be Africans in hell because of this boy you see standing before you."

My hands began to shake, and my legs trembled. In fact, I shook all over uncontrollably. I had seen horrible things and been tortured in this place, but nothing was as bad as this. I had broken the ultimate code of silence.

"You cannot serve both God and Satan, the Bible says. Wesley has tried. You cannot burn the candle at both ends without getting burned."

I don't know if what happened next was premeditated or just an evil idea of the moment. Whichever it was, Mr. Edwards ordered that a birthday candle be brought to him. He got out his pocketknife and trimmed the wick at the blunt end to produce a candle that could indeed burn from both directions.

"Here, Wesley," he said with a brightened face. "You want to serve both God and Satan? Try it!"

I took the candle between my cold, shaking fingers. Standing there in front of my friends, I remember the total silence. Nobody dared to breathe. Striking a match, Mr. Edwards lit both ends of my trembling candle. I stared incredulously as I contemplated what this would mean in just a few moments.

He turned his back to me and continued his lecture, assuming I would drop the candle before long. I heard only the first few words because of the pounding of my heart and the blood pulsing in my ears. My fear was deafening. As the flames flickered closer and closer to my skin, the children's eyes grew wide. He looked back at me, showed surprise that I still held the candle, but then continued speaking all the louder and faster.

Suddenly I again found myself. In a brief flash of reality, I saw the great evil that was going on. I was not Satan's tool; I was just a little boy with a broken heart who had tried to be rescued from this evil place. I loved Jesus and was my daddy's partner in ministry in the villages. Mr. Edwards was lying, and all of my friends were but frightened little lambs.

I dug deep into my soul and said to myself, *Not this time. They won't win this time. No matter how much this hurts, I am not...I will not let go of this candle! I won't give them the joy of humiliating me again.* I gritted my teeth, clenched my buttocks, and prepared for whatever amount of pain would come my way. Nothing, I mean nothing, was going to make me cry out or drop that candle...not this time...not this time.

I could only vaguely hear his words as I watched the skin on both sides of my fingers grow first red and then begin to bubble. In the background,

I could hear vaguely, "Satan's tool...Africans in hell..." Now a trace of smoke came up from my fingertips. The flames were touching my skin.

"No!" I exclaimed through clenched teeth. "No!"

Just then a first grader in the front row jumped up and slapped the candle out of my blistering fingers. It was over. The meeting broke up as the children rushed forward to hold and comfort me.

I honestly cannot remember what happened to Mr. Edwards at that moment. But his meeting was finished. At last the children had had enough. They could bear no more. They had recognized the evil at last.

A FATHER'S LOVE

When the dads arrived two months later, in early December, to take us students home for the three-month vacation, I was surprised to see my father among them, because it was not his turn in the rotation. He did not tell us why.

It was decades later, after his death, that I pieced together from yellowed documents and letters on onionskin paper how he had been hard at work on our behalf. As I read between the lines, it seemed he went to the annual conference the Conservative Baptist missionaries held every October with a stern message: something is wrong at Bandulo, and we must find out what it is. By the end of that conference, three decisions had been made: (1) Ken Stafford would join the other dads for an on-site inspection at the end of the term; (2) they would push for the Conservative Baptist children to be moved to different living quarters with different houseparents starting with the very next term in March; and (3) the ultimate solution would be to launch a brand-new boarding school at a more accessible location that could be more closely watched. My father was named to the executive committee for this effort.

But he was never one to boast about his work. When Carol and I arrived home for vacation, little was said. My mother seemed up and down, cheerful on some days and apprehensive on others. We passed the weeks enjoying family life together. The biggest thrill of this vacation, I remember, was that our house in Nielle now had electricity.

When we returned to Bandulo in March, we and a dozen or so other children were overjoyed to transfer into what was called the villa about half a mile down the hill from the main campus. Our new houseparents, Rolf and Clara Rose Parelius, were a delightful couple who had volunteered for this post. They were full of smiles and compliments, even as they maintained necessary boundaries in our lives. School life began to be more tolerable.

But our mother, back in Nielle, continued to wobble emotionally until in July my father finally sent her back to the States for help. She spent nine months there altogether, receiving counseling and some physical treatment for hypothyroidism. She also had a hysterectomy, which meant she was not at home when Carol and I returned for the next vacation.

Dad told us about the progress for the new school in Bouake, a much more accessible city in the middle of Ivory Coast. The process of raising funds, building a campus, and recruiting qualified staff would take awhile, of course. But he was excited about the potential. He was pushing things along as fast as possible.

My eighth-grade year brought for me the fruit of his labors: I got to transfer to the brand-new Ivory Coast Academy, an oasis of love by comparison. When he and I, as a thirteen-year-old, descended the gravel driveway of Bandulo for the last time, a shudder went through my body. I locked away all the dreadful memories and turned to face the future.

For many years as an adult, I would tell people nothing about Bandulo. I would only state with pride that I had the distinction of being in the first graduating class of Ivory Coast Academy. As if that wasn't honor enough, I would go on to brag that I had graduated second in my entire class. Okay, there were just two of us, but I was still right up there near the top! Just Janice Mills and me. That meant I had to answer every other question the teachers posed that year—most of the time with Janice's hand already waving wildly in the air as she exclaimed, "I know, I know!"

My parents were having talks of their own about the future. As we prepared to come to the States for the next furlough, they announced to the mission that they could not be separated from my sister and me for our high school years. They had already sent Carol back to Denver early to live with relatives and start tenth grade. They would resign if necessary. The mission persuaded them to stay on board but this time in the United States, working with the Navajo people of Arizona.

We never talked much as a family about the past abuse. I do recall, though, that in the year 2003, when my seventy-seven-year-old father lay dying of pulmonary fibrosis, he returned to the subject. One day I was sitting beside his hospital bed holding his hand when he, with cloudy eyes, said, "Wess, I'm so very, very sorry that you had to pay such a high price for our ministry in Africa."

With that, he stopped. His lungs couldn't get enough air to keep talking. I squeezed his hand and said, "Dad, I'm fine. I love you, and by God's grace, I'm okay. Really..." He died a week later.

THE MAKING OF AN ADVOCATE

More than forty years have come and gone since the candle incident. It was a defining moment for me. It turned me in the direction of my life's work as a passionate advocate for the hurting children of the world. I refuse to be defeated. I refuse to give in to the powerful forces that would violate the downtrodden and oppressed among us. It is the reason I write and speak with such fervor. Here I am past the midpoint of adulthood, and I'm still holding onto that candle and gritting my teeth as I battle for the value and importance of little ones. They shall have a defender, a champion, an advocate after all!

Why did God let me suffer the agonies of that boarding school? Why did he not intervene when I cried out to him night after night for relief? I have imagined at times my guardian angel pulling on God's sleeve saying, "Don't you hear little Wesley? Don't you see his pitiful tears? Can't you do something to deliver him from this monstrous evil?"

If that ever happened, I believe God replied, "I know. I see his pain; I hear his cry. But he needs to go through this. I have plans for his life. Out of his pain, I will save others. Trust me."

I'm not saying it was God's plan for the abuse to occur. But I do believe he can redeem anything and bring good out of evil. He was shaping me for an epic fight on behalf of abused children. When I address that issue these days, it is not just an academic topic for me, the subject of a doctoral dissertation. I've *lived* it. I have experienced firsthand that when children are not deemed important in our world, some very ugly things can happen.

But when adults speak up for the vulnerable and the weak, working and demanding that safety and respect prevail, God's little lambs are protected and nourished. They know they are not abandoned; they are loved. And the world becomes a little more like heaven as a result.

The Gospels show us that Jesus' blood never boiled quite like when he fired off these stunning words: "Whoever causes one of these little ones who believe in Me to stumble, it is better for him that a heavy millstone be hung around his neck, and that he be drowned in the depth of the sea. Woe to the world because of its stumbling blocks!" (Matthew 18:6–7, NASB). Let us never, never find ourselves in that dreadful category. We absolutely must battle with every bit of determination we can muster to root out the harm that would warp the souls and spirits of children in our world.

PART
TWO

BACK TO "CIVILIZATION"

As I lay on my cot in Nielle that last night before furlough, just a few weeks before my fourteenth birthday, the village drums were playing, and the balaphones pounded out a harmony across the tropical night. I recognized once again the sounds of a memorial for a child who had died.

How many of these had I listened to over the years? Why was I still alive? Why was I so privileged to have that small inoculation dent in my upper arm, while my friends had no such immunity to measles, to malaria, to smallpox? It wasn't fair. Nearly half of the children of our village who had touched my life were now gone. I had listened to the drums and cried myself to sleep literally dozens of nights.

Saying good-bye to my best friend, Alezye, the next morning at the crack of dawn was the most painful part of leaving Nielle. We had been through so much together. Like a big brother, he had taught me a great deal. As the others were saying farewell near the house, Alezye and I wandered, brokenhearted, to "our tree." In spite of the fact that we had planted and cared for hundreds of little seedlings since our earliest years together, this was still the only tree of any real size. Securely anchored in its branches was the tree house we had built together years before. I had heard so many stories and learned so many lessons up in those branches.

It was still Alezye's dream to become a pastor, maybe even pastor of Nielle's fledgling church someday. It was still my deepest desire to put the tools into his hands to do that. I was going to return one day and finish the Bible translation my father had so valiantly begun, much of it with Alezye at his side. He was so smart, was such a natural leader, and loved God so profoundly.

We stood under our tree, faced each other, grasped each other's arms, and looked straight into each other's tear-brimmed eyes. "Alezye," I began, "I don't know if I will ever see you again. If I do, it will be a long, long time from now. Thank you for being my friend. Thank you for teaching me so much."

He shifted his weight as he replied, "Well, a lot can change over many years. A lot of young men lose their way. What can we do to be sure that doesn't happen to us?"

"Let's promise each other," I answered, "that we will never let anybody or anything get between us and God. We'll study hard. We'll stay on track. Let's determine to be all we can become for God. I'm so proud of you. And I'm so sure you're going to be a great pastor."

With that, we both said, "I promise," in unison. We then hugged each other and silently wept.

Soon my parents and I climbed into our truck. The sun was just cracking the horizon as we drove down the bumpy road. Tears welled up in all three of us. Nobody could talk for a long while. This was the only home I had ever really known.

The Pearls of Poverty

I had a lot of time to think on the trip back to America. I wasn't mature enough, of course, to frame my thoughts into any kind of eloquent presentation. But I knew I had gained a wealth of understanding and experience in Nielle that would mark my life forever.

Now when I speak to audiences, I often say that everything good I really need to lead a worldwide child-development ministry I learned from the poor themselves, in the fields and around the campfires. They taught me what matters most, and I use those values to try to shape the culture of the present.

These most precious values I have come to call the "pearls of poverty," given to me by the peasants of West Africa. The pearl is a jewel, like the ruby, the diamond, and the sapphire. But unlike the others, a pearl comes originally from suffering. The oyster gets a grain of sand inside its shell. This is uncomfortable; it hurts the oyster. Over time, the oyster begins to protect itself from that irritant by coating it with a secretion, layer upon layer, until it becomes a smooth, brilliant, shining treasure—a pearl! Wealthy women wear strings of them around their necks and wrists, seldom remembering that some little creature suffered greatly to provide such beauty.

The lessons my village gave me were just such treasures. Many of them came from the suffering, hunger, sickness, and vulnerability of the peasant eking out a living for himself and his family in the harsh, rural African environment. Here are a few of the precious pearls I still carry in my heart today.

The pearl of love. Nothing is more powerful in the world today. It cannot be bought; in fact, it belongs to the very poor as much as to the very rich. My village taught me in so many ways that you may not have anything else to give, but you can always give love. The great mystery, of course, is that though you give it away, you will never run out.

Sometimes in the midst of famine or disease, when the villagers had virtually no money, no medicine, no answers, all we could do for one another was to give love. Nobody died alone in Nielle. As much as it broke our hearts, we would be there for each other's final moments of life. When you hold a friend in your arms and feel that final tremble as he or she slips into the arms of the heavenly Father, you can never be the same again. You become compelled by love.

The pearl of joy. The poor comprehend that joy is not dictated by the circumstances of life. Joy is a decision, a very brave one, about how you are going to *respond* to life. We in the West tend to be joyful when things go our way and good things are happening in our lives. For the poor, such good fortune and good things almost never come. Yet laughter and smiles abound.

Over the years as I have hosted dozens of Compassion's "vision trips" to the developing world, I've observed that Western visitors are greatly surprised by this. They simply can't believe how much joy thrives in the midst of harsh realities. If the poor chose to respond with anger or frustration, the world would be a much more dangerous place. Since the poor make up nearly two out of every three people on earth, imagine the ramifications if they had not learned to glean joy from the harshness of their everyday lives.

The pearl of hope. This is another courageous decision. Even when life's harshness and injustices pile up, the poor cling tenaciously to hope. They will humble you with their absolute belief in a loving God who can be trusted to sustain and bless them. We tend to be hopeful when we have more assets than liabilities. The poor always have more liabilities than assets. Yet their hope is consistently and amazingly strong.

Their prayers in times of overwhelming crisis have both humbled and strengthened me over the years. I love nothing more than to sit listening to a peasant pastor as he unpacks the Scriptures for his little congregation. He holds out nuggets of truth. The handholds for hope are there for all of us but are made plainest to those in poverty, for whom survival actually depends on hope in their God.

The pearl of time perspective, which I wrote about in chapter 5. The poor understand that time is to be our servant, not our master, and as a result they manage always to have time for one another and what is important. The tyranny of time, I find, is a dreadful disease, especially for the wealthy; among them it is a nearly fatal condition and horribly contagious. I feel this dichotomy keenly in my frequent world travels. When I get on a plane in Paris and get off five and a half hours later in Ouagadougou, Burkina Faso, I find that the obsession with time has been left somewhere up there at thirty-five thousand feet.

Another pearl the poor have shown me is the reality that *people matter; things don't.* Here in the West, the general name of the game seems to be "use people to get things." We even have bumper stickers that are humorous but all too true to our values: "He who dies with the most toys wins." If we stop and put the values of eternity into perspective, we realize that we take nothing with us. Our only legacy is the lives of people we have touched in Jesus' name.

Don't get me wrong. There is a place for making money and acquiring things, if that is how God has gifted you. But their only ultimate purpose is beyond this temporal world. A few years ago I took Cy Young Award–winning pitcher Orel Hershiser on a trip to Central America. We were sitting together with national staff members, who one by one went around the circle telling their stories and why they now worked with the poor.

When it came around to Orel, he pulled a baseball out of his backpack and stared at it. Everyone in the room knew of his fame, of course. "Listening to all of you here today," he said softly, "I think about what I do, which is to throw this. It seems kind of silly. But to some people in America, that's very important, because they give me lots of money to do it. So as a man of God, what I must do is throw this ball the best I can, take what the world will give me for that, and pass it along to the kingdom of heaven."

I will mention one more pearl of poverty: *knowing how to give and receive.* It has often been said, "You cannot out-give God." That is true. And the corollary is this: "You cannot out-give the poor." They, like God, will overwhelm you with generosity if given a chance.

To give selflessly is truly one of the greatest joys in life. Unfortunately, much of our giving here in the West tends to be in the form of *investment.* As we write our check, we inwardly question, *So what's in this for me?* In contrast, the poor widow who gave her last coins that day in the temple touched Jesus' heart, because she gave all she had with absolutely no idea that the Lord of Glory was standing right there observing her. It would have blown her mind to be told that two thousand years later, her quiet act of giving would be used as a noble example and would underlie a common expression, "the widow's mite."

An even greater challenge is to receive graciously, especially from the hands of the poor. The Scriptures teach that it is more blessed to give than to receive. In my experience, it is also *easier* to give than to receive. We in the developed world are generally very awkward about it. If there is one great pearl I have witnessed in my years of ministry among the poor, it is their ability to be truly and joyfully grateful.

In my village, selfishness was considered a tremendous evil. I witnessed amazing displays of the strong using their strength to lift up the fallen, to carry more than their share of the load—and doing it modestly in ways that honored those they were helping. I watched peasants work not only their own fields but silently move across the boundary to work large portions of their weaker neighbor's plot. When thanked, they would smile and mutter something like, "I guess I lost my place."

The same was true of courage. If God wired them to be brave and not frightened by things that scared others, they believed this was meant for more than their own comfort and security. I watched women and even children lag behind on the path to accompany the elderly who couldn't keep up on the evening hike back to the village, knowing full well the dangers of the night and the fear that can so easily grip the elderly and weak. Strength and courage were meant to help others.

These "pearls of poverty," taught quietly and consistently by the people of Nielle, made deep impressions in the wet cement of my spirit. You can live and succeed in the everyday whirlwind of life without them, but where they show themselves, they are recognized and still valued in our hearts. We know the kind of people we all, deep inside, want to be.

ANOTHER WORLD

After a long flight to Europe and then a ship crossing to America, we landed in New York harbor—the point at which I began this saga back in chapter 1. I survived the culture shock of the Manhattan taxi driver and then scored my great triumph with the slingshot at Coney Island. We spent about a week in the city doing what the mission called in-processing before we could venture west across this great land to our new home.

The mission owned a residence building in the heart of New York that, as I recall, looked an awful lot like the houses children now see on *Sesame Street*. It was red brick, probably four stories tall, and had a fire hydrant out front. At the foot of the stairs by the street was a cluster of grimy garbage cans just like the one Oscar lives in on the television show. The street was an endless stream of cars, horns honking, sirens blaring, and jackhammers pounding.

Immediately across the street was the chain-link fence of an inner-city schoolyard. The school towered six stories, all of its windows covered in rusty iron mesh. Everything my eyes took in seemed a world apart from my little quiet village on the plains of West Africa.

Except the heat. It was late June, and fans whirred in every window in the sweltering summer. The heat was all anybody talked about. It made for tension and short tempers in the streets and shops around us, and I couldn't help thinking it was still about fifteen degrees cooler than most any day in Nielle.

The sky was a slender ribbon of light high above the red-brick canyons of the city. I couldn't get a sense of where the horizon was supposed to be. The people were of many colors and cultures in that neighborhood, and I knew they were speaking English, but I could hardly understand a word as I tried to talk with them.

From my perch in the third-floor window of this tenement house, I sat one day and watched kids playing across the street. As with children everywhere, there were a lot of shrieks, laughter, and running, and like in my village, all these children happened to be black. I smiled and watched them. At least here was something I could understand in this confusing city. The boys were playing a kind of baseball, only they called it stickball. On the brick wall was chalked a rectangle, which I later learned was the strike zone. A little, black rubber ball was thrown at great speed toward the hitter, who stood next to the white rectangle on the wall holding a sawed-off broom handle. The object of the game was to see how high up the side of the opposite wall you could hit the ball.

We had played a kind of baseball at Bandulo, so I knew the gist of the game. We, too, used a bat, except ours was a whittled tree branch we called the caveman's club. We had no rubber balls; instead, we used green grapefruit, which we picked from the trees that surrounded our field. A green grapefruit, unripe and hard, was good for a half dozen or so pretty good hits. The first few hits could seriously sting your hand or leave a bruise on whatever part of your body it hit. But soon the grapefruit softened until, with one mighty whack, it would explode all over the infield, spraying pulp and seeds on everybody. We would just get a new one off the tree. The girls, I remember, always preferred to play in the outfield, away from the exploding "baseballs."

Now here in New York, the school was closed for summer vacation. A dozen or so boys played stickball on the playground, and I felt like joining them. It never occurred to me that my being white would matter in the least.

I found an old straw broom in the closet and set off across the street.

The game came to a sudden halt as I approached the schoolyard. The gate was padlocked, but I had seen several guys just climb over it, so I did the same.

"Can I play?" I asked.

These boys had apparently encountered very few white children, much less one who wanted to play stickball with them. There was an awkward moment as I stood there, broom in hand. Then the biggest kid, the leader, said, "Yeah, sure. C'mon."

I soon took my turn at bat. Not wanting to destroy mission property, I was the only kid on the field whose broomstick still had the straw bristles attached. It made everyone laugh and cramped my style a bit, but I didn't care. Soon I was laughing and swinging as hard as anyone else.

Suddenly out of nowhere half a dozen police cars converged on the schoolyard, lights flashing. "The fuzz! The pigs!" the boys all yelled and scrambled in an instant over the chain-link fence, leaving their broomsticks behind. In a flash, there was only this white kid standing alone in the batter's box, broom in hand, with a bewildered look on his face. Why had they run away? Who were all these men in uniform, and why were they here?

One apparently had a key to the padlock. It clicked open, and a huge man swaggered in. "Ya can't play here, kid," he growled.

"*Mais, pour quois pas?*" I stammered in the first language that came to mind.

He looked at me like I was some sort of smart aleck he was going to have to rough up a bit.

"Ooops...why not?" I said in English.

"Ya just can't. It's against the law. Now gimme your broom."

He grabbed it from my hand and, to my horror, stuck it along with all the other confiscated sticks in the bottom holes of the chain-link fence. He then proceeded to go down the line, stomping each one with his boot, breaking them all in half.

The policemen then stood back a moment, obviously trying to figure me out. Who was I and why on earth was I still hanging around? Shaking their heads, one of them muttered, "Get outta here, punk, and don't come back."

I stood there forlorn as they climbed back into their cars and drove off. In stunned silence I picked up my broken broom and went back across the street. How would I explain to the mission manager that I'd done something bad to his equipment?

This was my first exposure to law and order in this new country. I was baffled that doing something so perfectly fun and innocent could be not just wrong but illegal. I was amazed at the street savvy of those kids and the harshness of the authorities. It was Bandulo all over again. Here I was in my first week in this new land called America, and already I was a "juvenile delinquent!" I had a lot to learn.

Lucky for me, my father was gone that day. Hearing the story, my poor mother had no idea what justice would look like. I had gotten in trouble with the NYPD. That had to be bad, really bad. But what exactly was the crime of this new "immigrant"? She couldn't figure it out either.

THE ASSAULT

That evening my father was still at a meeting across town. In fact, he would not return until the next day. My bedroom was on the third floor overlooking the street, above the entrance to the building. My mother and I went to sleep around ten o'clock.

Suddenly at two in the morning, I was awakened by the sound of a woman shrieking in the street below me. "Help! Get away from me. Stop it! Somebody help!" she cried.

I sprang from my bed and rushed to the window. I had never seen anything like this before. Down among the row of garbage cans outside our building was a woman being attacked by two guys. They were slapping her and tearing at her clothing.

Everything within me compelled me to dash down there to her defense. I pulled on my jeans and ran from my bedroom toward the staircase—just as my mother rounded the corner. Out of the darkness, she grabbed my shirt and yanked me back.

"Mom," I gasped, "they're hurting a woman down there! I've got to help her!"

"Not here, not now, not in this country," she ruled. "Wesley, you *cannot* go down there! They'll kill you!" She corralled me in the bedroom overlooking the street. The screaming and pleas for help went on unabated.

All the lessons of the village ordered me to go to that woman's rescue. Someone was in trouble, which meant we all were in trouble, right? I was trembling inside, torn between my instincts and having to obey my mother.

We crept to the window and watched the scene below. Nobody ran out to intervene. In fact, windows began to squeak open on the opposite side of the street. I heard a man shout, "Hey, shut up already. We're trying to sleep up here!"

Soon more windows slipped open, and more voices shouted for quiet as the mugging continued. My mind raced. *What kind of a place is this? Why doesn't anybody help? Why doesn't anybody care?*

I suppose we should have at least grabbed the phone to call the police, but it was on the bottom floor of the building, and none of us had yet even touched it. We knew nothing about how to use the local "drums." (The invention of "Dial 911" was still seven years away at this time.)

In the distance a siren wailed, and the noise below subsided. Trash can lids rattled on the stairway for a moment, and then there was silence. When we again peered from our window, the men and the woman were gone. We never saw where they went.

I returned to my bed trembling with much to ponder. Between the "good guys" breaking my broom that afternoon and the "bad guys" getting away with whatever they wanted to do, I thought to myself, *That's it. I don't belong in this country. These are not my kind of people. I'm getting out of here and back to Africa as fast as possible.* Not that I had any way to follow through on that pledge as a young teenager. But if I had, I would certainly have done so.

The next day, still shaken from the trauma of the night, I took a walk around the block. Halfway around, I saw people walking along with large bags full of food. Backtracking, I discovered the source: a huge grocery store. I walked its aisles in amazement. Around the next corner was another, similar store.

Suddenly it hit me like a blow to the gut. *There's plenty of food in this world for everyone! Look at it all! My friends who died of hunger didn't need to. Why didn't these people send us some of this food? They sent us their used clothes; why didn't they send us what we really needed?*

On the same walk around the block, I entered a drugstore. Again the horrible reality hit me: *There's plenty of medicine, too!* It just wasn't in my village, where it was so desperately needed. I stumbled on in a blur of tears and sadness.

For most of my teenage years in America, I lived with a broken heart. I was from a precious place nobody had ever heard of. I carried deep scars of both pain and sorrow. Few people cared to hear much about it. Anyone who had the means to help and didn't do so became, by definition, my enemy. I was an angry young man, just biding my time in a strange land until I could get back "home."

WHY DOESN'T POVERTY
JUST GO AWAY?

I n time, of course, I worked through my teenage resentment. I came to realize that while millions of people didn't care about the plight of the poor, a fair number of others did. The inequities that gnawed at me while walking around the Manhattan block that day frustrated them as well. They wanted to help—but how?

Poverty, you see, is a lot more complex than it looks. Too many people assume it's just a shortage of money. If the poor had an adequate supply of money, they'd quickly solve their problems, and the world would be a beautiful place. So let's think up another fund-raiser, another benefit concert, another charity drive...

Any response to the needs of the poor certainly involves money somewhere along the line. But it is not the cure-all by any means. Billions have been spent by governments and nonprofit organizations alike to relieve poverty. At the time my family and I had just returned to America, President Lyndon B. Johnson was aggressively pushing a national "War on Poverty." It did some good, but it certainly didn't solve the problem forever. Today, forty years later, one of out every six American children *still* lives below the poverty line.[1]

Worldwide, it's more like one out of every two.[2] Think about that for a minute. This globe, with all its resources and efforts at getting organized to meet the need, still fails to provide adequately for *almost half* of its precious little ones. On the test of caring for the next generation, we're scoring a lowly 54 percent, which will get you an F at any school.

The world's greatest economic minds have studied, researched, analyzed, and written thick books on the subject. Still, the world's rich seem to get richer, while the poor get poorer.

Is this truly an unsolvable puzzle?

Under the Wheel

On the basis of my lifetime spent living and working with the poor, let me unpack for you what lies beneath the surface. To do so, I will employ a simple diagram. Think of a wagon wheel with six spokes:

The hub in the middle represents abject, unrelenting, bone-grinding poverty. These people have absolutely nothing. They live in the garbage dumps of Caracas and Cairo and Calcutta, clutching their stomachs in hunger, shivering in the rain.

The outer rim of the wheel represents wholeness, adequacy, "enough." Notice, I didn't say "wealth" or "riches" or even "abundance." (That condition is another subject for another time.) I simply indicated the condition of having one's actual needs met.

Now, going around the wheel, we can see what those needs are. Yes, one spoke is, of course, named "economics." If you don't have very much money, your options are severely limited. While in my late twenties and early thirties, I spent four years working in Haiti, the poorest nation in the Western Hemisphere. The average peasant family at that time could earn about $140 (U.S.) *per year* by trying to grow coffee or cotton on the hillsides, long since drained of nutrients by overfarming and erosion. Not much has changed since then. The average parents still have next-to-zero education to pursue any other line of work. They're stuck doing what they've always done.

They would like a better life for their six, seven, or eight children, however. To send just *one* of them to school costs around $50 a year in fees. So they take a deep breath, choose one child, and send him off to learn, tightening down the screws on life's other necessities even further. This child is called their *baton vieillesse,* their "cane for old age." He will grow up to get a better job, they hope, and will support the parents when they grow too old and infirm to work the land, since there is no Social Security or retirement program for them. Otherwise, they will starve.

One of the hardest things for this peasant to endure is when he walks to town and gets almost pushed off the roadway by a passing Rolls-Royce or Mercedes. Yes, Haiti has some extremely wealthy people. The poor person's agony is doubled by having to witness the opulence of others who can afford almost anything they see.

In daily life a lack of money translates into *a lack of options,* which is perhaps a more accurate definition of poverty. The world's poor look at a situation and cannot say, "Well, I could pursue choice A, B, or C. Which one makes the most sense? Which would turn out best for me and my family?" No, under the circumstances, there is only choice A. That is the reality of poverty.

The next spoke of the wheel is called "health." I have already told you of the needless deaths I saw as a boy growing up in Africa. Children suffered and died of something as simple as chickenpox or other problems you or I can easily handle with a quick trip to the pediatrician's office, which would be covered by health insurance that is subsidized by our employers. But in Nielle, none of those systems was in place.

A big part of health maintenance, of course, is getting adequate nutrition. Some people think the earth can't keep up with the food needs of its population. That is not true. In fact, the UN Food and Agriculture Organization (FAO) declared at a World Food Summit in Rome that the planet could produce enough food for every one of us to have a daily diet of 2,720 calories.[3] The average six-year-old needs only 1,800 calories a day. The average fourteen-year-old girl needs 2,200, and the fourteen-year-old boy needs 2,500.[4]

So why is a third of our world battling obesity and spending huge sums to burn off excess calories, while the other two-thirds yearn to get more of them?

The likelihood of a little Haitian child making it to his or her fifth birthday is so small that many parents do not even entrust their child with a name until then. They refer to the toddler as *ti chape,* "my little escapee." In other words, this little one has dodged death up to now, but who knows if he will actually survive? So why bother giving him a real name? We can always do that later, if needed.

Poor health is a major component of poverty and not disconnected from the first spoke, economics. As you will see in our journey around the wheel, the spokes are interdependent. Every one must be strong. A deficiency in any one of them will quickly make the others crack under the strain.

The next spoke is called "learning." The old saying "What you don't know can't hurt you" is a lie. Poverty is greatly aggravated by the absence of information and acquired skills. Without these, the big world swirls around you like a dust storm, bombarding you from all sides with surprises that you have no way to comprehend or process, let alone overcome.

One of the biggest killers in the world today is diarrhea. I didn't just say it was uncomfortable; I said it could take your life. How so? Because the message has been passed from grandmother to mother to daughter for generations: "Look at that child with diarrhea. What's the problem? Obviously, too much water inside! We need to stop the drinking for a while and dry out this little one. Then it'll be okay." And children go on dying of dehydration by the hundreds of thousands.

That is what you call a tragic lack of information.

In our Compassion programs, we've tackled this by teaching our sponsored children in science classes that the most common cause of diarrhea is contaminated water. We talk about how to protect themselves and their families. We show them how to mix salt and sugar into water right there at home so they can keep pushing fluids packed with the necessary electrolytes that will alleviate the problem. In so doing, we believe we've saved thousands of lives. All it took was a modest amount of education.

Obviously the ability to read and write and do math is mandatory in today's world. So are practical job skills. Too many of my African buddies have now grown up to spend their days and years chopping grass or hunting for animals that are rapidly dwindling, without ever reaching the potential God placed within them. Poverty will never be erased without learning.

The beautiful thing is, an educated child in the developing world becomes a multiplier of learning, creating a ripple effect. He or she goes home and teaches Dad or Mom or Grandpa to read. As children move toward the outer ring of adequacy in this area, they often bring whole families along with them.

The fourth spoke is called "environment." I know that some people in the West view this as a sideline concern. Well, it is no sideline issue in Nielle, where the life-giving marsh has now almost completely dried up. No longer can you fish, bathe, grow rice, or even cool off. This affects daily life for everyone in the village.

Ivory Coast has cut down and exported so much timber (mainly to Europe) that it competes in volume with Brazil, a country twenty times as large. Since 1975, Ivory Coast has suffered the highest deforestation rate in the world. The herds of elephants, lions, hippos, leopards, antelopes, and many other animals have been decimated as a result, which has changed things for humans as well.

When Christopher Columbus landed on the north coast of what is modern-day Haiti back in December 1492, he gazed at its rich forests and called it the Mahogany Queen. Trees covered 80 percent of the terrain. Today, the figure is 5 percent and still dropping, as desperate people chop down the few remaining trees to make charcoal for fuel. Any fuel that is petroleum based is too expensive for them. As a result, Haiti is an ecological disaster. The sun beats down on the bare, parched earth and radiates upward again. I have watched rain clouds form over the land, be driven upward by the heat, then push off toward the sea, there to drop their precious moisture where the thirsty people cannot access it.

The fifth spoke is termed "social" or "sociopolitical." Poverty is, among other things, a function of being powerless in the halls of government and the social structures that administer our lives. I am not making excuses here or looking for scapegoats. I am simply acknowledging that if you are fairly sure your vote won't count and that whatever taxes you pay will only end up financing a war or maybe increasing the governor's personal fortune, it is very easy to get discouraged and become fatalistic. When jobs and infrastructure improvements go inevitably to the tribe or region of the party in power, while other sections of the population are ignored, resentment grows. Corruption bleeds the meager resources that average citizens can muster, making it harder and harder for them to get on their feet. Nothing saps the peasant's initiative faster than a sense that the system is stacked against him.

The final spoke of the wheel is called "spiritual." Religious bondage can suffocate the poor in excruciating ways. I have seen hungry Africans forgo the nutrients of a chicken because they felt they must obey the witch doctor's directive to sacrifice it to ward off an evil spirit. I have watched followers of certain Asian religions decline to help their desperate neighbors because they believed it would interfere with their karma. The starving child in the street, they tell themselves, is working out some issue from a previous lifetime, and so that process must run its course.

Jesus asked one time, "What good will it be for a man if he gains the whole world, yet forfeits his soul?" (Matthew 16:26). All the dollars and euros and pesos and shillings and rupees in the world will not equal the peace that comes from knowing a God who loves you. He's not out to get you or destroy you. He is, in fact, on your side. He's more powerful than the evil spirits around you. He sent his Son for your liberation, and "if the Son sets you free, you will be free indeed" (John 8:36).

At one point in my life, I was recruited to leave my ministry position to work for USAID, the government agency that combats global poverty. It was a marvelous job that would have paid four times what I was making at Compassion. Actually, make that five times, since the salary would have been earned overseas and thus would have been tax free. But I will never forget the interviewer asking in half a dozen different ways, "Now, of course we know you're a Christian, and that's an important part of who you are. Do you feel you could do this job without, uh, letting the spiritual side of things get in the way? We have to remain nonsectarian, you know."

I replied, "Well, Christ is at the center of who I am. Part of what I've always done in my work with the poor is to bring the hope of Jesus Christ into their lives. If that's out of bounds in your operational scheme, then I guess I'm not the guy you're looking for."

In spite of that answer, they offered me the job anyway. I turned it down. I don't tell that story to boast about myself but to reinforce that the spiritual dimension is crucial to understanding poverty. You can't just sweep it to the side or view it as an optional add-on.

IT'S *ALL* SPIRITUAL

In fact, far from being peripheral, the spiritual aspect is essential to the other five spokes of the wheel. Some churchgoers may not realize it, but God's concern touches all parts of our lives, seven days a week.

Does he get involved with economics? Absolutely. "All hard work brings a profit," he says in Proverbs 14:23, "but mere talk leads only to poverty." Scripture is full of instruction about labor and money.

Does God care about health? Absolutely. Page after page of the Old Testament law spells out what kinds of animals to eat and not to eat, how to handle blood in meat, and what to do with infections. At one point, believe it or not, God even gets down to the messy details of sanitation rules for human waste (see Deuteronomy 23:12–13). Why? Because if we don't pay attention to these things, we'll have epidemics on our hands. To cite just one example, our world still has a new case of cholera—a disease spread by contaminated water—every three minutes.

Does God care about education? Certainly. His entire revelation to us comes in the form of a book, which he fully expects us to read and to help others read. Teaching is even listed as one of the special gifts of the Holy Spirit (Romans 12:7).

Does God care about the environment? Is he concerned about irrigation systems or reforestation? Does animal life matter to him? Listen to this passage from the majestic Psalm 8:

> You made him ruler over the works of your hands;
>   you put everything under his feet:
> all flocks and herds,
>   and the beasts of the field,
> the birds of the air,
>   and the fish of the sea,
>   all that swim the paths of the seas.

O LORD, our Lord,
how majestic is your name in all the earth! (verses 6–9)

It is his earth, after all; he made it in the first place. He put this planet together to serve the needs of his highest creation, human beings. When we interrupt or corrupt the systems that should sustain us, he is not happy about that. He wants to see the created order restored to its highest and best uses.

Does God care about our sociopolitical world? Definitely. The writings of the Old Testament prophets and poets are full of his concern for justice, equity, and cooperation. "A poor man's field may produce abundant food, but injustice sweeps it away," says Proverbs 13:23. How often this proves true! It breaks the heart of God. He gives a stern warning in Proverbs 22:22–23:

Do not exploit the poor because they are poor
and do not crush the needy in court,
for the LORD will take up their case
and will plunder those who plunder them.

If we are serious about helping overcome poverty, about moving people from the dark hole in the center of the wheel to the sunshine at the perimeter, we must care about all areas of their lives. It is not enough to concentrate on our favorite—say, health or education—and assume this will cure the rest. That's like coming out in the morning to find a flat tire on your car and saying, "Oh, well, just this one section is flat. The rest looks fine. I'll just drive on the other five-sixths of the tire today." Sorry, but that won't work.

When Jesus left this earth, he gave his followers the Great Commission: "Go and make disciples of all nations, baptizing them…and teaching them to obey *everything* I have commanded you" (Matthew 28:19–20). He meant for our work on his behalf to cover a broad range. Of all the topics he dealt with, we're supposed to include 100 percent. He didn't give us the choice of concentrating on just one or two or three.

Poverty is a large complex of issues, and Jesus spoke to every one of them. Our response must not be simplistic. It must cover as much ground as he covered.

It is at this point that someone is sure to protest, "Well, didn't Jesus also say something about 'the poor you have with you always'? This problem has been with us for centuries, and it's never really going away."

Don't stop in the middle of Jesus' sentence! His point was *not* that poverty is chronic in our world so don't worry about it. What he actually said that day in the temple was, "The poor you will always have with you, and you can help them any time you want. But you will not always have me" (Mark 14:7). He was *pro-help* all the way. He assumed they would help the poor since this was in line with one of the bedrock mandates of the Jewish faith: alms for the poor. The Law of Moses had made it abundantly clear: "Do not be hardhearted or tightfisted toward your poor brother. Rather be openhanded and freely lend him whatever he needs.... Give generously to him and do so without a grudging heart; then because of this the LORD your God will bless you in all your work and in everything you put your hand to" (Deuteronomy 15:7–8, 10).

We do not have the option of ignoring poverty. We are called to be Christ's hands, Christ's feet, and Christ's voice. Even a simple cup of cold water given in his name, he said, is like a gift given directly to him. Who would skip *that* opportunity?

Answer: Only those who fail to see the One who stands in the shadows behind the poor child or teenager or adult, waiting to observe our response. For those people, the sobering day will come when

> the King will reply,... "Depart from me, you who are cursed, into
> the eternal fire prepared for the devil and his angels. For I was hungry and you gave me nothing to eat. I was thirsty and you gave me
> nothing to drink. I was a stranger and you did not invite me in, I
> needed clothes and you did not clothe me, I was sick and in prison
> and you did not look after me." (Matthew 25:40–43)

The shocked people on that Judgment Day will of course protest that there must be some confusion, some mistaken identity involved here. But the Lord will have none of it. A rebuff to the poor equals a rebuff to him personally, he will insist. A faith that excludes generosity and compassion is apparently, from this passage, not a saving faith after all. And now the heavy price must be paid.

WHAT IS THE STARTING POINT?

If the stakes are this ominous, we had better get busy understanding how to make a dent in the suffering of the world's poor. This leads us to ask, "What is causing this misery? What is at the very root of poverty?"

I have good news! The answer is something every one of us can understand. We might not be medical, economic, or political experts, but we are human beings with hearts, souls, and spirits.

At its very core, poverty is a mind-set that goes far beyond the tragic circumstances. It is the cruel, destructive message that gets whispered into the ear of millions by the enemy Satan himself: "Give up! You don't matter. Nobody cares about you. Look around you: Things are terrible. Always have been, always will be. Think back. Your grandfather was a failure. Your parents couldn't protect or take care of you. Now it's your turn. You, too, will fail. So just give up!"

More than any other emotion, the poor feel *overwhelmed*. Without financial resources, shelter, food, education, justice, or skills to address their plight, they succumb to the downward spiral that leads to hopelessness and despair. That, my friend, is the essence of poverty.

Tragically, it can happen at a very early age. The sparkle in the child's eyes goes dull; the posture slumps; the countenance is downcast. I remember studying the faces of kids as young as three and four years old in Haiti. If you asked them a question, they would mutter instantly, *"M'pa kone"* ("I don't know"). Before they even considered what was being asked, they would hang their heads and surrender to their sense of ignorance.

If you asked them to do the simplest thing, they would respond, *"M'pa kapab"* ("I can't" or "I'm not capable"). They might as well have added, "Can't you see I am nobody? What makes you think I can do anything?"

Another common phrase was *"M'pa gagne"* ("I don't have," meaning "I don't have anything you need or would want").

After a while I learned to sit quietly instead of trying to talk them out of their apathy. I would wait for any sign of hope or self-worth. But most often what I got was the addition of an odd little gesture I've rarely seen an American child use. They would start wringing their tiny hands. They would look at me sadly and say, *"Pa fot mwe"* ("It's not my fault!"). I used to see that gesture through my tears. Sometimes it reminded me of Pontius Pilate washing his hands in a basin as if to say, "I can't do anything. I'm not responsible."

When a child would accidentally spill a glass of water at a meal, he or she would look at the mess and say with all sincerity, "The water spilled itself." The child wasn't being defensive but was merely expressing his or her honest perspective. In other words, "I have no control over my circumstances and certainly not my life. All control is outside of myself. I am nothing; I can do nothing; I am a victim—pa fot mwe."

Unless there is an intervention of love and hope, these seeds of apathy lead inevitably downward to an even lower death sentence called fatalism. The very word stinks of death. It is the bottom—as low as a human being can sink. When the human spirit becomes truly fatalistic, it is almost impossible to retrieve. This is complete and utter poverty, the end of the road.

One doesn't sink to fatalism easily or lightly. It doesn't happen overnight. It gradually encroaches on one's spirit like a thief over the years and even generations.

We in the United States and other lands of opportunity struggle to understand this. "Why doesn't that poor person just get up?" we snap. "He needs to grab his bootstraps, pick himself off the floor, and get on with it."

After living on both ends of this bridge, among both the rich and the poor, I can tell you that nobody sinks to this depth of hopelessness by choice or by lack of courage or resolve. It is a logical conclusion to life's harsh realities.

It may seem easy from our perspective to give a pep talk. But if any of us were stripped of our heritage, our can-do spirit, our education, our money, our health, and the justice we take for granted, we, too, would rapidly come to the conclusion that "I don't know what I need to know. I can't do what I need to do. I don't have what I need to have. And it's all beyond me. It's not my fault!" That is the heart and soul of poverty.

When I first arrived in Haiti back in 1977, the whole country was in the grip of a terrible drought. It had not rained in nearly eighteen months, and this was a country where 90 percent of the population tried to make their living as peasant agriculturists. The people of the northwest had been particularly stricken and were reduced to eating tree bark or even pulling out bits of their own hair to consume.

I was on my way to that region one day, bouncing along the rocky road in a Land Rover, when suddenly from the corner of my eye, through the dust cloud my vehicle was making, I saw an old man. He squatted at the base of a huge, beautiful mango tree. In his hand was a worn machete. Slowly, stroke by stroke, he was chopping down the tree.

Such trees were rare in Haiti. He had made quite a dent in one side of the tree when I slammed on my brakes beside him. Before the dust had cleared, I jumped from my truck and grabbed his hand in midair.

"What are you doing?!" I gasped in Creole. (It's fairly close to French, which I had learned as a child.)

"I am chopping down this tree," he replied matter-of-factly.

I looked at his wrinkled, weather-beaten face in disbelief. "Why?" I cried. This was the only green thing growing for miles around.

"I am going to make it into charcoal," he replied patiently.

"Why?" I asked again.

"Because I need the money to buy food. My family and I are very hungry."

Getting my emotions and heart together with my head, I took a deep breath. I decided I would need to carefully and patiently counter his logic at this madness. "Does this tree still produce mangoes?" I asked.

"Yes."

"How many times a year does it produce a crop?" I inquired.

"Twice a year—every six months."

"When did it last give you mangoes?"

"It gave me a harvest of mangoes just last month."

I pushed on. "When you sell the mangoes at harvest time, how much money do you usually get?"

There was no question in his mind about that answer. He had done it many, many times over the years. "Seventy-five dollars," he replied.

"When you have turned this tree into charcoal, how much money do you think you'll get for it?"

He stood up, craning his neck to survey the branches of his tree. He wrote with his finger on the palm of his callused, gnarled hand. Then he looked up and said, "About seventy-five dollars."

I had him right where I wanted him. "But that will be your last harvest from your precious tree that has taken care of you for so many years," I announced with a touch of triumph at winning the debate. "It will be gone forever!"

He looked sadly to the dusty ground and shuffled his bare feet, his machete hanging loosely at his side.

I plunged onward in my logic. "Don't you see, if you let the tree live and are patient for just five more months, it will give you another seventy-five dollars. In fact, it will give you that much money again and again in the future! I beg you, don't chop it down."

His tired, bloodshot eyes looked at me for a moment. Then, without a word, he stooped back down and began to chop away rhythmically at his tree once more.

I went to grab the knife again from his hand. "Don't you see?" I implored. "If you kill it now…"

"No, don't *you* see?!" he suddenly shouted at me, his eyes brimming with tears. "I don't know that my children or I will even be alive five months from now! All we have is today. I barely have that!"

I stood and watched his rhythmic chopping for a while longer. Behind his hand was the hand of an enemy at work. Satan's fingerprints were all over the tragedy I was witnessing. He had defeated yet another life with one of his favorite tools: poverty.

I couldn't bear to watch the tree fall. I heard the crack as I drove away. Another precious piece of Haiti's hope and future crashed to the parched ground.

GETTING AT THE ROOT

If we are going to strike poverty at its root, we must take aim at this condition called fatalism. This is what keeps people penniless, sick, ignorant, vulnerable, oppressed, and without God.

I know this is perhaps a different perspective of poverty than you have typically heard. Most people see only the circumstances and conditions. But poverty is an inside-out issue. It does its greatest damage on the inside, where it often cannot be seen.

Don't get me wrong; when it comes to the poor, I believe it is "good to do good." But not all good is of equal value or is strategic enough to attack poverty at its core and reverse its deadly effect. If we are going to do good, why not also be strategic? Henry Ford once said about the poor, "The only thing you can give a man without hurting him is an opportunity." He knew that no amount of handouts or doing good things on a person's behalf gets to the heart of the matter, which is the inner, destructive message of "Just give up." An opportunity, on the other hand, cuts to the very core by saying, "I believe in you! You can do it. Don't you dare give up!"

Think of a grapevine that consistently produces sour, bitter grapes. Nobody wants to eat them. What should be done about this? I suppose it would be a good thing (at least better than doing nothing) to pick off the destructive, bad fruit and throw it away. It feels good to do that. You feel like you're making a difference.

But the next season, the same bad fruit will be back—maybe even more of it. This will go on season after season until someone finally decides to get at the underground sewage system that is causing the bitter fruit. Only then will this grapevine become useful, producing the sweet fruit you would expect.

On the bitter vine of poverty are all kinds of sour fruit. Poor housing.

Contaminated water. Injustice. Economic limitations. A harsh environment. Lack of infrastructure. Poor health. War. But these are not poverty. They are merely its symptoms. They are deplorable and should be addressed by caring people. But the mere elimination of poverty's symptoms will never win the war.

We should have learned this lesson long ago in the United States. Some thirty-five years ago I myself was deeply and passionately engaged as a young student at Moody Bible Institute. Chicago's Juvenile Court put me to work as a community aide in the most deplorable ghetto of the city, Cabrini Green. My fellow students and I worked hard at tutoring and befriending at-risk children. All around us, big government programs were addressing everything but the human element at the core of the problem.

Sadly, today the high-rise housing of Cabrini Green, the basketball courts, and lighted parking lots are being torn down. They didn't work. Poverty didn't get defeated. The violence, crime, hatred, and hunger persisted. More than three decades have come and gone, and we have lost another entire generation! That is because deep in the ground of such deplorable conditions, at the base of the bitter grapevine, the roots of poverty keep producing the same destructive results year after year.

Albert Einstein once defined insanity as "doing the same thing over and over again and expecting different results." The battle against poverty has fallen into this trap more than a few times.

Several years after the Cabrini Green experience, I was doing my doctoral studies at Michigan State University. By this time I had seen more than my share of poverty and its destructiveness, not only in the lives of West Africans but also in Haitians. I sat through one graduate course after another analyzing the various aspects, causes, conditions, and strategies to address poverty from the perspective of many experts, bilateral and multilateral organizations, and governments.

Once in a while I would annoy and challenge my fellow students by leaning back in my chair and saying, "I still say that the most loving and strategic thing that can be done for children in poverty is to bring them to their heavenly Father."

They would groan and reply, "Ah, Wess, there you go putting a spiritual Band-Aid on the hurts of the world!" They sounded really informed and knowledgeable with their dismissal of my perspective.

I'd just smile and say, "Yeah, you got a problem with that?" After a good-hearted laugh, I would explain that when you understand poverty's root, its core, as a destructive mind-set that says, "I don't matter. There is nothing special about me. Why should I try? Why should I dare to hope? Who cares about me?" you have stumbled right into the very heart of the gospel. Every Christian who has experienced the love of God in his or her life is in a perfect place to understand the centrality of this perspective.

Sometimes when I speak with pastors, I find them a little bit hesitant or awkward with this whole issue of poverty. *Is it within our mandate?* they wonder. What about the struggle between spiritual and physical? Is it part of their discipleship calling?

I tell them that nobody is in a better position than they to understand the very root of poverty or to champion the most strategic path out of it. When a poor child comes to understand that God Almighty, maker of heaven and earth, knows her name, that God cares deeply about her, that he knows how many hairs are on her head, that he etched the unique design of her fingerprints, that he gave her a unique and delightful way of laughing, and that he sent his own Son to die on the cross to save her, that leads to an epiphany that changes everything. "I guess I matter after all!"

When a child in poverty says, "I matter," he has just taken the first teetering step out of poverty! The outer circumstances with which he struggles may not have changed at all, but the inner core, the root of his personhood, is vastly altered. The healing can now begin, from the inside out.

How? The child begins to think, "Well, if I matter, what I think matters, and what I feel is valid and important." This step enables a child to leave some of the worst abuse behind. No longer will the little girl in Bangkok acquiesce to selling her precious body for a few dollars to any pervert on the street. No longer will the little boy in Port-au-Prince shrug and say, "The water spilled itself." A sense of value has been regained.

When a child in a Compassion project gets to this important stage in personal development, he or she is surrounded by caring people of the church and the consistent message, "That's right, sweetheart. You *do* matter. So tell me, what do you think? What do you feel? Here, can you paint it for me on this easel? Can you play it on this guitar? Can you sing it for me? Can you write it in a letter to your sponsor?" Day after day, week after week, this awakening moves consistently and lovingly forward. The twinkle, that almost-extinguished sparkle, reappears in the child's eyes. His or her posture straightens up. Confidence is restored. That long-lost smile and that desire to give a hug or hold trustingly to your hand slowly blossom like a flower. Mom and Dad start to notice, and joy fills their faces.

As the years pass, they experience success upon success. A well-drawn picture. Applause for a beautiful dance. Getting from first grade to second after passing a difficult exam. A pat on the back when their soccer or volleyball team excels. The blue ribbon for Scripture memory or a tapestry well done.

Faraway sponsors watch their progress over the years and join in the applause and affirmation of the children's progress. It's magic to watch!

Then comes a day, usually in adolescence, when the youth will look you in the eye, straighten their shoulders, and say, "You want to know what I think and feel? I'll tell you!" (This may come in the form of an essay, a speech to the community, or a quiet conversation under the mango tree.) They look around at their surroundings and say boldly, "I don't think my community should look like this." Or they see an injustice or cruelty and say, "I don't think it's right that people treat each other that way." Eventually they'll say, "See what's going on over there? That's wrong—and I can fix it!"

The immediate response of the caring adult is, "You know what? I think you're absolutely right! You could do that. Go fix it. Make your world a better place!" At such a wonderful moment, a productive life is launched. Now the adult's role is to watch, help, and applaud.

It all begins, I maintain, with that powerful and underutilized thing called love. God's love for the individual is displayed by those people who reflect his love in their words and deeds. It ultimately gets understood and accepted by the child in poverty, and through that individual's love for others, the world gets changed.

One changed child eventually changes a family. A changed family will influence change in its church. Enough changed churches will transform the community. Changed communities change regions. Changed regions will in time change an entire nation.

The Runner

This, my friends, is the path out of poverty! And it happens one child at a time. I know that has become a cliché, but it is absolutely true if you understand that poverty, an overwhelming global tragedy, occurs one life at a time. It destroys lives one at a time. And it is defeated one life at a time.

Curiously enough, the poor seem to know this instinctively. All over the world I've found that if you ask a poor man or woman, "What can I do to help you?" the answer is the same. It doesn't matter whether you're in Asia, Africa, or Latin America, conversing in Tagalog, Lingala, or Spanish. Whatever the circumstance, the poor do *not* request money or personal things. They invariably look back at you with hopeful eyes and say, "If you want to help me, help my children."

If throughout this book you have discounted my passion by saying to yourself, "Well, Wess Stafford is a sentimentalist toward children; he's the kind of guy who gets all mushy around little kids," let me tell you, it's a lot more than sentiment. I truly believe in this cause for hard-nosed, objective, strategic reasons. I'm not just looking to feel good or assuage my conscience. I believe this is the *smart* way to combat the poverty problem.

Notice, I didn't say the *fast* way. The child-centered strategy takes several years to produce fruit. It's not as quick as whipping out your checkbook and changing an external condition in a poor neighborhood. But it is a lot more permanent. It gets results that will last.

Some approaches to poverty are microwave solutions. I'm talking instead about a Crock-pot approach. It may take longer, but the taste at the end of the day is far better and the food more nutritious. It feeds the soul.

So there is something for everyone to do. We who know God's love and have some money in our pockets can reach out to lift up the child in poverty. That child, once awakened to his or her value to God, proceeds to change the local circumstances. It is not an either-or. The responsibility is not entirely on one set of shoulders or the other. We work together.

I come back to my premise that merely addressing the circumstances and conditions of poverty at the community level is not enough. There are simply too many corrupt levels of society for benefit to "trickle down" to the neediest. It just doesn't work—or at least not often enough to make it worth my life's effort! But when the poorest of the poor are the ones changed, they come alive and "bubble up" through their community. That breaks the back of poverty and brings a sustainable transformation, by transformed people, that cannot be taken away. While changed circumstances sometimes change people, changed people always change circumstances.

One of my favorite stories of the power of child sponsorship didn't happen in the realm of my organization; it was some other effort whose name I have lost. But to me, it epitomizes the wonderful power of a concerned adult to change a child's life. In this case, it was a British schoolmarm who sometime around 1970 began to sponsor a little boy in Kenya. Every month she sent her modest check. But she did more than that. This teacher understood child development, and she could tell right away by his early letters that he was trapped in hopelessness.

"Dear Sponsor," he wrote in the beginning. "Here is a picture of me. You can see that I am not very handsome."

His British sponsor smiled warmly and wrote back. "I think you are wrong about that. I have your picture on my desk. I look at you every day, and I think you are very handsome."

The next letter from Kenya said, "Well, thank you, but you can see from my report card they sent you that I'm not very smart. I'm so sorry."

Again she smiled. "Well, I promise you that you are as smart as God wants you to be to do whatever he wants you to do," she wrote back. "Just do your very best!"

In time this little boy began to sense that his sponsor actually believed in him and was committed to him. He was eight years old when he sat down and wrote, "Guess what I just learned? I discovered that I can run faster than anyone else in my classroom. There are five of us, and I am the fastest!"

Knowing how important the taste of success is to any child, but especially to a child living in poverty, the woman wrote back, "Well, it is good to be good at something. I'm proud of you. Be the best runner you can be!"

The little boy listened to her and began to run. A few years later a letter came that said, "Guess what? I now run faster than anyone in my whole school!"

Her reply came a few weeks later. "Wow! That is really something! I am so proud of you. Keep on running and be the best you can be!"

The years of their friendship rolled by. The woman retired from teaching and settled into a little cottage in the south of England. Meanwhile, the lad remembered her words of encouragement and ran everywhere he went: to the store, to church, to school, and back home again. Soon he was winning community-wide races. In time as a young man he sat down and penned this letter to his now-aging sponsor: "Guess what now! I run faster than almost anyone in, not only my community, but all of Kenya. In fact, I have made the Olympic team!"

With tears glistening in her bespectacled eyes, she bowed her head and breathed a prayer for her young Kenyan friend. The year was 1988, and the Olympics would soon be held in Seoul, South Korea. She watched the news reports eagerly.

The day came for his long-distance race. She sat glued to her television set back in Britain, watching for her young man. And when the exhausted racers crossed the finish line, she wept as he captured the silver medal. Her sponsored child, who originally had felt he could do nothing, had grown up to impress the entire world.

Soon news came that the young man's route back home after the Olympic Games would include a plane change in London. He couldn't go home, he said, without first seeing this dear lady. When the day came, this lanky Olympian had to stoop to get through her cottage doorway. There before him, in a wheelchair, sat his champion.

He stood for a moment with tears filling his eyes. Then the handsome young man held out his Olympic medal by its ribbon. "This is for you," he finally managed to whisper.

"Oh, no, no, no," she exclaimed. "I got to watch you run this time on television. You were right all along. You were so fast! I am so proud of you. I am so very proud of you!"

"No, stop," he gently interrupted her. "If you hadn't believed in me when I was eight years old, if you hadn't told that little boy to run, I never would have accomplished this. This is your medal. This is your victory."

I wish I could promise every person who cares about a child in poverty that an Olympic medal awaits. Not every young boy or girl is genetically put together by the Creator with that ability. But I am absolutely convinced that each and every child is lovingly knit in the mother's womb with the gifts, talents, and potential to accomplish great things—if only given a chance. Every child matters to God. Once that child, through our intervention, comes to understand and believe the awesome truth, the cold fingers of poverty are pried loose once and for all.

THE CHILDREN'S CHAMPION: A RIGHTEOUS RAGE

As you can tell by now, I am passionate about the needs and nurture of children. It is my mission in life. Some people mistakenly assume that youth workers are just paying their dues until they can move up to a more prestigious job. For me, working on behalf of children is all I want to do for the rest of my useful days. My understanding of the priorities of God's kingdom presents no higher or more strategic calling.

If I seem a little overwrought about this at times, well, I don't apologize. I got this passion, this fire, from a worthy source. I'm not just talking about my boyhood experience of growing up among the poor or of being personally abused. I'm talking about the intensely held values of the greatest man who ever lived, Jesus of Nazareth.

Everyone knows the account of how Jesus welcomed the little children into his arms—but not everyone notices the story behind the story. The day he said, "Let the little children come to me, and do not hinder them" (Matthew 19:14 and its parallels in Mark 10:14; Luke 18:16) has inspired painters, sculptors, poets, and songwriters down through the ages in virtually every language and culture. As I have traveled the world, I have seen just about every interpretation of this incident in art galleries, churches, and homes.

What Jesus did and said that day were extraordinary. After all, he wasn't a political candidate out on the stump, kissing babies for the television cameras. He had no ulterior motive for his action. He simply reached out to children for their own worth, and it no doubt startled everyone. The newsworthiness of this event is evident in the fact that all three Synoptic

Gospel writers felt compelled to include it in their accounts of Jesus' life. Luke, with a doctor's eye, used a different word from the one Matthew and Mark used to describe these little ones. He called them babies (in Greek, *brephos*), the same word he used earlier in his Christmas scene ("You will find a baby wrapped in cloths and lying in a manger," Luke 2:12). The other two gospel writers called them *paidion* (young children). Probably the group ranged anywhere from rambunctious six-year-olds down to infants in diapers.

It was, after all, just one incident on one day out of more than a thousand days of Jesus' public ministry. It was a single act and a few sentences. But apparently it was powerful enough to get written down.

Today most pastors, Sunday school teachers, religious broadcasters, and seminary professors have a sermon or lesson on this text. I've heard dozens across the world in many settings and languages. Yet I have rarely heard anyone capture the essence of what really took place that day. Few expositors dwell on the strong word in Mark's account that when the children were being pushed aside, Jesus "was *indignant*" (Mark 10:14). Why did the Son of God get *angry*?

After all, the religious leaders and Jesus were at that moment in the middle of discussing the important issue of divorce. The disciples felt this was no time for irrelevant *children* to appear on the scene and disrupt serious adult matters. I don't know how long Jesus tolerated the disciples' attempts at crowd control, but at some point he could stand it no longer. What made him snap? Was it the hurt expressions on the children's faces? Was it the transition from excitement, joy, and hope to disappointment, fear, and rejection? Were some of them crying? Whatever the case, Jesus, the Lord of Glory, the Creator of the universe, the Good Shepherd, almighty God, erupted with anger and came to their defense.

This is where every sermon I've heard depicting this moment falls short. Jesus did not lovingly and quietly coo, "Oh, just let the little children come over to me for a moment." This strong, powerful man, this brawny carpenter, filled with exasperation, anger, and even rage, apparently raised his voice with great passion. "Let the little children come to me! Don't you *dare* hinder them! My kingdom belongs to such as these."

Never in my research of the world's artwork have I seen *this* Jesus. He who not long afterward would wield a whip in the temple to drive out the moneychangers and turn over their product-laden tables was now equally incensed at *this* corruption. He shocked everyone, making a deep impression on those who would be charged with building his kingdom, and spoke passionately enough that his words ring down through the ages.

The children realized that this obviously in-charge adult was defending and protecting *them,* scolding adults on their behalf. Knowing they were loved and welcome, they came meekly at first, then boldly to him. No one would dare stop them now. He gathered them into his strong arms with a tender embrace. He placed his hands gently on them and breathed a blessing over them. How I wish a gospel writer had recovered from his shock in time to record the words of that blessing so that we might have forever, straight from the heart of God, an expression of his love, hope, and deepest desire for their lives.

What Set Him Off?

You might say that I'm making it sound as if Jesus lost his temper, and you've never really thought of him like that.

Granted, Jesus was not a hothead. I can find only three examples in Jesus' life when he was truly angry:

1. In a synagogue when a man with a withered hand needed healing, and the religious leaders sat silently daring Jesus to do so on the Sabbath (Mark 3:5)
2. This incident with the young children
3. In the Jerusalem temple overrun by corruption and commercialism (Mark 11:15–17)

Being fully human, yet fully God, Jesus felt all the emotions we experience—from love and joy to deep sorrow, disappointment, and, yes, even anger. His reactions were far from an abrupt flareup. They were premeditated, the result of reflecting on earlier events. Mark 11:11 says that Jesus went to the temple the evening *before* his invasion, saw what was going on yet again, but did nothing "since it was already late." How his heart must have ached all that night in Bethany. The next morning he could stand it no longer. He stormed the place, whip in hand, and drove them out.

There's an equally aggravating background to Jesus' reaction to the disciples who had shooed away the children. To understand Jesus' profound irritation that day, we must go back to an earlier conversation when he had made his Father's values about children perfectly clear. How could they have forgotten such a vital lesson? How could they have missed the kingdom principle of "Children *matter!*"

It all began, according to the previous chapter (see Mark 9:33), with an ugly conversation on the road to Capernaum. The disciples had exchanged some snippy remarks. It must have broken Jesus' heart to realize that they had not yet learned the importance of humility and servanthood. Later on, Jesus called them to account by saying, "What were you arguing about on the road?"

Of course, none of them would repeat their words to Jesus; the text says, "They kept quiet" (Mark 9:34). But he knew. They had been snarling at each other over status, namely, who among them was the greatest. We will never know what sparked the topic. Unbelievably, they were fresh from a spiritual high point, the experience of the Transfiguration. Maybe they wondered why Moses and Elijah had been chosen for that glorious encounter. Why not Abraham, David, or Samuel? Maybe they had passed a legion of Roman soldiers on the road and, seeing a proud centurion ride a spectacular white horse while a humble foot soldier walked carefully behind, got into a debate regarding hierarchy. Or maybe they were just starting to salivate over the prospects of their own future rise to power and prestige.

The argument sounds petty to us, even juvenile. But, of course, we weren't there. All of us could probably go back in our personal histories and cringe at some of the squabbles we've gotten into. I can imagine that Andrew may have made his case built on seniority; after all, he was the first disciple chosen. Philip could have noted that the kingdom is all about outreach, and he alone had recruited another disciple (Nathanael). Peter could have made a strong case about being the spokesman, sort of second in command. Can't you hear him saying, "Well, when Jesus is not around, I'm in charge, you know."

Matthew might have pointed out that as a former tax collector, he alone knew about fund-raising, and where would they all be without money? Judas, the treasurer, might have countered, "Yes, but what good are funds without stewardship?" John surely thought of himself as "the one Jesus loved," which was a pretty strong endorsement to his credit.

Thomas's best shot might have been, "I doubt…that any of you fully grasps my finer qualities!" Simon the Zealot could have claimed, "My name says it all." Meanwhile, James the son of Zebedee was probably quietly plotting how to get his mother to plead his case later for the right-hand throne. Timing was everything.

Whatever the conversation, it all led to the breaking of the Savior's heart. Time was running out, and after three years of teaching and modeling the qualities of his kingdom, this batch still seemed far off base. Was he really going to take a towel and basin of water later on and wash these unworthy feet? They had so much yet to learn.

All eyes were fixed on Jesus. Would he settle this pecking-order issue once and for all?

MINIATURE ROLE MODEL

At critical or awkward moments, Jesus had an odd habit of turning the tables in surprising ways. He could shock people—and then suddenly take the discussion to a far deeper level. For example, with stones poised to kill the woman caught in adultery, her accusers demanded an immediate pronouncement of judgment from Jesus. To their consternation, he calmly stooped and wrote in the dust with his finger. Then he raised the stakes on *them:* "If any one of you is without sin, let him be the first to throw a stone at her" (John 8:7). On another occasion he told a paralyzed man to rise and walk (and, oh yes, he said his sins were forgiven). He gave original meaning to the phrase "politically incorrect" by dining with sinful tax collectors and prostitutes. Jesus, a powerful teacher, was full of surprises at such pivotal moments.

Jesus' modus operandi was the same here. To the amazement of all, he called a little boy to come to him. Surely the disciples were perplexed and impatient. What did this have to do with the question? (Some historians have speculated that this took place in Peter's house and that the boy was Peter's son.)

Nobody had given the boy's presence a second thought. To the disciples, he was just part of the scenery—invisible, unimportant. Some people still have an attitude that "children should be seen and not heard." The tragedy is that today they are not only unheard but also unseen.

The child's sweet face must have provided Jesus with a momentary oasis of refreshment in the parched desert of grasping egos around him. The look on the boy's face brought up a flood of plans, dreams, and hopes for the kingdom—now seemingly remote and unattainable. How could these disciples have missed the centrality of his message? It had been the very model of his life: leaving the splendor of heaven to come to a manger in Bethlehem; choosing not to live among the rich and powerful but among the poor and powerless; coming not to be served but to serve; desiring not to be the greatest but a servant. The future of his church would hinge on the all-important concepts of humility, servanthood, and considering others better than oneself.

As the Master Teacher's eyes fell on that precious little boy, perhaps he got a surge of inspiration. The disciples had all been children once. Could he transport them back to how they were not so long ago? Could they remember having a childlike spirit? Could they recall how it felt to trust completely, to look up to nearly everyone around them and willingly follow the lead of others? He decided to give it a try.

Scripture tells us Jesus had this child *stand* in their midst. How long? Probably long enough for them to take a good look at him before he ran to Jesus' lap. Long enough for their eyes to fixate on him and for their mood to change as they silently studied his youthful spirit. Plucked from the fringes of power, he was suddenly front and center in the spotlight. They must have scrutinized him with undivided attention, as if they had never really looked upon a child before. What was Jesus trying to tell them?

At last Jesus spoke. "I tell you the truth, unless you change and become like little children, you will never *enter* the kingdom of heaven" (Matthew

18:3). And he could have added, "much less be the greatest in it!" The word *change* here is the same basic word that Peter used later on the Day of Pentecost when he confronted the crowd on their role in crucifying the Son of God: "Repent, then, and *turn* to God, so that your sins may be wiped out" (Acts 3:19).

Jesus was not talking to his disciples about a minor modification, a slightly altered perspective. He was calling them to be radically overhauled from the inside out to be even a part of his kingdom, much less a leader. He might have added, "You demonstrated out there on the road that you have the child*ish* part perfected. But what you need is to become child*like*!"

By this he did not mean they had to become perfect. Sinful nature manifests itself in children as well as adults. This was not a lesson in somehow earning a place in heaven by appropriate behavior (i.e., by being "good children"). No, this was an insight into their very core, their nature, as only the Divine Designer and Creator could possibly know. Jesus was speaking of humility. Lowliness of heart and mind. A teachable spirit. A willingness, even a delight, to learn. The kind of simple faith that wouldn't have walked tentatively on the water as Peter did but would have skipped and frolicked, completely secure in the Master's presence and protection. The trust that allows one to live contentedly by another's rules, even without fully understanding them. The need to love and be loved that simply cannot hold a grudge but is quick to forgive, confident that love can go on.

An entire book could (and should) be written about how the spirit of a child is central to the kingdom of heaven. Jesus was saying that the disciples at that moment were far from what they needed to be, heading in exactly the wrong direction. Time was running out. A radical change was in order.

Perfectly Clear

At that moment perhaps the boy squirmed a little in Jesus' arms. Or maybe the boy reached out to touch the side of Jesus' leg. In some way he seems to have recaptured the Master's attention, because Jesus continued: "Therefore, whoever humbles himself like this child is the greatest in the kingdom of heaven" (Matthew 18:4). A new topic took over at this moment. Up to this point Jesus had been talking about greatness in his kingdom, using the boy as an illustration. Now the child became the central focus as he forged ahead with renewed passion: "And whoever welcomes a little child like this in my name welcomes me" (Matthew 18:5).

Luke's account adds, "For he who is least among you all—he is the greatest" (Luke 9:48). Mark takes it even a step further: "Whoever welcomes me does not welcome me but the one who sent me" (Mark 9:37).

Well, that certainly derailed the roadside debate! No doubt the disciples were stunned and reeling as Jesus' words sank in. An act of kindness to a child is the same as doing that act to Jesus Christ—indeed, to God himself?

One would think that a great new respect and appreciation for children would have seized their hearts. A whole new theology should have arisen that placed children at the center of the work of the church. A new priority for programs, budgets, and strategies should have been established that very moment. The words of Jesus couldn't have been any clearer.

How unbelievable that they forgot all this within a few days. How unbelievably sad that the church would also forget it for the next two thousand years!

When Mark and Luke wrote their accounts (some four decades later), they apparently forgot the rest of the discussion that occurred that day. Their narratives revert immediately to "adult" concerns. Both report that John asked, rather out of the blue, about a guy who had been casting out demons in Jesus' name and what to do about it (Mark 9:38; Luke 9:49). The enlightening moment was apparently lost on these two gospel writers.

Matthew, however, was careful to complete the scene. In Matthew 18:6, Jesus seems stricken with the potential for harm that awaits this little boy before him. He speaks in a somber tone: "But if anyone causes one of these little ones who believe in me to sin, it would be better for him to have a large millstone hung around his neck and to be drowned in the depths of the sea." He paints the most horrifying picture possible to drive home the seriousness of such an offense. He asks his listeners to imagine themselves plunging, head first, arms and legs thrashing, deeper and deeper into the churning sea, dragged down to their deaths by the weight of a two-ton millstone. Jesus certainly had their attention now! Seeing their blanched faces, he might have added, "Have you got that? Can I make it any clearer to you that children matter to me?"

No doubt his mind raced with the many evils that history had perpetrated on little innocents, even the massacre of his Bethlehem peers after his birth. Next, he may have thought ahead to the coming harm of the child slave trade, child sexual exploitation, broken homes with fighting parents, child pornography, child soldiers, the scourge of AIDS. With a sob in his spirit, he plunged on in his powerful teaching for three more verses, saying that if you are inclined to any of these despicable sins, it would be better for you to cut off your hand, lop off your foot, or gouge out your eye. Better to be maimed on earth than to be thrown into the eternal fire of hell!

I think of this verse when I visit a country such as Guatemala, just south of Mexico. It's a small country like many others, struggling to get on its feet economically and lift up the more than 60 percent who live below the poverty line. One of its assets is its tourist appeal; Guatemala has mild weather year round, lovely ocean beaches, active volcanoes, low costs, colorful marketplaces, and three different World Heritage sites designated by UNESCO, including the stunning Mayan ruins at Tikal.

But some tourists these days have a different pleasure in mind. They come from Europe especially, but also North America, looking for twelve- and thirteen-year-old girls. The going rate for a night's "service" is a mere ten U.S. dollars. That, however, is as much as the girl's father makes in half a week of long shifts in a clothing factory. If he were trying to sell souvenirs on the street, he would net even less. When the family is hungry, some anguished and desperate parents are willing to send their innocent daughters out to help earn cash.

Imagine this young girl walking home in the early morning hours from the hotel, clutching in her hand a crumpled ten-dollar bill. But that is not the worst part of the atrocity. In some cases she doesn't know that she is carrying home something else as a result of this night: the AIDS virus. As a result of this ghastly trade called sexual tourism, Guatemala and its neighbor, Honduras, now have the highest HIV infection rates of all Latin American countries.

Once the young woman comes down with full-blown AIDS, the medical response will be far less than in the developed world. Antiretroviral drugs to keep her alive will be vastly too expensive for her family. Thus, death will come much sooner. Look at these two sets of figures for the same year, 2003:

- The United States, the third-largest country in the world with 290 million citizens, buried 14,000 AIDS sufferers.
- Guatemala, with only 11 million citizens, buried 44,000 AIDS sufferers.[1]

Does that not fire your sense of outrage? How disgusting that wealthy, promiscuous travelers from affluent countries should take advantage of these precious children! That's the kind of thing Jesus was fuming about in Matthew 18. No doubt his heart was pounding and his eyes flashing as he spoke.

And I'm sure the disciples agreed with him. Of course they would never deliberately hurt a child with such vicious sin, they told themselves.

Jesus, on the other hand, knew there was another whole side to the topic of children at risk. The sins that would break the heart of God didn't have to be sins of commission. Equally evil and far more prevalent in his kingdom would be sins of omission. Children could simply be looked upon as unimportant, second-rate.

Looking at the culture around him and, through time, to the present, Jesus was not willing to allow for that loophole. He pressed on in verse 10, "See that you do not look down on one of these little ones. For I tell you that their angels in heaven always see the face of my Father in heaven."

Now this was new territory. Don't even *look down on* these little ones? No society in history had given children equal footing to adults, and certainly not the dominant Roman or Jewish cultures of that day. But Jesus was talking about the values and passions of a new kingdom altogether—the kingdom these disciples were to proclaim.

I don't fully understand the pageantry and ceremonial worship that goes on in heaven. Even John the apostle was at a loss for words to describe its splendor to our mortal minds. But from what Jesus said here, there exists in the midst of the elders and the heavenly hosts a cluster of angels—"their" angels—who are attuned to the needs of little children. Theologians debate if there are actual guardian angels assigned to the care and protection of each of us. (If there are, I fear I will be presented with a massive bill upon my entry into heaven for my guardian angel's "overtime" service!)

What this verse seems to be saying is that the highest realms of heaven include angels who are representatives for these little ones, and therefore they should not be looked down on or treated as if they are not important.

Can you imagine a guardian angel suddenly raising his hand in the midst of worship, interrupting the echoes of "Holy, holy, holy," to say to God Almighty on his throne, "Excuse me, but we've just gotten a message from little Maria down in Fortaleza. She sounds upset. She's saying, 'O God, please don't let it happen again tonight.' It sounds like she's crying..."

The music abruptly stops. A great sadness mixed with a touch of irritation comes across the visage of the Eternal One. "Angel!" he suddenly commands. "Go down there immediately, and stand guard beside her bed all night. Make sure she sleeps in peace."

Such is the influence, the access, the "clout" of children in the courts of heaven. I'm convinced that one of the most powerful forces on earth is the prayer of a child.

Jesus closes this discourse on the priorities of his kingdom with the well-known parable of the lost sheep. Many preachers say the point of this story is to illustrate the value of each individual to the Good Shepherd, which is certainly true. You could get that generic application by reading the version in Luke 15:4–7. But here in Matthew 18, it is clear that Jesus is still talking specifically about his love for children. In verse 14 he concludes, "In the same way your Father in heaven is not willing that any of these *little ones* should be lost."

I can't help wondering if, as the disciples wandered away in stunned silence, Jesus lingered a moment with that little boy. The youngster might have looked up at him in awe to say, "Wow, I guess you told them! That's a lesson they will never forget! Your hands were even shaking!"

Reflecting, Jesus might have nodded and said, "I hope so. I felt my heart would burst. I don't remember ever teaching anything more passionately."

The boy's mother may have looked at Jesus gratefully and breathed a quiet "Thank you," understanding that something very important had just happened for her son. Jesus probably slept soundly that night, having taken care of one of the key principles of his kingdom with finality.

Or so it seemed.

DISTRACTED?

Soon afterward, Jesus and his disciples headed down the road south from Galilee toward Perea, a section east of the Jordan River, where "some Pharisees came to test him" (Matthew 19:3). Thus began the complicated discussion of divorce, with children and their mothers hanging around the fringes.

I highly doubt this was the first time Jesus' attention had turned to little ones. I can imagine this happening repeatedly with the Son of God. Children have an uncanny ability to read whether an adult likes them or not. They can tell what's in the spirit of a grownup. They can predict whether the tall people will welcome them with a smile or brush them aside in frustration. I have no doubt that Jesus looked like the kind of person whom kids would love to approach.

Perhaps the disciples knew this about their Master. They'd seen it happen before: he would be engaged in a serious adult issue, and then a child would show up, derailing the group's whole concentration. "Why can't he stay focused? This is such important stuff, with so much at stake," they may have muttered to themselves. I can just picture the scene this particular day: Pharisees all around Jesus in the closest positions, with disciples in the next circle, leaning in to hear every momentous word. They still loved being in the proximity of power.

Then a little boy with a gap-toothed grin peeks out from behind the robe of Peter and gives Jesus a timid wave. A few feet away a little girl holds up a flower with a stem that is starting to bend over in the heat. Then a baby on his mother's back coos and reaches out his chubby arms toward the Master...

He, midsentence on the serious topic at hand, falters just a second as he winks at a mischievous little face. He raises his eyebrows to acknowledge the girl's flower, knowing that it is a gift for him. He can sense the love and admiration of the young mothers who wait patiently, still on the fringes.

Things are unraveling fast. The disciples feel responsible to regain order, lest this important dialogue get sidetracked. *There he goes again with kids,* they think. *Doesn't he realize the power and prestige of the men around him? This is a moment of high influence.* They start to stir, turning to motion with their hands and say, "Shhh!" with their lips. "Not now, ma'am. Can't you see the Master is occupied?"

This is the poignant moment that Mark 10:14 reports: "When Jesus saw this, he was indignant."

Again, I would love to see artwork that captures *this* explosive moment, about twenty seconds before the scene that is normally painted. It would portray not just the face of a distressed and agitated Savior but how all of heaven's and hell's witnesses must have jumped back in stunned silence. Hell suffered a humiliating defeat in that instant. I can only imagine that all heaven broke into cheers! The least of these—so easy to attack, so vulnerable, so unprotected—had, in a flash, been elevated to a place of significance and prominence, championed and shielded by God himself. In that moment it was abundantly clear that the disciples had been honoring the wrong people.

The next words were heard loudly and clearly by all: "Let the little children come to me, and do not hinder them." Those few recorded words speak volumes about what Jesus was like as a human being. He did not say, "*Bring* those children to me now. It's 11:20, the scheduled time in the morning service when we customarily turn our attention to children—briefly." No, Jesus said, "Just get out of the way and *let them come.* All you have to do is stop obstructing them. Look at them; they already feel drawn to me. Don't you dare hinder their coming."

Jesus was too merciful to humiliate his disciples further, but he could have added, "Don't you remember anything from our discussion the other day?! I told you as clearly and forcefully as anything I have ever taught you that the kingdom of God belongs to such as these." Even without such a scolding, I can picture the disciples, disarmed and deflated, watching in silence as an avalanche of triumphant little children surge past them into the embrace of their Master. Jesus instinctively takes them into his arms, hugs them tight, and blesses them. Giggles and laughter fill the air. Tears well up in the eyes of grateful young mothers.

I believe Jesus needed those moments of unbridled love and joy as much as the children. People always came to Jesus to *get*, to take away something for themselves—healing, information, food, blessing. Rarely was Jesus given anything. But when he was on the receiving end of a relationship or a gift—a cup of cold water, a broken vial of perfume—it moved him deeply. On this particular day, to his great delight, the children came only to give. They didn't have much, but they gave everything they had.

We don't know how long Jesus lingered there with the children, but I suspect he stayed awhile—for them and for himself. He needed that sweet, generous love because it had to last him. Very soon, in the midst of his suffering, he would draw much-needed strength from these moments of simple, sincere love.

ENCORE

Only one or two chapters later the gospel writers tell us about Jesus' triumphal entry into Jerusalem. A large crowd—fathers, mothers, and children—line the streets to wave palm branches and shout in excited voices, "Hosanna to the Son of David! Blessed is he who comes in the name of the Lord! Hosanna in the highest!" (Matthew 21:9). Jesus is the hero of the day.

Only a few people are irritated by this whole celebratory scene. "When the chief priests and the teachers of the law saw…the children *shouting* in the temple area,…they were indignant" (verse 15).

Jesus immediately defended the young ones. He quoted Psalm 8:2: "From the lips of children and infants you have ordained praise." No doubt he could have added, "Oh, yes, I hear them! And so do the massive hosts of heaven and hell. Nothing pleases God more. If you try to silence them, the stones will cry out."

At least the disciples kept quiet that day. Apparently they had finally learned what we all need to learn: *children matter.* Jesus will make time for a child regardless of what else is calling for his attention. He loves children passionately. They are too precious to hurt and are right at the center of God's heart and kingdom.

13

WHEN "FOLLOW
THE LEADER"
ISN'T CHILD'S PLAY

Having promoted children in the last chapter from the outer shadows of life to the front row, having pressed Jesus' point of "Do not look down on one of these little ones" (Matthew 18:10), I want to go out on a limb even further in this chapter. I honestly believe—and will demonstrate from Scripture—that on certain occasions God uses children *instead of adults* to accomplish strategic things in his kingdom.

That sounds far-fetched, I know. But hear me out.

So far as we see in reading the Gospels, Jesus never admonished children to become more grown-up. He did, however, exhort grownups to become more like children (Mark 10:15). How often have you heard an exasperated parent (maybe yourself!) growl at a child through clenched teeth, "Would you just grow up?!" Jesus said the opposite to his adult followers: "Would you please grow down? That's what it will take for you to enter my kingdom."

I consider it a partial victory when I hear Christian leaders speak about children as "the church of tomorrow." It's not the most enlightened viewpoint, but at least it's a step in the right direction. Maybe in time these leaders will come to see children as part of *the church of today,* too. In more powerful and dramatic ways than most of us can imagine, God delights in using children to build his kingdom precisely because they *are* children, unsoiled vessels in his hand.

Along the way to becoming adults, children pass through stages that at various points make them exactly what God can use. In fact, a walk through the Scriptures shows several times when the perfect tool needed in the hands of almighty God was a child—precisely *because* he or she was a child. The task could not be entrusted to adults. They think too much. They know too much. Or at least they think they know! For sure they doubt too much, fear too much, are too selfish, too eager for glory, too... well, adult! Isaiah described this phenomenon well in his depiction of the upside-down kingdom of God. It's different, he concluded: "The wolf will live with the lamb, the leopard will lie down with the goat...and a little child will lead them" (Isaiah 11:6).

Here are some incidents—both from Scripture and from current times—where God seemed to pause, rub his hands together, smile warmly, and say, "I need someone really powerful for this task. I know—I'll use a child."

NEEDED: COURAGE AND CREATIVITY (EXODUS 2)

It took a very smart girl to save the life of a great leader of Israel while he was still a baby. She was his protective big sister. Her name was Miriam, and he was Moses.

When I hear or read this story, I always picture the marsh just outside our African village. That was where we kids caught frogs, fished, and hid among the reeds at the exact spot we knew the wild animals would come for water. It was also where the tribe came in the evening to bathe. Such a place was the setting when God used a slave girl to read the heart of a princess and save her brother's life and her nation's destiny.

The wicked Egyptian pharaoh who had enslaved God's people had decreed that all Hebrew baby boys were to be taken at birth and thrown to their deaths in the Nile River. Moses' mother and father could not bear to do that to their beautiful baby son. At great risk, they hid him for three months, caring for him in their home.

When the child's whimpers grew to loud outbursts, the frightened mother hatched a desperate plan. Miriam must have held little Moses often as her mom fashioned a basket of papyrus reeds and covered it with tar so it was "marsh worthy" (or worse, "Nile worthy," if it should float downriver to some unknown fate). Mother and daughter must have prayed as each reed was woven into place. Surely every possible terrifying scenario played out in their minds: the basket snatched by crocodiles, a huge snake squeezing out the baby's life, a swift machete blow somewhere downstream by an angry Egyptian. But also perhaps a miracle somehow?

Possibly they even thought through the legal loopholes. "Oh, we're sorry, Officer. Did the king say to 'throw' him into the river? We thought the word was to 'place' him in the river. The boat? What boat? That's just a little old basket we brought along. So sorry for the confusion."

The baby's cries grew louder and more frequent. There had been too many close calls. Perhaps the neighbors, though understanding and supportive, grew nervous as they increasingly risked their own lives to help keep the secret.

Finally the basket was ready. At daybreak Moses' parents quietly made their way to the river's edge with their precious bundle. There must have been the most heart-wrenching farewell—a mother's anguished prayer, a father's quivering hug, a sister's silent sobs at the water's edge. "Miriam, hide in the reeds," the mother whispered, "and keep an eye on your little brother. I can't bear the thought of him out here all alone. Be brave." Miriam's mother knew that a child "playing" by the river would draw far less suspicion than a hovering adult.

Miriam did as she was told. We don't know how long she hid in the reeds. But soon the morning stillness was broken by the approaching sound of giggling and then singing. A procession drew nearer. Girls! They were coming down a path to the river's edge, headed right for the little hideout.

Then from the parted grasses stepped the most beautiful young woman Miriam had ever seen. I'm sure that in all the terrifying scenarios of what might happen, the family had never imagined their precious son being discovered by the princess of Egypt and her band of maids. Nothing had prepared little Miriam for this.

The princess's eyes fell on the basket in the reeds, and with great curiosity she sent a servant to fetch it. From Miriam's hiding place she could see it all. Her heart pounded as she watched the dripping basket being placed before the daughter of Israel's greatest enemy—in fact, the most hateful and wicked man in the world. Surely everyone in his family was like him. What horrible torture was about to end the life of her baby brother? The crocodiles and snakes sounded pretty swift and merciful compared to this turn of events.

This is where most of us grownups would have failed. We would have sunk into despair based on what we "knew" about Egyptians, our experiences and hearsay of their cruelty. With hearts poisoned by preconceived opinions, we would have been blinded by our righteous indignation. We would have seen only what we were preconditioned to see.

But not so a child. Children are ingenuous. They are also blessed with an uncanny ability to read a person's character instantly. Even though they are inexperienced and unsophisticated, they often know instinctively who can be trusted and who is the charlatan.

It took the spirit and savvy of a child to understand what she was seeing as the princess opened the basket. There was initial shock, surprise, and then a face aglow with delight and tenderness for the beautiful infant fugitive. The princess, recognizing her newfound treasure to be a Hebrew baby, sized up the situation quickly. Miriam caught every nuance on the face of her enemy. She watched as the princess's eyes darted up and down the river to see if her discovery had been witnessed.

Next the princess's eyes fell on each of her maids. The laughter and song were long gone. What would she do with this baby, they wondered, who had instantly captivated her affection?

In that heart-stopping moment, Miriam's bright mind seized upon an ingenious plan. Risking her own life, she stepped out of the reeds to pose a brilliantly framed question. "Shall I go and get one of the Hebrew women to nurse the baby for you?" There was a powerful meeting of hearts and minds that transcended culture, wealth, and position.

"Yes, go," breathed a relieved and grateful princess.

Wouldn't you love to have witnessed the arrival of little Miriam back at her home? "Mom, guess what? You're not gonna believe this!" Not only had she correctly interpreted the wishes of a foreign princess and saved her baby brother's life, but she had also managed to get her mother paid by the government to raise her own child!

When God needed courage, a perceptive spirit, and inspired creativity to save the life of one of the greatest leaders the world would ever know, only a girl would do.

NEEDED: A PURE CHANNEL IN A CORRUPT ERA (1 SAMUEL 3)

Fast-forward three hundred years to a time that was not exactly Israel's finest hour. The delivery from slavery in Egypt, the miracle crossing of the Red Sea, manna in the wilderness, and the conquest of Canaan were becoming dim memories. As the people of Israel settled in and got organized, their faithfulness and fervor cooled. The priesthood became a disaster.

Eli, the high priest, was now an old man, and his two sons, Hophni and Phinehas, were corrupt and arrogant. They made a mockery of their priestly position. While Eli was a mediocre high priest, he was a terrible father. He knew all about the sins of his sons but didn't do much more than sigh, complain, and nag them to be good.

Israel's enemies, the Philistines, sensed that the fire had gone out of those once powerful people of God. It had been a while since their last drubbing at the hand of Samson. They were beginning to feel their oats again, positioning to attack.

Okay, I'm depressing myself and likely you as well. I imagine even God must have felt the same dismay. It was time for a breath of fresh air, a new beginning, an awakening. It was time for a child!

His name was Samuel. His godly mother, Hannah, brokenhearted by her inability to conceive a child, had made a deal with God. She had prayed in Eli's tabernacle and, through anguished sobs, promised that if God would give her a son, she would give him right back for a lifetime of service. God was moved, had a plan in need of a child, and granted her petition.

So her son, Samuel, was raised in the tabernacle, surrounded by the things of God. He was Eli's helper. His bed was near Eli's so he could come on a moment's notice to help the aging priest. All Eli needed to do was call out "Samuel" day or night.

Then one night God decided to use Eli's trick. God broke his long silence by speaking not in a public way but privately to a child: "Samuel!"

Instantly the boy responded, "Here I am."

It took two separate callings, but to sleepy Eli's credit, he finally realized that something divine was happening. He instructed Samuel to say next time, "Speak, LORD, for your servant is listening."

How long God had waited to hear those words from his comatose people. This little boy was the perfect pure and humble channel he could use.

In this case God wanted the child to carry a message not just to anyone but to the highest spiritual leader in the land. And if that wasn't daunting enough, it was a very adult and powerful message! It said, in essence, "You've been a terrible father, your sons are a disgrace, and big trouble is on the way. You're all fired." Ouch!

This gives me an eye-opening insight into God's perspective and the value he places on children. God didn't say, "Oh well, it's just little Samuel. I'll start him off with a simple, pleasant message." No, God saw this child as capable and worthy of doing a major intervention in the life of a powerful man. He didn't shade the assignment at all. And in fact, Scripture says the next morning that young "Samuel told [Eli] everything, hiding nothing from him" (verse 18). He let fly with the full message God had given him in the night.

I ask you, would you entrust such a message to a child? Of course not—but God did. Obviously he feels differently about children than we do. How far we are from understanding God's perspective on children and their place in the priorities of his kingdom.

God needed a pure, credible channel to send a powerful message to wicked leaders. He knew that only a child would do.

NEEDED: GREAT FAITH (1 SAMUEL 17)

The older we get and the more education and experience we collect, the harder it becomes to retain one of God's greatest values—faith. But without it, it is impossible to please God (Hebrews 11:6). Out of a large array of positive qualities, this one made the "final three": faith, hope, and love

(1 Corinthians 13:13). What is so tough about retaining great faith is that it flies in the face of everything we call adult. We are now too sophisticated to be "sure of what we hope for and certain of what we do not see" (Hebrews 11:1). That sounds naive to us.

No story in the Bible highlights the triumph of faith over strength, intellect, and strategy more than the showdown of David and Goliath. This was the most grown-up of situations. Armies were lined up in full array facing each other across a narrow valley. The order of the day was to prove superior strength, skill, and courage. Hand-to-hand combat would soon erupt, a fight to the death, with everything at stake—and the losers would become the victors' slaves.

David's father had sent the teenager off as a mere courier: "Just take this food to your warrior brothers and see how they are doing." Once he arrived in the camp, David's oldest brother, Eliab, got irritated. "Why have you come down here?" he sneered. "And with whom did you leave those few sheep in the desert?" With the cruel, soul-piercing thrusts that only an older brother can deliver, he continued, "I know how conceited you are and how wicked your heart is; you came down only to watch the battle" (1 Samuel 17:28).

Other warriors told David of the lavish rewards that awaited whoever would slay the giant, perhaps just to tease him. The thought that David would earn those rewards never so much as crossed their minds.

The story grows increasingly weird. That King Saul would even speak to the shepherd boy, much less give him a shot at Goliath, defies logic—aside from a divine plan at work in this future king's life. David tries on Saul's too-big tunic, coat of armor, bronze helmet, and massive sword. Once again we are reminded that David is a boy, not a man. The giant Goliath dishes out the final insults: "Am I a dog, that you come to me with sticks?"

What a moment! With two mighty armies as witnesses, fate rests on a giant and a boy. A hardened mountain of a fighting man, and a small young sheepherder. A foul, blasphemous bully, and a lad full of faith in what his God could and surely would do.

From that moment on there was nothing childish about what David said or did. "You come against me with sword and spear and javelin," he called out, "but I come against you in the name of the LORD Almighty, the God of the armies of Israel, whom you have defied. This day the LORD will hand you over to me, and I'll strike you down and cut off your head."

I can hear Goliath's retort: "Oh yeah? You and whose ar-r-r..."

When good met evil on the battlefield that day, God called on a child. All the other military might and strategy were useless. What the situation required was not faith in human strength but faith in God's. That had been sadly lacking for forty days among the warrior grownups, but it resided in full measure in a little shepherd boy. Only a child would do.

NEEDED: A COMPASSIONATE AND FORGIVING HEART (2 KINGS 5)

We don't even know the name of one of the most remarkable little girls in the Bible. All we know is that she was a slave. She had been captured, savagely torn from her parents and her home in a brutal raid on northern Israel by Aramean marauders. These were treacherous, terrifying, bloody attacks that occurred each spring in the region where this precious child lived. Her age when taken captive is not reported, but her faith, character, and spirit were well entrenched by her loving family before the tragic invasion.

She found herself in the home of one of the most powerful men in the new country. His name was Naaman, the commander of the army. This man had it all—success, reputation, wealth, influence—and, oh yes, did I mention leprosy? Personally speaking, I know the horrors of this disease. I saw its devastating effects on the parents of my friends back in Nielle: grotesque nubs of fingers and toes, ears eaten away, and little holes in the middle of faces where once there was a nose. It's a frightening malady that slowly drains a person of beauty, dignity, and hope.

Money was no object, of course, and the dignified military commander Naaman had tried every possible cure in Aram to rid himself of this dreaded curse. He would have traded everything he had for deliverance from this one foe he was powerless to conquer.

His salvation lay right under his nose, in his own household. The godly

Israelite slave girl apparently had a child's ability to forgive. With her own heart still aching for home, she watched the agony of her mistress and the lady's increasingly hideous husband. These people were the enemy who had devastated her young life; yet still she cared for them.

One day when all hope seemed gone and her mistress lay heartbroken, perhaps sobbing into her pillow, the little girl took the woman's face into her hands and whispered these precious words: "If only my master would see the prophet who is in Samaria! He would cure him of his leprosy."

That triggered a series of powerful and dramatic events. The king of Aram wrote a letter to the king of Israel. A military squadron was assembled for the journey. Lavish gifts were gathered to reward the prophet who could cure Naaman—750 pounds of silver and 150 pounds of pure gold. Talk about being worth one's weight in gold—this little girl certainly was!

In time, the cure prescribed by Elisha was literally "child's play," yet it required such humility that this great warrior could not bring himself to do it. Dip himself seven times in the disgustingly muddy Jordan River? Naaman smoldered with pride and outrage as he packed for home. If there was to be any river dipping, he would do it privately in his own Damascus rivers! Why did he ever listen to that child? What was his wife thinking, anyway?

Naaman's troops, having marched all this distance (at least 130 miles), were not thrilled with the idea of just turning around and going home again without at least an attempt to fulfill the mission. They urged him to follow Elisha's instructions. Swallowing his pride, the commander did so. I can only imagine his growing anxiety with each nonproductive dip. Three, four, five, six...he skimmed the disgusting scum from his arms after each one. Then down he went again...

Oh my, what a moment! When Naaman came sputtering back up the seventh time and wiped his eyes, his whole world had changed. The Bible says, "His flesh was restored and became clean like that of a young boy." His faith, too, had become like that of a young servant girl. "Now I know that there is no God in all the world except in Israel," exclaimed the grateful general.

That is the last we hear of this compassionate little girl. I wish the Bible told us more about her. I guess the sequels live all around us, if we only have eyes to see them.

NEEDED: GREAT GENEROSITY (JOHN 6)

A massive crowd had gathered for the day to hear Jesus teach—bigger than the attendance at many a professional basketball or hockey game. Scripture says there were five thousand men plus women and children. The day went on until the sun sank low in the western sky. But there were no concessionaires around the edge of the crowd selling (kosher) hot dogs or Pepsi. Not even bottled water.

The disciples could sense the developing problem here. "This is a remote place," they said quietly to Jesus, according to Mark's account (6:35–36), "and it's already very late. Send the people away so they can go to the surrounding countryside and villages and buy themselves something to eat."

That made sense, right? This was a reasonable, practical suggestion. Good adult thinking here.

But the Son of God had a better, outside-the-box idea—one that involved a child. Jesus challenged the disciples to come up with an on-the-spot solution so people could be fed right away.

The practical disciples said that just wasn't going to work. This was far beyond the means of their humble treasury. How in the world would they ever...

And then Andrew said something like, "Well, I did see one boy here with a lunch bag. During the last break, I asked him what he had inside. He looked at what his mother had packed and then said proudly, 'Five little barley loaves and two little fish!'" The rest of the disciples no doubt shrugged.

New Testament scholars tell us that the mention of "barley loaves" is significant here. This was the food of the poor, those who needed to eat cheaply. Jesus, the friend of poor people, no doubt felt right at home taking this food in his hands, giving thanks, and then pulling off the amazing miracle of multiplication right before their eyes. All because of the generosity of a little boy.

He could have fed the crowd any number of other ways, obviously. He could have snapped his fingers and had massive truckloads of food drop out of the sky. For that matter, he could simply have waved his hand and made everyone's hunger pangs vanish with no external food whatsoever.

But he didn't. He used the lunch of a child.

I wonder what would have happened if Andrew had approached an adult instead. The man would possibly have said, "Well, I planned ahead for this day by bringing my lunch. If others weren't that foresighted, it's not my problem, is it?"

Or perhaps he would have negotiated: "Okay, I'll split it with you. I'll give you three loaves and one fish so I still have something left to eat myself." In contrast, the open-hearted boy freely gave his all.

Part of discipling children, we have found in our ministry's work, is to help them know that if you give God all you have, you will be amazed at what he does with it. It sounds counterintuitive. You would think that if you have very little, you should hold tightly to it, not knowing how or when you'll ever acquire more. But in fact, Jesus changes all those equations. He takes our small lunch and creates enough to feed an arena full of people.

Children "get it." They don't argue back about needing to preserve their assets. They freely give to Jesus, and he blesses them for it—along with everyone else.

I wonder what the boy's mother said when he got home that evening. "So how was your lunch, Johnny? Did you have enough to keep you going all day?"

He probably just smiled and said, "Yep, sure did. More than enough!"

NEEDED: THE STRAIGHT TRUTH (MARK 14)

One of the beautiful things about children is how they often get right to the point. They haven't yet learned to weave and dodge around the uncomfortable facts. They are not artful enough to gloss over things, even if adults would prefer that they keep quiet.

Such a moment happened not once but twice in the wee hours of the morning as Jesus was hauled before the accusing priests and elders. The disciples were scared to death. All that they had feared now seemed to be crashing down upon their heads. The closest Peter could get to the scene was the campfire out in the courtyard, where an assortment of people stood rubbing their hands together and trying to get warm.

He had been told earlier by the Master that he would embarrass himself this night. But Peter would believe none of that. He was still going to be brave and courageous...until, as Mark records, "one of the servant girls of the high priest came by. When she saw Peter warming himself, she looked closely at him."

Peter's blood froze in his veins in that moment. He didn't want anyone staring at him, especially not a teenage (or younger?) employee of the high priest. He kept studying the orange flames as they leaped up from the wood.

Then the girl spoke. "You also were with that Nazarene, Jesus."

Peter tried to keep his shoulders from jerking upward. Words caromed off the sides of his brain. What should he say? Anything at all?

He had to say something. "I-I don't know or understand what you're talking about," he stuttered, trying to keep his voice calm even though his heart was pounding. He had just been nailed by a young girl! Peter swiftly pivoted toward the exit.

This was a test of Peter's commitment. The Lord was giving him an opportunity to prove his mettle. Yes, it was a hard test, but then again, is it so scary to speak the truth about your faith to a young girl? If you can't share your faith with a child, whom can you talk to?

Peter shivered in the cold and darkness, wishing he could return to the fire but afraid to increase his visibility. Occasionally he would glance that direction. She was still there, eyeing him. The Bible says in Mark 14:69, "When the servant girl saw him there, she said again to those standing around, 'This fellow is one of them.'"

Look, miss, will you just shut up? Again Peter shook his head, perhaps a little too vigorously, and denied her statement.

God needed someone to force the big fisherman into self-honesty. He needed someone to puncture Peter's bravado and let the hot air out so he could start to become real. His future service as an apostle depended squarely upon his finding out how weak he really was and how much he would have to rely upon God's strength.

To accomplish such a personal meltdown in a proud man, only a child would do.

Needed: Alertness to Danger (Acts 23)

Adults normally protect children—but once in a while, children protect adults. The Bible tells about the apostle Paul returning to Jerusalem after many years of ministry to Gentiles—a notably unpopular idea in that hotbed of Judaism. He was in the city just a week when a mob surrounded him at the temple and would have lynched him on the spot had not the local Roman commander intervened with his troops. Paul did a masterful job of explaining his work to the crowd that day, until he got to the part about the Lord sending him "to the Gentiles," and again the place exploded in rage. "Rid the earth of him! He's not fit to live!" the irate people screamed (Acts 22:22).

Fortunately, the Romans hustled him away to protective custody. He was taken the next day for a court hearing before the Sanhedrin, but that hearing also deteriorated into a shouting match. Paul's opponents were so livid that the following morning more than forty of them made a death pledge to each other: "We will totally fast until we kill this scoundrel. Not a bite of food until then." They even worked out an elaborate ruse to get access to him during his transit to the next court appearance. It reminds the reader of how Jack Ruby exploited a transfer in the Dallas police headquarters basement to shoot Lee Harvey Oswald two days after the John F. Kennedy assassination.

But for such a treacherous moment in Paul's life, God had a boy in place.

Paul's young nephew just happened to be in the right spot at the right time. He alertly picked up on the whispers and furtive glances. He figured out the code language. His uncle was in major danger, far worse than he or the Roman authorities knew.

Says Acts 23:16–17, "But when the son of Paul's sister heard of this plot, he went into the barracks and told Paul. Then Paul called one of the centurions and said, 'Take this young man to the commander; he has something to tell him.'" Within an hour the kid was face to face with one of Caesar's finest, and the cover was blown. By nine o'clock that night the Romans had Paul on a horse surrounded by 470 troops headed out of the city for an overnight trek to safe haven in Caesarea.

What if this boy had not been around? What if Paul had indeed been caught by the death squad and killed that week? What if his ministry had been cut short in A.D. 59? He would never have gone to Rome. Most seriously for you and me, here is what our New Testaments would be missing: Ephesians, Philippians, Colossians, Philemon, 1 Timothy, 2 Timothy, and Titus. What a loss that would have been!

God had a lot more for Paul to accomplish in the years following, even if Paul was behind bars. To make sure his plan was not derailed, God put a sharp young guy on duty to safeguard his uncle. He was exactly the scout for the occasion.

NEEDED: A HEALING PRAYER (ALBANIA, LATE 1980S)

Such stories from the pages of the Bible inspire us with their drama. We haven't covered the whole roster by any means. We could go on to spotlight other young people God used: Joash, who became a godly king of Judah at age seven; Josiah, who ascended the same throne at age eight and eventually brought a sweeping revival; young Shadrach, Meshach, and Abednego, who resisted the king's idol of gold and bravely went to the fiery furnace for their integrity; Rhoda, the servant girl who broke up a prayer meeting with the news, "Peter is at the door!" and wouldn't let adults talk her out of it; even the unborn John the Baptist, who though still in his mother's womb sensed another unborn child in the room, the coming Messiah of God, and leaped for joy in response.

But what about today? Does God still use children to accomplish his strategic goals in the current era? Absolutely.

During the Communist period in Albania, this little Balkan country was isolated from nearly everyone except its one ally, faraway North Korea. Travel was next to impossible. Radio and television broadcast signals from the Western world were jammed all across the country.

A little group of children in that dismal society was playing in an attic one day and found an old radio covered in dust and cobwebs. They somehow got it to work again, and lo and behold, it could pick up a Christian radio station! How this signal missed being jammed, nobody ever learned. The kids began to gather secretly in the attic and listen, with the volume turned way down low, whenever an Albanian-language program would come on.

In time the gospel message got through to them, affecting their fertile hearts with great power. One by one they prayed to accept Jesus as their Savior and Lord. Now the secret programs became discipleship lessons as they learned to pray and slowly grew in their walk with Christ. This remained a strictly "No Adults Allowed" club, because the children knew their parents, in great fear of the authorities, would take away their precious radio and probably destroy it if they knew.

One day as they were listening to the speaker, they learned a new thing about God—that he was the Great Physician. Jesus had healed the sick, the man said, and apparently could still do it today. Looking at one another, the kids said simply, "Well, we know where the sick people are. Let's go!"

This little band of courageous and compassionate children found their way down the city street and into the state-run Marxist hospital. They decided to start at the top floor, the third floor. Peeking inside the first room, they saw a very sick man. "Lord Jesus," they prayed in the hallway, "here's one. Please heal him."

They shuffled off to the second room and, discovering yet another sick person, repeated their childlike prayer: "Jesus, you can do this. Please heal her," they said quietly.

At the third doorway, their hearts were touched by the sight of a child about their age. "Oh, Jesus," they prayed, "please heal that little boy. He needs you very much."

As they worked their way down the hallway, door by door, a commotion began to build up behind them. Starting back at room one, patients were discovering that they had been healed and were getting up out of bed in wonder. Oblivious to the distraction they were creating, the children continued their prayer trek down the hallway. Door by door they prayed, and miracles kept happening.

The bewildered nursing staff was too consumed with trying to get rejoicing people back into their beds to notice the little prayer band of children. They got to the end of the third floor and then disappeared. As the patients kept telling a common story of a little group of children in their doorways for a moment followed by healing, a search was launched for the kids. But they were nowhere to be found.

Besa Shapalo, the wonderful Albanian child worker who told me about this, said she eventually got word of the miracles at the hospital, recognized the description of the children, and caught up with the little band.

"Do you know what was happening back there at the hospital?" she asked them with excitement and wonder in her voice.

"What?" replied the children.

"People were getting healed! God was answering your prayers. Many people were healed that day. Did you know that?"

The children looked at her with innocent eyes and said, "Yes, Jesus is the Great Doctor. He can do that."

"I know, I know," she replied, "but why didn't you keep going? Why didn't you pray on the second floor and then the first? You could have healed everyone in the hospital!"

Looking sheepish, they replied with the utter innocence that comes only from little children. "Oh, we kinda got tired of doing that. We just wanted to go do something else"!

Needed: An Evangelist in the Village (Ecuador 2004)

Compassion's South Korea director, Dr. Justin Suh, and members of his board of directors were visiting our work in Ecuador and arrived at a certain project one evening. They were scheduled to see the program the next morning.

"We are so grateful for your visit to us," the pastor said when they climbed out of the minibus. "But I'm so very sorry to inform you that tomorrow will not be a typical day at our project. I know you want to meet the children and see what we are trying to do for them in this desperate community, but..." At this, the man's throat began to tighten. "The children will not be gathering as usual tomorrow. Instead, we will have a funeral."

He took a deep breath before continuing. "Two of our little boys, brothers, were crossing the busy street to come to the project yesterday and were struck by a huge truck. The eight-year-old was severely injured and is in intensive care at the city hospital. But the little six-year-old was crushed and died in the dirty street. He was a wonderful little boy. We are all brokenhearted."

Justin Suh replied, "Oh, my brother, we are so very sorry."

The pastor wiped a tear and continued, "In our culture, children do not generally attend funerals, especially tragic ones like this. So I'm afraid you will not see among us what you came so far to see."

The South Korean leaders conferred and then offered, "Would it be all right if we came anyway, sat with your congregation, and just grieved with our Ecuadorian brothers and sisters in their great loss? We know something of such great sorrow in our own land."

The next morning when the Korean delegation arrived at the little church, the sanctuary was filled to capacity. To their surprise, some sixty of the mourners sitting on the coarse wooden benches were children. The pastor met the visitors at the door and just shrugged his shoulders; he had no explanation for why so many children had shown up for a funeral.

While waiting for the service to begin, our national staff members began to move among the children, quietly talking with them in Spanish. Eventually Justin and his group heard the report. Child after child had said, "He was my friend. He is the one who told me of Jesus' love. He helped me invite Jesus into my heart. I'm sad, but I've come today to send him to his heavenly home."

This little Ecuadorian child had led over fifty of his friends to Jesus! His life's work was gloriously accomplished by the tender age of six. God needed a great evangelist for that village. He needed a child.

FIT FOR THE JOB AT HAND

What these stories illustrate is that God is interested not as much in our *ability* as our *availability.* He does not require talent and experience; he is looking mainly for a willing spirit. Even if it comes in a small body.

The apostle Paul reminded the Corinthians that "God chose the foolish things of the world to shame the wise; God chose the weak things of the world to shame the strong. He chose the lowly things of this world and the despised things—and the things that are not—to nullify the things that are, so that no one may boast before him" (1 Corinthians 1:27–29). That certainly includes children. They are intrinsically "weak" and "lowly." They are sometimes "foolish." In today's world they are often "despised."

Watch carefully the children around you. In precious moments you will catch a glimpse of your Savior's face. Listen intently and you will hear his voice. Walk gently among them; his footprints are all around you. Embrace them, for you are embracing him. Respect them, because they are sometimes God's agents—exactly the kind of instruments he needs. At such times, only a child will do.

14

IMAGINE...

I realize I am stretching the envelope rather vigorously here. I am portraying children in ways you may never have considered before. Some readers may find this preposterous or at least exceptions to the general rule.

As long as we remain in our rutted assumptions, however, we never realize what we're omitting. The Kennedy brothers were fond of quoting a line from a George Bernard Shaw play: "Some men see things as they are and say, why. I dream of things that never were and say, why not." Yes, it is awkward to think outside the box. We don't do it naturally. But we need to stretch ourselves.

We are all too often like the football coaches my first year back in America as a ninth grader at Lakewood Junior High School in Denver. I eagerly showed up for tryouts that fall, and when asked what position I'd like to play, I knew exactly what to say: "Center!" After all, this was the most demanding position in the *futbol* game I'd played so much in the village and at boarding school. The center forward, or striker, had to be the fastest, most nimble player on the field. He nearly always kicked in the most goals. I was lean and quick on my feet, so I was sure to qualify, I thought.

The gym erupted in laughter. "Center? Are you crazy, Stafford? You'll get slaughtered." In just a few minutes I learned that *American* football requires a center who is a big, stocky guy and can hike the ball to the quarterback and hold his ground without getting bulldozed.

I did find out, however, that one or two players in this strange game actually used their *foot* to advance the *ball*! The head coach mentioned that he needed a place-kicker, and I told him I had scored goals from fifty yards out. Surely I was the answer to his kicking needs. "Fair enough," he said, marking me down on his clipboard.

The only trouble was, this was 1963, the height of the George Blanda era in the National Football League. Blanda used a heavy, square-toed boot to power the ball through the uprights; it even had a leather thong from the toe back around the ankle. I stared in confusion as an assistant coach strapped one of these contraptions on my foot, set the odd-shaped football up on a tee, and said, "Okay, let's see what you can do."

Well, I could hardly walk in that monster boot, let alone kick. All my life on the soccer fields of Africa, I had hit the ball off the top of my foot (for distance) or off my instep (for short passes). My results with this new boot were pathetic, and the coaches shrugged as they scratched my name off their rosters.

Just a few years later, by the time I reached my senior year of high school, the soccer style of kicking emerged in the NFL. Today every place-kicker uses it. The old Blanda boot is nowhere to be found.

Thinking back, I wonder what would have happened if those coaches had had the creativity to think outside the tradition? What if they had said, "All we want is to see the ball go off your foot and between the posts in the end zone. We don't really care how you get it done." I could have been the school hero! I could have gotten a college scholarship and gone on to fame and fortune in the NFL...well, maybe not. But a willingness to dream, to experiment, to allow for a different approach would have made a big difference.

Will you join me in imagining what our world could be like if it valued children? Let your assumptions go. How could our nation, our cities, our churches, and our families be different if we truly believed that children matter? What new things would we start doing? What old things would we stop? How would you and I think and act if we were truly mindful of the precious little ones God has given us?

What follows are only a few ideas, the tip of the iceberg, to stimulate your mind as you think about *your* world. Close your eyes and imagine...what if?

A WORLD WHERE KIDS COUNT

- What if we could actually see the guardian angel standing on duty behind each little child—a huge warrior, the kind of powerful presence that, in numerous Bible incidents, triggered instant panic in strong adults? If just one of these angels revealed himself at our nearby schoolyard or neighborhood park, we would begin treating the little ones with a newfound awe and respect. Gone would be our world's pathetic pattern of child abuse, cruelty, and even neglect. The globe and its priorities would be turned upside down. Imagine...

- What if every child was immunized against all known childhood diseases? We can do this—if we care. Take measles as just one example. The World Health Organization reported that 745,000 children died of this disease in the year 2001, and the total cost to vaccinate them would have been only $558,750. We spend *five times that much* on chewing gum each and every day of the year. It's all a matter of priorities.

- What if world leaders put the care, nurture, and protection of children as a checkpoint for every new law? Imagine if a huge banner reading "What About the Children?" hung in the United Nations Assembly Hall, the United States Senate and House of Representatives, the Pentagon, and every corporate boardroom. Even though children cannot understand the complexities of government decisions, they are drastically affected by them. Lawmakers need to think about that as they deliberate.

- What if we put some real teeth into enforcing the provisions of the Geneva Convention regarding children in war situations? We all piously signed this treaty way back in 1949 (the year I was born!). Are we obeying it? We agreed that "parties to a conflict must respect children, provide them with any care or aid they require, and protect them from any form of indecent assault." We promised that "children under 15 must not participate in hostilities and must not be recruited into the armed forces." We said that "warring parties must try to make local arrangements to allow the removal of children from besieged or encircled areas...must allow the free passage of medicine, food and clothing intended for children under 15...must ensure that orphans or lost children are not left alone, and that they are taken care of and allowed to practice their religion and pursue their education in their cultural tradition if possible."

Did we *mean* any of this? Or was this just political hot air? When little children are taken as slaves for combat or used as human shields, not to mention sexual playthings for the troops, it is hard to defend our sincerity. What if at least our nation declared that we will take the above protections at face value and refuse to tolerate those who violate them? "Fight if you must, but don't you dare touch the children!"

My memory is forever seared by a day shortly after Rwanda's massacres when I held stunned little boys and girls in my arms at a camp in Kigali, the capital city. I asked our staff members why the children seemed so passive. They told me these little ones had been forced to watch as their pregnant mothers were savagely raped, then cut open and the fetuses of their little unborn brothers and sisters pulled out to be roasted on an open fire. Finally, the waiting children had been forced to eat the meat. I stood there shaking with tears and rage at this unspeakable depravity. Why doesn't the entire civilized world rise up and drive this level of evil from the face of the earth? It should have no place to hide!

• What if the men of the world consciously viewed themselves as God-appointed guardians of children? What if every culture said to its men, "It's part of your job in life, as strong, tall adults, to make sure children are safe from hunger, deprivation, and all kinds of abuse." This would mean sticking with families instead of abandoning them. It would mean providing for financial, emotional, and spiritual needs. Women rarely ditch their children, no matter how severe the circumstances. What if men saw it as part of their manhood to match or even exceed this commitment?

A NEW NATION

If the above is too much to imagine, perhaps we can bring our dreams a little closer to home. If the idea of a child-friendly planet is out of reach, what about our own country?

After all, we're a pacesetter for the world. America sets trends—both good ones and bad ones. We're committed to justice and liberty. We have freedom of expression to debate national directions and behavior. If we determined to make this a nation where children flourish, what would be the results?

- What if we automatically doubled the penalty for any criminal conviction that involved harm to a child? It would be the same concept as construction zones on the highway, where if you get caught speeding, the fine multiplies by two. What if the fine or jail term for any misdeed affecting a child was doubled? If you set fire to a house with a child inside, if you hurt a child while burglarizing a store, if you injure a child while driving under the influence, you spend twice as long behind bars.

- What if our education system found fresh and effective ways to recruit and retain men in the elementary classrooms of our nation, thereby balancing the ratio with the heroic women who already teach there? I recently spoke to a college group of future teachers: There were thirty women in the room and one man. Don't get me wrong; I'm not saying that men can teach little kids better than women. I'm just saying we should present our children with a roughly equal faculty.

- Speaking of schools—will we ever deal with the long-overdue money issue? When the average elementary school teacher is earning between $25,000 and $30,000 for a year's work, while baseball pitcher Pedro Martinez is making that much for *every out* he gets on the mound (three outs per inning, twenty-seven outs per complete game), something is desperately out of whack.

- What if we stepped up the requirements as well as pay for those (outside the family) who provide childcare? My goodness, in this country you can't even clean someone's teeth or cut their hair without securing a state license, which usually hangs in a frame on the wall. If dental hygienists and barbers have to complete a mandated course of study, how much more those who care for our children! And what about the salary scales? Don't those who care for children, our most precious possession, deserve more than minimum wage?

- Imagine if parents mobilized to put pressure on the entertainment industry (film, television, radio, music) whenever it degrades the nation's moral fabric. What if we all covenanted to reject violence as fun, sex as recreation, drugs as escape, and greed as simple ambition? Those advertisers who persisted in supporting such trash would pay a swift price in the marketplace as their products went ignored. If we truly believed that children (and adults) are affected by what they see and hear, we would not sit still for the unending rivers of filth that come our way.

- What if every household took its children to the nearest nursing home for a visit once a quarter to make friends with elderly residents who desperately need to be needed? Each generation would learn from the other and grow to love each other. Some care facilities now bring puppies and kittens to brighten the lives of their residents. Why not also children?

NEW NEIGHBORHOODS

If even the nation seems too big a challenge, let's bring the focus down another notch to the cities, towns, and neighborhoods where we live, work, shop, pay taxes, and vote. What would make a genuine difference for children here?

- What if every Parks and Recreation team, whether baseball, soccer, or football, had an enthusiastic and dedicated coach? What if the Scout and 4-H programs had waiting lists of adult volunteers eager to invest in children?

- What if on game days the bleachers filled up not just with parents but with other residents of the town as well who came for no other reason than to show their interest in the next generation? Instead of sitting in front of the television for another wasted set of hours, people would choose to attend a youth event. No school play or concert should ever happen in a half-empty auditorium. Kids should sense that adults are cheering for them in whatever forum they attempt.
- Imagine newspaper and local television coverage of children showing bravery, kindness, generosity, or courage. The features would go beyond kids just being cute; they would spotlight kids making a real difference in their society.
- Could we ever revive the tradition of years past when adults felt free to watch out for other people's kids, correcting them appropriately if necessary? Now we seem afraid to say a word for fear of parental backlash. What if we admitted to one another that parenting is a complex, round-the-clock job and that we all need help from one another to do it well?

AN AWAKENED CHURCH

If children really mattered to God's people, it would affect numerous areas.

- We'd start making thirty-year plans instead of three-year plans. We would launch courageous, long-range strategies to affect the next generations. We would ask ourselves, "What effect will this current action, initiative, or expansion have by the time our kids are grown? What should we be doing *now* to prepare the way for their ministry era?"
- Christian colleges and seminaries, like the governments mentioned earlier in this chapter, would reexamine every academic discipline in light of the question "What about the children?" Pastors, for example, would not be allowed to graduate without taking a series of child-focused courses. Missions, social work, communications,

and other majors would likewise deal with the strategic place of children.

- In light of the fertile harvest that awaits among the young, what if church boards earmarked 40 percent or more of their budget to reaching children and teenagers?
- What if every senior pastor was absent from the pulpit two Sunday mornings a year because he was working in the church nursery? Wouldn't that send a novel message to the congregation!
- What if all the children in the church were provided with personal champions or sponsors, adults who committed to remembering their birthdays, taking them out for ice cream after every performance no matter how minor, inviting them to special outings together, and praying daily for their growth in the faith? Can you imagine the impact of a man saying to a ten-year-old boy, "I'm going to a college basketball game next month. Want to come with me? Want to bring along two of your best friends?" Or something like, "I don't know what you want to be when you grow up, but I'm a mechanic. Would you like to come to my garage for a day and see what I do? I've got stuff you can help me with." In this day of so many single-parent households, the influence of a godly adult on a young boy or girl could be dynamic. How many churches would step up to organize such a contact?
- What if Children's Day was as big a deal in our churches as Mother's Day and Father's Day? Do you even know when Children's Day falls on the calendar? The United Nations says November 20, while other traditions point to the second Sunday of June. All in all, it means we're unfocused on honoring the young. Virtually nobody celebrates the holiday. But what a day it could be if, across the country, pastors preached on the place of children in God's kingdom, children's workers in the church were honored with gift certificates, and reports of the church's success among children were celebrated. A special offering could be taken for a children's project. How about a potluck luncheon afterward with nothing but desserts? (Just kidding!)

- What if mission organizations decided to do what's best for the sons and daughters of their career missionaries, even if it made waves in the overall program? God does not expect his work to be built on the slender backs of neglected children. This topic is, as you know, close to my heart. The days of expecting missionary kids to put up with the leftovers must stop.

ENERGIZED FAMILIES

While churches and their mission organizations are powerful entities to bless children, no place has more impact than our homes. The nineteenth-century lawyer and poet William Ross Wallace had it right when he wrote, "The hand that rocks the cradle / is the hand that rules the world."

Imagine for a moment what would happen if the following occurred in homes all across our land:

- What if moms and dads alike made an unbending commitment to the magical moments of bedtime, utilizing the important rituals of stories, conversation, hugs, kisses, songs, and prayers to bond with their children? Kids learn more about a parent's heart and values at bedtime than any other hour of the day. No infant is too young to catch the intimate rhythms and cadences of a bedtime prayer. This window of opportunity is open for only a dozen years or so; we need to use it wisely.
- What if parents deliberately arranged their leisure time with a view to minimizing absence from their kids? Moms and dads need time for themselves, to be sure, but why not slot that time when the kids are in school or sleeping? Young fathers, do I dare say it? Don't take up golf until your children are grown. Like no other sport, it takes you away from them for large blocks of weekend time when they need you most. A little forethought and strategic planning can make a real difference.
- In a similar vein, what if parents refused to let media push them aside? Young children may clamor for cartoons, but the comfort and security of face-to-face contact with Mom or Dad is a genuine

treasure. If we don't watch out, the minivan's backseat DVD can monopolize time that parents and children could be talking about real things in the real world that matter greatly. Love unexpressed is all too soon a mere shadow of itself.

- You would expect this next one from someone like me, but I'll say it anyway: What if every North American family sponsored a child in poverty? What a huge impact this would have on the child— *and* on the sponsoring family. Whenever I ask Compassion sponsors why they do what they do each month, I get answers such as "Well, we really care about the little guy in Kenya, but we also do it for our own children. More than anything we want our sons and daughters to grow up compassionate, caring, and warm-hearted. We know that won't be learned by our lectures. They won't pick it up at the mall or on television. They'll learn it by how we use our money, what we pray about, and the relationships we build through the letters back and forth. So, to be honest, we're using your program to disciple our own children."

    Sponsoring a child is certainly not all we should be doing for the world's poor. But it's hard to imagine doing less. And the benefits run two directions.

- What if every Christian family blocked out one night a week to enjoy each other and pass along their values to their children through a "family night" tradition? It sounds like a big commitment at first. But what else, truly, is more important? Nothing we can give our kids equals in value the gift of time. It's what kids crave most, and families that do this can testify to the major impact it makes. Fortunately, an abundance of resource material is now available to help make the experience alive and exciting.

GOD'S PART, OUR PART

The previous ideas are not entirely far-fetched and utopian. We could make at least some of them happen if we summoned the will to do so. If we truly cared about children and the world we are passing on to them, we could make some sizable improvements.

I remember as a young child in Africa coming upon a wild tulip in the jungle at the side of the road. A cement block had apparently fallen off a truck and rolled down the embankment to the jungle's edge. Now the stem of the wildflower was twisted and gnarled as it had struggled to grow from under the cement block. It had contorted itself first this way and then that, seeking the light of day, until it had at long last found the edge of the blockage. Once freed, it had taken off as best it could in an upward direction. Its struggle had produced a tulip, but it was stunted, small and weak, exhausted. A flower alive, but barely. Its early struggle to overcome its blockage had sapped its strength, potential, and growth.

As I think back on that tragic flower, I now realize that God had done his part. He had built a perfect design into the DNA of that little tulip bulb, a potential for beautiful color, size, and fragrance. The Bible tells us God has also done that in the life of each child. Each is beautifully knit together in the mother's womb. Though some children are born with defects and imperfections that break a parent's heart, none are beyond God's ability to work in that new life and receive great joy and glory from what he has created. No mistakes!

Likewise, children were made to grow, develop, thrive, and reach the fullness God knit into them. He lovingly said in Jeremiah 29:11, "I know the plans I have for you,...plans to prosper you and not to harm you, plans to give you hope and a future."

As God's agents, his hands and his feet in this hurting world, it is our mandate to remove the "cement blocks" that suffocate children: poverty, abuse, neglect, and injustice of all kinds. We are called to provide safe, nurturing environments for them. It is our job to "train a child in the way he should go" (Proverbs 22:6). In these ways God's plan can be wonderfully realized in their lives.

As much as I might want a plant to grow, I cannot simply grab the seedling between my fingers and pull it upward to make it rise faster. I cannot beg, shout, or threaten it to get going. If in my zeal or impatience I pull too hard, its fragile roots may lose their grip on the life-giving soil it so desperately needs. The design and the path are ultimately in the loving, capable hands of each child's creator God. Our role is to provide a conducive environment so that every opportunity to grow and thrive can be fulfilled.

We can do this if we will! All we are missing are the vision and the heart. The world doesn't have to be like this for our little ones. There are enough of us who do care that this kind of evil does not have to prevail. It is in our hands to stop abuse and neglect and inspire nurture. Imagine...

15

"Just" Children:
A Call to Arms

We have come a long way together in the pilgrimage of this book. If we had been sitting all this while around the campfire in Nielle, the last flickering flames would be dancing in the red coals. We would stare quietly at the glowing embers and the wisps of smoke rising. Thoughts of getting up and heading home would be creeping into our heads.

But I am reluctant to leave. Maybe you are too. My heart wants to linger a few more moments to ask, "So what will we actually do?" Knowing what we know, having been through what we've been through, we cannot simply put the book down, sigh, and walk away.

Jesus clearly and solemnly stated, "From everyone who has been given much, much will be demanded; and from the one who has been entrusted with much, much more will be asked" (Luke 12:48). We normally think that verse refers to money. Maybe it does, but I think it means even more. It can just as reasonably be talking about knowledge, experiences, insights, and a stirred heart. In this book we have journeyed together to a point of no return. We cannot go back to how things used to be.

Let me speak for myself before the fire is gone. I have no choice but to keep pressing the battle for "the least of these," the children. My personal journey has taken me through both the horrors of poverty and the devastation of child abuse. I've learned that poverty and abuse speak the same language—a message that says, "You don't matter. Give up!" Both are completely opposite to the wonderful message of the gospel, which says, "You *do* matter. You are of immeasurable value. You are deeply loved by God himself."

For many years I dreaded putting my life and thoughts on paper. Others told me I should write a book, but I kept putting it off. I knew it would be painful. My greatest fear was that it might cost me so dearly, and yet nothing would change.

You see, I know that feeling. I've felt it before. I remember once spending time in a desperate slum in Haiti. It was, ironically, called Cite Soleil, "City of the Sun." But it was a terribly dark place. An epidemic of measles had swept into the shacks and was stealing the children, the ti chapes ("little escapees"), one at a time. Cries of anguish rose from peasant parents as one by one their little ones died. There was altogether too little money, too little vaccine, too little hope.

I had held a tiny six-month-old baby in my arms that last day. So small, so vulnerable, so sick. He wore no diaper, just a pair of blue underpants. I looked down to notice a cruel irony: the shorts were decorated with yellow smiley faces. I assure you that nobody was smiling this day. His mother, in desperation, had handed this tiny, withered body to me, hoping something, anything, might change his certain fate. Maybe the touch of a stranger with white skin would make a last-minute difference.

I cradled the child as I prayed and wept helplessly, watching his rib cage rise and fall. The limp little boy gave a tiny shudder...and then went still, dead in my arms. His mother, watching anxiously, fell sobbing against me. I will never forget the anguish of her cry. It came from deep within her.

That very night I had to fly from Haiti to New York State, where I was scheduled to speak at a Christian music festival. It was summertime, and the festival was being held on the grounds of a huge amusement park. I was the first speaker of the morning.

As I walked onto the stage, it was less than twenty-four hours after I had brokenheartedly handed that tiny Haitian baby into the arms of his heavenly Father. I saw in front of me a small, distracted crowd sitting on the grass. Most of the festival attendees were still sleeping in, exhausted from the late concert the night before. I could hear others shrieking and giggling as a roller coaster rumbled along its track. A huge, colorful Ferris wheel towered over us, and we were showered good-naturedly with popcorn from on high.

The transition between opposite worlds had been so abrupt that I found myself speechless before this little group of people. I didn't know where to begin. What to say? How could I possibly connect them with where I had just been?

I stood there silent for an awkward length of time, tears blurring my vision. What hope was there that I could possibly find the words to help them understand the world and their place in it? How could they feel what I felt and grasp that it was only a night's flight in our world from this carnival grounds to the Haitian slum? A runaway Frisbee skittered across the stage in front of me. I hung my head in despair.

I don't remember how I finally started my talk or what I eventually said. The words felt like sawdust in my mouth.

It is the cry of my heart for you that, as a result of our time together in this book, you will not disconnect. I hope you will search deep in your heart, remember your own pilgrimage, and join me in this battle for children. We need an entire army of us who will commit ourselves to "speak up for those who cannot speak for themselves, for the rights of all who are destitute" (Proverbs 31:8). That scripture is emblazoned above the main entrance to Compassion's headquarters in Colorado Springs. It captures what this battle is all about. It is worth whatever amount of passion and energy and resource you pour into it.

RIPPLES OF INFLUENCE

Let me ask you: What children has God placed in your life on a regular basis? Whom has he entrusted to your care and influence? Take a minute to actually list them on a piece of paper. Then, next to each name, jot a note of what you could say or do to lift them up and invest in their spirits the next time you see them. What a wonderful world it would be if every child was loved, protected, and nourished by the adults in his or her life.

Every child needs to have at least one person who loves him or her unconditionally. Not "if only you were…" or "I love you when…" or "I love you because…" Instead, someone who will say, "I love you and always will. Nothing you could ever say or do would lessen my love for you."

The whole concept can be overwhelming, because there are so many children, so many needs. It is easy to get paralyzed by the magnitude of the task and wind up doing nothing because we can't do everything. One of the most intelligent men who ever lived, Albert Einstein, said, "The world is a dangerous place to live. Not because of the people who are evil, but because of the people who don't do anything about it." What is needed is an army of us who understand this and commit to action. It takes a plan and a daily resolve to be that kind of person.

I have a rather crazy way to remind myself of my calling to be an advocate for children. For nearly five years now, I have had tinnitus, an intermittent ringing in my left ear. It makes a very high pitch, an A on the musical scale. Some people have gotten so distressed by this condition that they have actually committed suicide to escape its overwhelming annoyance.

I have prayed fervently for healing from this "thorn in the flesh." I've reasoned with God that I have enough responsibility and stress in my life without this. In spite of all my research for a cure, visits to specialists, and pleading with the Almighty, the condition persists. If it were a broken arm or something else obvious, I might get some pity. But this is an invisible infirmity, and I have to behave normally in meetings and conversations as if there were not a telephone constantly ringing in my ear.

Since God has not chosen to take this condition away, I have decided to use it in my life as a kind of wake-up call for children. Whenever I am aware of the ringing, I take it as a cue to look around for a nearby child whom I can somehow bless. I will say a kind word, give a kind assistance— anything to lift the child up. If no children are in the vicinity, I use the moment to pray for the cause of children in the world. Doing this must irritate Satan, because in no time at all, the ringing in my ear subsides!

I don't know what kind of reminder system will work for you, but I challenge you to find something that will regularly make you aware of the children around you and across the world. It doesn't have to be a dramatic intervention, just a little act of love. With enough of us doing that, the world actually would become a better place. As Mother Teresa liked to say, "We cannot all do great things, but we can each do small things with great love."

What we are doing is forcing ourselves to see children specifically, not just as a nebulous population subset. One of my favorite stories about Jesus is in Mark 8:22–26, when he healed a blind man in Bethsaida. He applied saliva to the man's eyes, then asked him, "Do you see anything?" The man replied that he could see only the fuzzy shapes of people that seemed more like trees in motion.

"Once more Jesus put his hands on the man's eyes. Then his eyes were opened, his sight was restored, and he saw everything clearly" (verse 25).

To the Messiah, the Lord of Glory, people looking like blurry trees was not good enough! He had created each human being in a unique way, and he would not rest until the man saw what he himself saw: precious, distinct individuals made with dignity and in the image of God.

That is how it is with children in today's world. We must see them one child at a time. We must reach out to them one child at a time. If enough of us do this, great things can be accomplished!

Every one of us has a "sphere of influence," people in our immediate world whom we can influence with our words and deeds. Some of these people have considerable ability to bless children, once their eyes are opened. If we can make child advocates of these people, many children will be helped whom we would never otherwise reach and in ways we might never be able to bring about.

It is the mandate of the church to be salt and light in the world, bringing healing and hope wherever it is planted. Just as I argued earlier that societal change can start at the very bottom with the life of one child, I also believe in taking this cause to the very top of society. The church—that is, all of us who love our Lord—needs to challenge our governments and cultures and make them accountable for the welfare of the youngest and most vulnerable citizens. Imagine the amazing good that could be accomplished systemically if powerful individuals, both nationally and internationally, could be motivated to use their influence on behalf of the little ones.

To do this, church and mission leaders must grasp the significance of elevating children as a priority. Theologians and missiologists must influence seminaries and Bible colleges with a powerful theology of children's ministry. This will spawn bold initiatives that will transform what happens in our churches and on the mission fields of the world. Are you one of these leaders? Are you married to one of them? Do you know one of these gate-keepers? Then you can start the process.

Does your pastor champion the cause of children? Do the missionaries you support seem to understand the strategic importance of ministry to children? Do the telecasts you tune into seem to grasp the place of children in the kingdom of God and use their powerful media to stir up their sphere of influence on behalf of children? What about the radio programs you listen to or the magazines you read or the organizations to which you donate funds? You have a golden opportunity and also great responsibility to influence these prominent people, whom God has entrusted with much, to join us in the battle for children.

We also have a sacred duty to honor and support those already ministering to children, from Sunday school teachers to midweek club workers to those heroes who operate your church's nursery. In all these places, the cement of little souls is being molded for good. These workers need to be supported in prayer as well as recognized, honored, and thanked for their strategic ministry. They already have the hugs and hearts of children, but they need to be stroked by adults as well. They need to be provided with quality training, equipment, encouragement—and an occasional rest. This means stepping in and giving them a hand so they can have a weekend or even a summer to refresh their vision and passion.

I remember a poignant moment a few years ago when I had the honor of speaking at my alma mater, Moody Bible Institute in Chicago. As I stood before a thousand students in Torrey-Gray Auditorium, I asked the soccer team, which had been quite successful that year, to stand. After all, I was one of the missionary kids back in the late 1960s, when soccer was not widely played in America, who had formed Moody's first soccer team. We had all grown up playing soccer in our villages.

Now on this day, the athletes stood up. The place erupted in wild applause, whistles, and cheers. They basked for a few moments in the admiration and adulation of their fellow students.

When they were seated again, I then asked all the Christian education majors to stand. You could almost tell that the crowd was thinking, *Huh? Did I hear him right?* The C. E. students looked sheepishly at one another and then, one by one, stood to their feet quietly and self-consciously. The student body looked at them awkwardly. I had to call for a round of applause.

I then said to the students, "There are your true heroes. These are the people who are going to do most strategically what all of you came to Moody to prepare for—to build the kingdom of God. They will be working with the most powerful demographic group, having the most dynamic and lasting impact, ultimately bringing in the greatest harvest for Christ!" At that, the students volunteered a standing ovation for these future ministers to children.

I wasn't just blowing smoke; a 2004 study showed that 43 percent of Americans who accept Jesus Christ as their Savior do so before reaching age thirteen. Another 21 percent do so by the age of eighteen, and another 13 percent by age twenty-one. That leaves only 23 percent who decide to follow Christ as adults.[1] So who's pulling the greatest weight in bringing people to the foot of the Cross?

When the bewildered Christian education students sat back down, I said to them, "I am so very sorry, but given the messed-up values and priorities of this world and even the church and mission organizations, this may be the last time you get a standing ovation for what you do—at least this side of heaven. Just know this: What you will do among children is as close to the heart of God and central to his kingdom as anything we could mention."

On that occasion I went on to tell the story I often tell of Dr. Tony Campolo, well-known author and sociologist at Eastern University outside Philadelphia. He grew up in that city, and one day while downtown he got the notion to drive by his old boyhood church. He knew the demographics of the neighborhood had changed several times since his childhood, and the congregation had gone from white to black to Asian to...now, nothing. He drove up to the familiar address to see plywood covering the windows of the sanctuary. Deterioration was on every side.

Dr. Campolo was sad—but also curious. He began to muse, *What kills a church? What makes a once-thriving church wither away and die?* He decided to make his boyhood church a case study.

Finding the last group of elders, he introduced himself and then said,

"I'm interested in the life cycle of this church. Do you still have the records? May I study them?"

They told him where to find the archives—in the basement of the building in a vault behind a door nailed shut. Dr. Campolo showed up a few days later with a crowbar and managed to pry open the room. Sweeping away the cobwebs, he stared at the stack of annual reports. *Where do I begin?* he wondered.

I know, he said to himself, *I'll start at the year I gave my life to Christ as a boy.* He rustled through the stack until he found the report. Opening its yellowed pages, he began to read.

That had not been a particularly good year for the church, the author admitted. Giving was down from the previous year. Mission activity was subdued. Attendance had declined. There were only three conversions over the course of the year, and they were "just children."

Dr. Campolo stared at the page in disbelief and irritation. "Wait a minute!" he said out loud. "I was one of those three! And I know the other two. One spent his life in mission service in Africa, while the other became president of a seminary here in the United States. And I've given my life to Christian higher education. What do you mean, just three children came to Christ that year?"

The sociologist had found the answer to his research question. A church begins to die when it says, "They were just children." If that is the mind-set, decline and decay will surely follow.

One of the great professors at Dallas Theological Seminary, Dr. Howard Hendricks, has written, "It is my deep conviction that no effort in Christian ministry is more enduring or more stabilizing in our Christian faith than outreach to children." Francis Xavier, early Jesuit in the 1500s, is well remembered for his bold claim, "Give me a child until he is seven, and I will give you the man." The rationale here is the same as in the battle against poverty around the world. Children will ultimately change the churches in which they worship. Changed churches will produce changed communities. In time, changed communities will change nations and ultimately the world. It all begins with the young.

When you poke your finger into wet cement, you get instant results.

You don't have to push very hard. The indentation is there for all to see. That's what it is like to bring the imprint of Jesus to a child's soul.

Later on, as the cement begins to set up, you have to push harder to make an impression. So it is with ministry to teenagers and college students. The fact of their unique culture creates greater resistance.

When it comes to full-scale adults, the concrete has become like rock. If you want to reshape the spirit at this point, you need a hammer and a chisel.

This is why it makes good strategic sense to concentrate our efforts on the most receptive stages of life—the early ones. Otherwise, we'll miss the golden opportunities…which leads me to tell you one final story before we leave this "campfire."

THE REUNION

The year was 1985; I had been serving as a young executive with Compassion International for about eight years. We were helping about a hundred thousand sponsored children at that time. Those were the tragic days of the Ethiopian famine that caught the heart of the whole world. Secular and Christian musicians alike wrote songs and raised funds to help the starving.

Our president, Wally Erickson, asked another young man named Mark Yeadon (now our vice president of child ministry) and me to travel to that country for an audit of our assistance. Was the money getting through properly? Was it actually saving lives? And was everything being done, as our mission statement claimed, "in Jesus' name"?

Since this was my first trip back to the continent of Africa in twenty-two years, I was given permission to take a detour on my way home and swing by the Ivory Coast. I arranged to ride a truck up to Nielle to see my own village. As we rumbled into town, I could barely recognize where I was. The village was no longer a little cluster of mud huts; it was now a full-blown town. Our little mission compound was no longer outside the village; the town had grown around it and had encircled our home.

I found our driveway, and as I walked down it, suitcase in hand, I was smitten by the big, beautiful trees. Sure enough, those little seedlings that

Alezye and I had so lovingly planted, watered, protected, and nurtured had now become a lush, tropical forest. I learned later that Nielle was such a pleasant place that missionaries came here for vacation—to rest and renew amid the cool shade of our trees.

Other buildings had been added to the compound over the years. At the end of the road I found the little house Dad had built, surrounded now by flowers, bushes, and fruit trees. I smiled again as I remembered my childhood fantasy that I had played a major role in constructing that house.

The missionaries now living in our home were kind and gracious. They allowed me to stay with them and even sleep in my own little room. I will never forget that night. I lay there listening once again to the village drums. I hadn't heard them in more than two decades, but it was as if time had stood still. They were closer now, since the town had encroached all around us. I heard the same tropical symphony I had loved as a boy: the crickets, the croaking of the tree frogs, the sounds of the village at night. I was home again!

At breakfast the next morning, the missionaries told me how things had changed. The Sahara Desert had encroached to the south, the sands and wind taking over the once-fertile fields. Little boys no longer had to guard the crops against marauding bands of monkeys, because even the animals had moved on in search of a more reliable food supply. Nobody shot slings anymore, because there was no game big enough to need such a powerful weapon. Even slingshots around the necks of little boys were a rare sight.

The marigot, our little marsh, had long since dried up into a useless dustbowl. There were no more fish, and the rice paddies had been gone for more than a decade. Poverty was worse than it had ever been, since the little boys who had trained to be hunters had nothing to hunt, the fishermen had nothing to fish, and the peasants could barely feed their families, much less have anything left to sell in the marketplace. My heart ached for my people and how harsh life had become for them.

I asked about the Senufo Christians. "How is the church here these days?" I said brightly.

Again, the report was bleak. "Oh, it is a very tough place to minister," they replied. "Not only do we fight against the animism, the Satan worship of your parents' era, but now the Muslims have moved in with great influence."

"How big is the church?" I asked.

"It's still pretty small," they answered. "Maybe forty people."

"Really? Only forty—children and all?" I asked incredulously.

"Oh, well, if you count children, there's probably closer to a hundred in the church."

I moved on to quiz them about Alezye. Twenty-two years had passed since we had gripped each other's arms and pledged to remain faithful to God and prepare ourselves to be tools he could use. We had exchanged a letter or two after that. But like most young men, the letter writing dwindled, and by now I had no idea what had become of him.

"Do you know Alezye?" I blurted out.

"Oh, yes. In fact, he will be here today. He knows you are here! The drums are still faster than the trucks. Before you arrived, the people knew you were coming back."

I was so excited that I decided not to spoil the reunion by asking all kinds of questions about him. I was sure he was a pastor or maybe a mission leader by now. I would see him soon enough, and he could tell me everything himself. How my heart soared as I walked outside amid the trees and tropical floral scents.

I crossed the field to "our" tree, which was still standing. It wasn't the tallest tree anymore, but as I approached its base, I looked up into its branches—and there was our tree house! It had been attacked by termites over the years, but it still existed. I was surprised at how low it actually was. I remembered a dizzying height, so high you could fall to your death from way up there. Now as a grown man, I discovered I could almost reach up and touch it. My heart and mind filled with wonderful memories.

Then I heard a rustling in the grass behind me...footsteps. A familiar voice said, "Wesley..."

With tears welling up in my eyes, I whirled around to face my dear friend. But there stood an old man. His hair was turning white; his skin was wrinkled and worn. I looked deeply into his eyes. Yes, it was Alezye—

stooped over, in worn-out clothing, and holding in his weathered hand a machete. Actually, it wasn't much more than a dagger now, having been resharpened so many times.

I raced to give him a huge hug. Through his clothing, I could feel his ribs. I told him excitedly in French that I had at long last come back to Africa. I said I'd just been to Ethiopia and had arranged to come by to see him!

I could see in his eyes that he wasn't following my words. He shook his head and told me in Senari that he didn't remember very much French.

A great sadness draped itself over me. I felt my knees go weak, and my stomach clenched within me. Something was desperately wrong here. Rags…machete…wrinkled skin…forgotten French. This man before me was clearly not a pastor. It was Alezye, all right, but the fire had gone out of his eyes and his spirit.

We slumped down and sat together at the foot of our tree. "Alezye," I finally stammered, "what happened? What went wrong?"

He looked at me kindly. "Wesley," he finally said, "all that is left of our dream…is that I still love my Lord. You can see that I'm not the Nielle pastor. That didn't happen. Do you know what I do to feed my family?"

"No, my friend," I managed. "What do you do?"

"I chop grass on this mission compound—with this." He held up his worn-out knife. I remembered how we had chopped elephant grass together as kids to feed the chief's horse. We used to say how much we didn't like the job…that our life paths would take us far above this menial, lowly work.

But here was my best friend—a peasant grass cutter. I sat silently as we both wept beneath our tree…beneath our dreams.

"Why?" I finally whispered. "Tell me…"

With a faraway look in his eyes as if he were talking about someone else, he told me that shortly after our departure from Africa, his family had fallen on hard times. His father had grown sick and had died in about a year. The expenses of the illness and then the funeral had forced the sale of his family's land. Clearly there had been no money for the modest school fees. He had been forced to drop out.

For many years now they had been peasants without land. "But I am fortunate," he added, "to at least have this job. It means I can still take care of my family. Now tell me what you do."

I told him of Compassion and that God had led me to serve the poor, especially children in poverty. He nodded and said he was genuinely proud and happy about that.

But after a few minutes, my dear friend gave a sigh and stood up. "I know you've come a long journey to see me, and I am so sorry you have to see me like this, but I must get back to work now, Wesley. This job isn't much, but it's all I have, and I can't risk losing it." I knew he wouldn't be in jeopardy for spending time with me. But he was worried nonetheless.

In stunned silence we hugged one last time. He touched my cheek with his callused hand and slowly walked away. I slumped back against the bark of our tree. I could barely breathe in my grief as I watched this amazing man go. Soon he bent over in the middle of the lime orchard we had planted together and began rhythmically swinging his machete in the hot, tropical sun.

I sat a long moment, helpless and in great anguish. This was so horribly wrong! There I was, Dr. Stafford, an executive with a large and wonderful international ministry, while a far superior man in every way was bent over in the trees cutting grass, just barely able to feed his family. It was so unjust, so unfair. Suddenly I was angry with everything. Where was this loving God we both had so solemnly promised to serve? Where were the mission and the church that should have kept this from happening? Why was it he and not I? My head dropped between my knees, and I gave way to my grief, anger, sorrow, and bewilderment. Huge sobs racked my body and stole my breath.

With my head down, my face wet with tears, I suddenly heard a voice. It was as clear as if someone were sitting beside me. *Wess, don't you see what I have done?*

I jerked my head up to see who had spoken. No one was there. Could that have somehow been the voice of God?

You have to remember that my roots are Conservative Baptist. We don't expect God to speak directly to us—at least not very often, and certainly not out loud!

When I got over my shock, I began to ponder the words. "Lord, if that's you—no. I don't see anything here that you could have done. All I see is waste and destruction, injustice and evil. Nothing here has your touch on it!"

Then I heard a second phrase. I don't know if I heard it with my ears or if it just roared through my head. Anyway, here it is: *I've given you one hundred thousand Alezyes.*

"What? What is that supposed to mean? One hundred thousand Alezyes?"

Then it hit me like a wave crashing on the beach. The ministry I served was at that very moment ministering to a hundred thousand little children around the world. I began to consider the words. What if Compassion had been here in my village when we were both children? How different things might have been. When Alezye's father had gotten sick, our ministry would have helped pay the bills. When his father died, our catastrophe fund would have kept the family intact through the financial crisis, keeping him in school. We would have stayed with him through high school and probably into seminary. He could have stayed on course and become the pastor his heart so desired to be. Everything that had dashed my best friend's dreams would have been prevented. This kind of work was going on worldwide, even at that moment, for a hundred thousand Alezyes, as I sat brokenhearted in my anger and grief.

I looked down the hill at my friend. Then slowly and deliberately, I said back to God, "Okay…okay…I think I understand. Who am I to doubt your ways? But you chose the wrong guy. It should be me in the hot sun with the machete instead of him.

"One thing I do know, Lord, is that I absolutely dedicate myself, my heart, my mind, my energy, everything I have, to use the life you have given me to see that this does not happen again…that, if I can help it, there will be no more little Alezyes doomed to destruction anywhere in the world—ever!"

To this day I carry a huge sense of responsibility for Alezye and all the other children with whom I was raised in Nielle. I fight poverty and its destructive evil on their behalf. Sadly, I now get reports that most of my generation of village children is gone. They've already died of old age. Life is so harsh that the life expectancy is only about forty-five years.

When I rode away from Nielle later that day, I paused for a moment at the end of our beautiful tree-lined driveway and looked back. Suddenly it hit me: What if we had invested in *children* many years ago the way we nurtured and cared for young *trees*? How different things might be today. Instead of a beautiful, tropical paradise, we might have had a strong, thriving, vibrant church in my village—with Alezye as pastor.

I came back to America and promptly sent my boyhood friend some money through a missionary who knew him well. A month or so later I did so again. But then I began to think about the African culture and realized that if I kept this up indefinitely, I would humiliate Alezye's pride as an adult. He wasn't a child I could "sponsor." I dared not offend him.

Another twenty years have passed since I made that pilgrimage to Nielle. I have not been back since. Instead, I have used that heartbreaking experience in 1985 to keep me faithful to my calling. For many years I kept track of the time zone difference, Ivory Coast being seven hours ahead of my home in Colorado. When I was getting up, I would think about the villagers coming in from a long day in the fields. When I went to bed at night, I knew Alezye was getting up, and I breathed a prayer for him as he started another day of chopping grass in the hot sun. No matter where I was in the world or what challenges my day held, I tackled them with a passion and a fervor I could only hope was worthy of the sacrifice I knew had been made to seal my calling.

Then in the year 2000, I learned in a passing conversation with a missionary that Alezye had died. I hadn't even known! Why didn't anybody tell me?

Of course, why would anybody think to tell the president of an international development agency that a "yard boy," a peasant in West Africa, had passed away? To most, he looked like any other poor peasant—ragged, thin, and worn. But to me...well, I knew his heart, his spirit, his potential, and his dreams. On the day of his death, a noble man in peasant's garb slipped quietly into the presence of God, faithful to the end.

My most fervent prayer is that I, too, will one day be found faithful to the calling on my life—the calling to serve those in every desperate village and town and city across this globe who are too small to ignore.

WHAT WILL YOU DO?

What are you thinking just now? What is happening inside your heart? Every human being needs a cause in life, a passion. If you don't have something in your life that can make your heart pound, that can move you either to tears of joy or tears of sorrow in about thirty seconds, then my friend, you are not fully alive. Life is too precious to go on in such a half-awake condition. You can do better. You deserve better.

If you don't have such a cause or mission in life, then please take mine! I implore you to join me in this battle for the hearts, souls, minds, and bodies of children. May you begin to seize every chance for saying or doing something that will lift them up. May your prayers include them on a daily basis. May you reach out to applaud the moms, dads, teachers, and others who struggle to guide their little lives.

I once complimented a young mother at a car wash on how well she was relating to her little boy. While we waited for our cars to be dried, I tapped her arm and said, "You're doing something really important, you know. And you're doing it very well. He is a lucky little boy. Way to go."

She paused, looked at me for a moment, and then tears began to fill her soft eyes. Suddenly she reached out to me as she said, "Thank you. Nobody has ever said that to me before. You have no idea how much I needed that!"

I wish I could promise you that every such gesture on behalf of children would be so warmly received. It would be nice to experience only joy, love, acceptance, and gratitude. But that is not the nature of our battle. In my experience, most of what we do to bless children enrages the hosts of hell. We are paddling our boat upstream against the swift current of a world that has lost most of its heart. But the rewards will last for eternity. Every child who enters the gates of heaven will trigger a cascade of cheers and joy.

I look forward to being part of that eternal extravaganza. I look forward to seeing you there too—and, oh yes, be sure to bring lots of little ones with you when you come.

Afterword

THE REST OF THE STORY

The tragic experiences I related in chapters 8 and 9 are not complete without telling you what unfolded much later.

One day after three decades had passed, around the time I was named president of Compassion International at the age of forty-four, I got a letter from one of my Bandulo Christian Academy buddies. Now a pastor in the state of Illinois, he poured out the agony in his spirit that he simply couldn't overcome. He told of many other mutual classmates who were still living lives of distress, unable to leave the hurtful past behind.

They were now adults and could no longer be silenced. They had begun to write to one another, sharing memories in the form of poems, essays, and letters. My correspondent informed me that they were still angry and damaged, to the point of organizing a class-action suit against the mission that ran the boarding school. The academy had been closed for more than twenty years at that point, but there was still unfinished business, they believed. They had somehow heard about my life and work, remembered my moment of determination with the birthday candle, and wanted me to help champion their cause.

I had not thought about all this in a very long time. My mind went back to a certain campfire at Woodbine Ranch, a camp in Colorado, where as a seventeen-year-old I had sat listening to a talk on forgiveness. Immediately, of course, I had thought about Bandulo. As the speaker continued that evening in the crisp Rocky Mountain air, I was saying internally, *Yes, but not a single one of those people has ever asked my forgiveness. They won't even admit that what they did to us was wrong.*

I stewed about that for a few minutes but then made a pivotal decision in my young life. *They will never ask me to forgive them, so I will simply do it without their request,* I told myself. *They all but ruined my childhood. But I don't have to let them ruin my whole life! I'm going to forgive them and leave them forever behind me. I'm going to live above all this.*

From that night on, I chose to interpret my childhood exclusively in terms of Nielle, the wonderful African village. The other place simply no longer existed for me. That mind game had worked pretty well for decades.

Now in 1993, I was sent a packet of my classmates' letters and poems as they poured out their pain. We'd never been allowed to write these things in our weekly letters to our parents. Here at last, the floodgates were open.

I stretched out on the living room couch one evening to read them. One by one, their desperately sad stories unfolded—fears, resentment, dysfunction in parenting their own children, broken marriages, even attempts at suicide. For the first time in decades, I found myself transported back to that painful place. My eyes filled with tears until I could no longer read. I stifled sobs that welled up from a long-dormant volcano of pain and hurt.

Across the room, my wife, Donna, was quietly reading in her favorite chair. She looked over the top of her book and was concerned to see her husband in great distress. As I struggled to compose myself and still keep reading the stories of destroyed lives of my dear childhood friends, she put her book down and came over to me. She said gently, "Something big I don't know about, right?"

That broke the dam. "Oh, Donna," I sobbed, "I thought I had left it behind. I didn't want it to still be a part of my life, much less ours. Yes, sweetheart, there are deep, deep hurts in the childhood of the man you married."

Over the next few days, Donna read the letters and came to know the rest of me. The silence was shattered at last. While she had picked up hints over the years, she finally understood the scope of my heartbreaking history, and she went through great grief for me, my sister, and my friends.

As I was debating whether or not to help my childhood friends fight this battle with the mission, the issue became more and more public. Newspapers and magazines picked up on it. The mission, feeling the pressure, felt compelled to explain themselves in their magazine to their constituents. Sadly, the gist of their story was that the MKs causing all this trouble were losers and probably would have been poorly adjusted to life no matter where they had been brought up. That was the straw that broke the camel's back for me. I simply could not bear to see the victims blamed yet again.

AWKWARD LUNCH

I asked the head of the denomination and his missions department director to meet me for lunch. They knew me only as the head of a child-focused Christian ministry. I felt like Joseph in the book of Genesis when his brothers came to Egypt to buy food. These men didn't know who I was!

I'm not sure what they thought the topic of the lunch would be, but I caught them completely off guard when I asked them to define *loser* for me. As they stammered, I explained, "Well, I sort of need to know because …apparently, I am one. I went to Bandulo Christian Academy for six years." The color immediately drained from their faces. I warned them that day not to deny that the abuses had actually happened or to attempt to blame the victims. If they kept doing this, I would join the cause and become their worst nightmare.

To make a long story short, I was able to serve as a bridge in getting the class-action suit put aside if the mission would conduct its own thorough investigation and hold the perpetrators accountable for their crimes. An investigative panel of outside child-development experts and board members was convened. Many of us submitted our painful stories in writing. The committee also invited a dozen or more of us to give live witness—with the perpetrators present.

My sister, Carol, and I both traveled to Florida to testify. I will never forget that day. I walked into a hotel conference room, and sitting at the table were Mr. and Mrs. Staber. My stomach churned as if I were a six-year-old again. Across from them were the committee members, counselors, and experts in child abuse. For close to two hours I sat within six feet of this elderly couple and recounted what I had been through at their hands. With virtually everything I said, they shook their heads, wrote furiously, and hissed, "Oh, that's a lie. That is a complete lie." The panel admonished them to be silent many times but to no avail.

At one point as I was describing the size and heft of the truck-tire sandal they used to beat us, Mrs. Staber glared at me and sneered, "Oh, it wasn't anywhere near that big!"

I paused a moment, looked at that diminutive, still-angry woman, and said, "You know, maybe you're right. In fact, you don't look that big to me anymore, either!"

When my testimony was over, my heart was shattered. I walked out of the room as calmly as I could, then fell to my knees in the hotel hallway. Soon my six-foot-one frame had collapsed flat to the floor, sobbing and sobbing anew like a little boy. People tried to comfort me, but all I could gasp was, "They aren't even sorry! After all they did, they still aren't even sorry!"

MELTDOWN IN DALLAS

That evening I had to fly to Dallas so I could give the keynote address to the American Association of Christian Counselors convention early the next day. I couldn't sleep a bit that night, so troubled was my heart. The next morning I walked into an enormous ballroom filled with twenty-four hundred psychologists and Christian counselors.

Dr. Gary Collins, the association president at the time, introduced me, and I stood up to deliver my prepared remarks. I intended to challenge them that, in the midst of their day-to-day concern for the hurts of humanity, they should include the poor. I would tell them that nobody quite understood the inside-out dynamic of poverty as they did.

I plunged into my talk, starting with a joke, of course—and halfway through the joke, my heart just broke. I stopped speaking. The room grew quiet. I looked across that sea of faces and finally said, "I have an important talk for you today, but I'm not sure I can deliver it. I am a suffering, hurting person today." Through my tears I told them the story of Bandulo and the previous day's testimony.

When I got to the part where those who had abused me had repeatedly accused me of lying, I stopped, hung my head, and gave way to my tears and sobs. There was total silence across the ballroom as they waited for the speaker to compose himself.

Then from far in the back of the ballroom, a woman's voice broke the silence. "I believe you!" Immediately a man's voice called from the other side of the darkened room. "Yeah, we believe you!" One by one, people stood to their feet and shouted out, "We believe you!"

Soon the entire convention was on its feet, ministering to the keynote speaker. They were doing what counselors do best, which is to care. By now, the morning program was in shambles. Nobody had ever seen a conference speaker implode quite like this. Dr. Collins came up and prayed a prayer of comfort for me. It was a precious moment.

When everyone was seated, I started again. I pointed out that our God is awesome. Here I had gone thirty-five years with a broken heart and never a single hour of counseling, and yet this morning, the first time I had spoken publicly of it and was overwhelmed by grief, God had provided not just one counselor but twenty-four hundred of them! The place broke into wild applause. This was exactly what their hearts longed to do, what their minds were trained to do—and they had done it when least expected. I don't remember much of what I said that morning, but even now, years later, I still get letters from counselors around the world who remember that as one of the profound moments of their ministry.

KINSHIP OF THE WOUNDED

When the investigation panel presented its final report in November 1997, a total of nine people were indicted: seven staff members and two students. Of this group, three had already died, two others had left the denomination, and the remaining four (including the Stabers) were formally reprimanded. From a legal point of view, the statute of limitations had long since expired, and besides, the crimes were perpetrated on foreign soil, not inside the United States. So no charges could be filed. But the panel did sanction the four as severely as they could within their power, stripping

262 TOO SMALL TO IGNORE

them of official clergy credentials and advising them never again to work with children. This, of course, was mostly a moot point, since all were now comfortably retired.

In May 1999, the denomination organized a weekend reunion for all the Bandulo MKs, at mission expense, to formally apologize and offer assistance to us. Parents and spouses were also invited to a retreat center in Georgia. It was, of course, one of the most powerful and emotional experiences of our lives. Some eighty of us classmates showed up, along with another seventy parents, spouses, and officials.

One by one we recognized each other through the wrinkles and graying hair, fell into each other's arms, and sobbed—sobs that welled up from deep within our spirits. The president of the denomination stood before us on Sunday morning and read an official apology. They offered to reimburse everyone's counseling expenses and encouraged the rest of us to get counseling if we ever felt we needed it. It was a gracious and clearly appropriate thing to do.

But the voices we "children" most needed to hear express regret were not there for us. Only the current mission leadership—a generation removed from the disaster—had the courage to deal with the devastation and try to make things right. Actually, there was one exception: the school nurse had made a videotape on which she admitted her guilt and requested forgiveness, and it had been mailed to our homes. We had sat in silence, listening to this now elderly lady pour out her heart, and one by one we forgave her.

Otherwise, silence continued to reign.

We did plenty of talking, however, to each other that weekend. We gathered in reunion groups to catch up on each other's lives. Those were sad, sad sessions, as life after life was unfolded amid grieving friends. Some had racked up tens of thousands of dollars in therapy bills. My childhood sweetheart was on her third marriage. She had found refuge in the Catholic church, which was just then battling horrendous abuse accusations of its own. Destroyed life after destroyed life was exposed.

My long-ago accuser Paul, now an insurance salesman, came up to me and said quietly, "It was me." I looked at him with puzzlement, until he continued, "It was my fingerprints in the cement. I've been dying to 'fess up for many years. I'm so sorry, Wess." I gave him a hug.

Adult women, through their tears, revealed for the first time what had been done to them in private. Stories came tumbling out to us, the only people who could possibly understand them.

Most of us fell into one of two categories: those who simply couldn't get over the hurt so that it destroyed their lives, and those of us who felt compelled to use the pain to become superachievers, which is a prison all its own. Many had endured a lifetime of destructive relationships, and some were angry, bitter, estranged from God, and felt they had nothing left to give to others. The pain was etched on their middle-aged faces.

For all of us, the pain had in one way or another absolutely dominated our lives. As in my own case, the pain was ever present right under the surface.

When it came my turn to tell my story, I saw expectant looks. What on earth had become of the boy with the birthday candle? I looked around the circle at my childhood friends and said, "Believe it or not, I serve as the leader of an evangelical ministry—to children."

A silence swept the room. Then through tear-filled eyes, the responses came one by one: "Why?" They went on to say, "You don't owe anything to anybody. We remember how they tried to destroy you. Why do you still care?"

I had never had to answer that to anybody, not even myself, until that moment. I felt such love for these people. This was the most profound question that could come from a group whose lives had been so torn by cruelty and abuse—the same abuse I had been through.

I wiped the tears yet again from my eyes and said to my dear friends, "It was probably the same rage and determination that made me hold that candle until it was slapped away. I simply refused to let them win again. They had stolen the joy of my childhood. I would not let them have the rest of my life too! Call it whatever you want; I simply chose to turn it for good."

By the end of the weekend, they were calling me Joseph. They would hug me and refer to Genesis 50:20, where Joseph tells his brothers, "You intended to harm me, but God intended it for good to accomplish what is now being done, the saving of many lives." They would continue, "Good for you, Wess. I'm so proud and happy for you!"

Just as I fight poverty on behalf of the Nielle children, I now keep my boarding school friends close. It motivates my battle against child abuse. Both are at the heart and soul of everything I do at Compassion. I am, by God's grace, a survivor of both.

But I must finish telling you about the Sunday morning meeting. The denomination had planned a worship service. A handful of us agreed to sing and lead as a worship group. We practiced on Saturday night, praying that somehow God would use us the next morning to comfort grieving hearts.

The room was set up that day to handle all 150 or so of us. When time came for the service, the room was nearly empty. Fewer than a tenth of my childhood friends cared to worship the God of this mission. Our forlorn little group sang bravely through broken hearts. One of the chosen songs was "You Are My All in All," which includes the poignant lyrics, "When I fall down, you pick me up / When I am dry, you fill my cup."[1] As I looked out at all the empty chairs, my eyes filled with tears. I couldn't keep singing. I grieved for the damaged souls of friends who had stumbled and couldn't find it in their hearts to get up again.

What is it with me? I thought. *What would it take for me to give up on this God we are singing about?* I felt not a tinge of condemnation for the absent ones; I could understand their reasoning all too well. But in my own heart, I clung desperately as I always had to the Jesus who defended the little ones and sternly warned grownups not to take advantage of them. This was the real Jesus, I assured myself, and I would keep loving and serving him, come what may.

STUDY AND
DISCUSSION GUIDE

Too Small to Ignore is filled with stories and ideas that lead its readers to think and more importantly, motivate them to act. This study guide will help you reflect on and personalize for yourself what Compassion International CEO and President Wess Stafford has to say about changing the world one child at a time. You can use it individually or as part of a group. For additional questions, journaling activities, and lists of suggested action steps related to each chapter, see www.toosmalltoignore.com.

CHAPTER 1: NOT SOMEDAY...TODAY

Bring the Chapter into Focus
Chapter 1 of Too Small to Ignore is about the importance of recognizing a child's present value, not just his or her "someday" value.

1. How does the author's youthful proficiency with a slingshot demonstrate the value children can have in society?
2. How would you characterize the difference between the way children in Nielle were allowed to contribute to community life and the way most children in Western nations are allowed to contribute?

Go Deeper into the Word
Read 1 Samuel 17, the story of David and Goliath.

3. What in this Bible story indicates that the adults around David

were at first more concerned with keeping the teen in his place than in discovering what he had to contribute?

4. What was the turning point in Saul's decision to allow David to face Goliath (see verses 34-37)?

5. Using the story of David and Goliath as an example, how would you say adults should go about discovering what children have to contribute?

Apply It

Stafford describes the frustration of youth and children who feel as though adults don't understand how much young people want to make a difference.

6. What was one experience in your childhood when you felt as though you had something to contribute but weren't allowed to? What did you think and feel while you were in that situation?

7. How does your church encourage children and youth to contribute to the life of the fellowship? How might your church sometimes inhibit their contribution?

8. What can your church or family do to be more proactive in receiving the contributions children can make?

Take Action

There are a number of ways to encourage children to contribute what they can or to encourage adults to accept what children have to offer.

9. Who are the children you have the closest contact with?

10. What do they have to contribute, and how can you help to bring out these contributions?

CHAPTER 2: BUILDING CASTLES IN THE CLOUDS

Bring the Chapter into Focus

Stafford offers a practical pathway to nurture children's dreams and to reaffirm their hope and worth in the second chapter.

1. What did you find most fascinating or most surprising about the interaction between adults and children in Nielle?

2. Think about how adults in our culture treat children. Where would you say we make our biggest mistakes?

Go Deeper into the Word

Read Deuteronomy 6, a passage about making God's commands a part of home and community life.

3. What kind of relationship would need to exist between an adult and a child for this passage to be fulfilled?
4. What might a modern-day attempt to fulfill this passage look like?
5. Describe several ways to impress the commandments of God on a child.
6. How can an adult use the commandments of God to both encourage and shape a child's dreams?

Apply It

How do you nurture the dreams of children? Stafford suggests that first you must enter a child's world, and second, bring the child into your world.

7. Which adults from your childhood nurtured your dreams? How did those adults enter your world and bring you into their worlds?
8. What kinds of shared activities can help to make an adult's presence in a child's world positive for both of them and for God's kingdom?
9. How can adults help youth cope with the frustration of being physically and mentally ready for life's challenges but not legally allowed to take their place in society?

Take Action

It's not always easy to develop the kind of relationship with a child where you have the privilege of nurturing dreams. But merging the two worlds, as Stafford says, can bring about that sort of relationship.

10. What do you know about the dreams of the children in your life?

11. What practical steps can you take to encourage them to fulfill their dreams in a godly way?

Chapter 3: It Really Does Take a Village

Bring the Chapter into Focus
Chapter 3 addresses the importance of community in the development of a child.

1. Review the section titled "In the Lap of Community" (page 57). What about the evening gathering shows the value that the community of Nielle placed on its children?
2. How does your community treat children differently than Nielle did?

Go Deeper into the Word
Read Luke 2:41-51, describing Jesus's trip to the temple at age twelve.

3. What does this passage indicate about the people who traveled with Mary, Joseph, and Jesus to Jerusalem?
4. Using this story as an example, describe the degree of involvement you believe a community of believers ought to have in the life of a child.

Apply It
The challenge of community is to surround children with love, attention, and support.

5. How did the community where you grew up affect your life?
6. How did your community of faith shape your life?
7. Consider your present community of faith. How does it contribute positively to the lives of its children?

Take Action
There are many ways for a community to contribute the love, attention, and support every child needs. None of us can help in every way, but all of us can help in some way.

8. If you could improve the quality of your community's care for children in three ways, what would they be?

9. What is something you can do now to make a difference in one of those three ways?

CHAPTER 4: GETTING THE FULL PICTURE—BODY AND SOUL

Bring the Chapter into Focus

Most Christians would agree that God cares about every area of a child's life—spiritual, social, physical, economic, environmental, and more. But translating that agreement into helpful action can be a challenge.

1. How would you characterize Ken Stafford's act of reconstructing a well in the context of his missionary work—as an interruption, a strategic move, or a necessary part of the job? Explain your response.

2. What could the Western church learn from this story of the Staffords and Kashongo?

Go Deeper into the Word

Read Luke 2:52: "Jesus grew in wisdom and stature, and in favor with God and men." In Luke's Gospel, this verse represents the transition between Jesus's childhood and his public ministry as an adult.

3. How does this verse reflect the holistic development of young Jesus?

4. What elements (for example, nutrition) would need to be introduced into a child's life in order to bring about the results cited for Jesus's development in Luke 2:52?

5. As you reflect on your own reading of the Gospels, do you think Jesus believed his ministry needed to engage the whole person (body, soul, and spirit) or not? Give examples to support your response.

Apply It

How can adults take a holistic approach to the development of the children around them? Keeping the big picture of a child's life in mind is a good starting point.

6. Identify a time in your youth or childhood when an adult surprised you with a positive interest in an area of your life beyond his or her normal contact with you. (For example, maybe a neighbor took an interest in your guitar lessons.) How did this make you feel?

7. What are the children in your life missing that would make them more complete individuals?

8. What can adults do to help kids grow into the full picture of the lives God wants for them?

Take Action

Jesus Christ came to save the whole person. Consequently, Stafford encourages an integrated approach to ministry that meets the needs of body, soul, and spirit.

9. How have you perhaps become unbalanced in your attempts to help children?

10. What changes can you make to pursue a more holistic approach toward helping the children in your life?

Chapter 5: Time: A River Runs Through It

Bring the Chapter into Focus

Chapter 5 shows how a hectic pace can rob both children and adults of the richness of today.

1. Review the story of young Pascal, which begins on page 81. Rather than putting Pascal on a high-pressure schedule, what might have been a better response to his interest in the clarinet?

2. Describe how you've seen adults' obsession with time impact the children around them.

Go Deeper into the Word

Read Proverbs 3:5-6: "Trust in the LORD with all your heart and lean not on your own understanding; in all your ways acknowledge him, and he will make your paths straight."

3. Give some examples of what it might mean to trust in the Lord with all one's heart, lean not on one's own understanding, and acknowledge God in all one's ways.

4. In what ways might God make our paths straight if we live as he desires?

5. How can an adult demonstrate to a child the impact of trusting God with one's time?

Apply It

Stafford concludes chapter 5 with encouragement to relax in the knowledge that God is in charge of our life and time and to pace ourselves appropriately.

6. Do you remember anyone from your childhood who had a God-honoring pace of life? How did you feel when you were around that person?

7. Describe the schedules of the children you're familiar with.

8. Does the schedule of your local church encourage a sane pace for children and their families? How about the schedule of your own family, if you have children? Explain your responses.

Take Action

Releasing someone from the tyranny of a schedule isn't easy. However, there are practical options that can help children (and adults) to live today completely and to trust tomorrow to God.

9. What needs to change in your life for you to have a more godly relationship with time?

10. What can you do to help children discover the value of relaxing their schedule in order to enjoy the life God has given them?

Chapter 6: When Is Enough...Enough?

Bring the Chapter into Focus
In chapter 6, Stafford explores the effect of materialism and culture on children. The acquisition of "stuff" is never enough to develop a child into a whole person, he believes.

1. What, if anything, do you admire about the attitude that the people of Nielle had toward money, possessions, and commerce?
2. How have you seen children affected when those around them put too much emphasis upon accumulating stuff?

Go Deeper into the Word
Read Matthew 19:16-30, a story about a rich young ruler. Sometimes those of us in affluent cultures face a similar choice to that of the young ruler.

3. What do you think was going on in the heart of the young man at the time of this meeting?
4. Is the difficulty that wealthy people face a problem with wealth itself or with how they deal with wealth? Explain your response in light of verses 23 and 24.
5. What biblical principles regarding wealth do you think are most important to remember? How would you explain those principles to a child?

Apply It
What does a child truly need? Stafford offers specific ideas on the subject, including this one: if we hope to influence children to take a healthy approach to materialism, we need to make sure our own approach to stuff makes sense.

6. How would you describe your own approach to keeping stuff in proper perspective?
7. Which of your friends, relatives, or associates seem to have the most healthy approach to deciding how much is enough? What are the signs of health in their approach?

8. How is your local church helping children and youth deal biblically with materialism and its effects? How might it do better?

Take Action

We need to ensure that the children within our reach have enough of life's basics to thrive. But we also need to teach our children the values they need so that they learn how to manage material things well, rather than being managed by the materialism that permeates our society.

9. What is one thing you'd like to change about your own approach to material things?

10. What are some lessons on materialism you can share with the younger generation? How will you pass along those lessons effectively?

CHAPTER 7: WHEN TRIUMPH IS DISASTER

Bring the Chapter into Focus

In chapter 7, Stafford differentiates between the kind of competition that spurs us on to excellence and the kind that promotes winning at any cost.

1. What aspects of the attitude in Nielle toward competition surprised you most?

2. Do you agree or disagree with the author's criticism of much of the competition urged upon children in the West? Explain.

Go Deeper into the Word

Read 2 Timothy 4:6-8, a passage Paul wrote to sum up his life as he was nearing death.

3. In these verses, what was Paul trying to convey to his original reader, Timothy?

4. Even though Paul used the language of athletic competition, he said nothing about winning against someone else. What might this suggest about the nature of competition as Paul saw it?

5. How would you explain these verses to children in a way that could help them understand competition that leads to excellence?

Apply It

Stafford suggests that we should teach and demonstrate that competition is not an end in itself but a tool for encouraging excellence.

6. Describe your past experience with and attitude toward competition.

7. How do you think your approach to competition affects the children you influence? What do you want them to learn from your example?

8. What are some practical ways that adults can show children the benefits of competition that promotes excellence?

Take Action

Now, more than ever, children need healthy role models who know how to deal with competition.

9. What do you think about Stafford's approach to teaching soccer?

10. What can you take away from his example? What other ideas do you have to help you guide children into a healthier form of competition?

CHAPTERS 8 AND 9: THE SILENCE OF THE LAMBS; BREAKING THE SILENCE

Bring the Chapters into Focus

Chapters 8 and 9 introduce us to the school for missionaries' children at Bandulo, where humiliation, beatings, and sexual abuse awaited the children. Chapter 9 demonstrates the necessity of adults speaking up for abused children.

1. Were you surprised that the kinds of abuse described by the author went on at a school run by missionaries? Why, or why not?

2. How common do you think physical, verbal, and sexual abuses of children are in our society?

Go Deeper into the Word

Read Matthew 18:1-6, recording the event when Jesus used a child to picture the humility required to enter God's kingdom and then went on to warn against harming children.

3. Describe the place you think children have in the heart of God.

4. What are some ways people can cause children to sin (verse 6)?

5. What does this passage suggest about how God views child abuse?

Apply It

Stafford brings a painful memory to light so that others can learn from it. Further, he suggests that his experience demonstrates the importance of adults confronting the evil that threatens children.

6. From what you've read, heard, or experienced, what are some signs that a child might be a victim of abuse?

7. Why do you think many abused children are silent about their abuse? What effect does their silence tend to have on them?

8. What is your church (or other community group you are affiliated with) doing to prevent child abuse?

9. Proverbs 31:8 says, "Speak up for those who cannot speak for themselves." What does it mean to you to "speak up" for children in need?

Take Action

You can play an important part in preventing child abuse and helping its victims.

10. How can you educate yourself about preventing child abuse, recognizing the signs that it is occurring, and helping victims to recover?

11. What groups are you a part of that include or affect children? Within these groups, what can you do to advocate for greater safety for the children?

Chapter 10: Back to "Civilization"

Bring the Chapter into Focus
Stafford shows how the poor can be in a better position than the rest of us when it comes to love, joy, hope, and one's perspective on time.

1. Identify some of the ways in which the "pearls of poverty" that Stafford learned in Nielle defined the community's life.
2. Do you think the experiences the author had as a youth in New York City—having his stickball game broken up and overhearing an assault where nobody helped—represent American attitudes toward community fairly? Why or why not?

Go Deeper into the Word
Read Proverbs 8:10-11: "Choose my instruction instead of silver, knowledge rather than choice gold, for wisdom is more precious than rubies, and nothing you desire can compare with her."

3. What might be some differences between a culture that values wisdom more than material wealth and a culture that values material wealth more than wisdom?
4. What are the children in your church or community being encouraged to pursue more: wealth or wisdom? Explain your answer.

Apply It
The author says that everything good he needed to know in order to lead a worldwide child-development ministry, he learned from the poor themselves. Stafford calls these the "pearls of poverty," because they are jewels that have been made precious by suffering.

5. What are the challenges of applying the values represented in the pearls of poverty in an affluent, developed society?
6. How can adults in our society give the pearls of poverty as a gift to our youth?
7. How might life be different for children if these pearls were more common today?

Take Action
The pearls of poverty are largely lacking in our society—but they don't have to be, if adults will learn them and introduce them to children.

8. Which of the pearls of poverty would you most like to introduce to the children in your life, and why?

9. How will you bless children with these pearls? Describe at least one specific step you will take.

Chapter 11: Why Doesn't Poverty Just Go Away?

Bring the Chapter into Focus
In this chapter, Stafford further unpacks the complexity of poverty and also builds a case for defeating poverty through changing the lives of children.

1. What contact do you have with poverty, especially poverty that affects children?

2. Do you agree with Stafford's assertion that an effective fight against poverty must bring about a change in the people trapped in poverty as well as a change in their circumstances? Explain your response.

Go Deeper into the Word
Read Deuteronomy 15:7-11, one of the many biblical passages emphasizing that those who *can* give to the poor *should* give to the poor. In the Bible, it's that simple.

3. What practical actions do you find commanded in this passage? What attitudes of the heart do you see addressed?

4. What are the best ways for people of faith to fulfill this mandate today? To what or to whom should we give?

Apply It
The author champions the idea of investing in individuals who need release from poverty.

5. Both giving to change people and giving to change circumstances are crucial in fighting poverty. What are the similarities between

these kinds of giving? The differences?

6. Would you agree that poor children are even more appropriate candidates for help than are poor adults? Why or why not?

7. How would you like to see our society address poverty differently?

8. What might be some advantages for you if you decide to give to an individual in need? What might be some disadvantages?

Take Action
Chapter 11 makes a compelling argument for giving to the poor in ways that will change people as well as change their environment.

9. Think about the author's explanation of poverty as a wheel (page 176). How can you invest in children or youth in a way that will bring their lives into balance?

Chapter 12: The Children's Champion: A Righteous Rage

Bring the Chapter into Focus
Taking another look at Jesus's encounters with children in chapter 12, Stafford concludes that Jesus was a champion of children, to the point of being outraged when they were treated as second-class citizens.

1. Based on this chapter's Scriptural review, how would you describe Jesus's attitude toward children?

2. How does your community's or culture's attitude toward children measure up to the way Jesus treated them?

Go Deeper into the Word
Read Mark 10:13-16, a passage describing how Jesus became indignant at his disciples for preventing children from coming to him.

3. How do you think Jesus expressed his indignation in the presence of children?

4. What phrase in Jesus's response to his disciples most startles you? Why?

5. What do you think it means to receive the kingdom like a little child?

Apply It

The reality check for this chapter's study is how we treat children in everyday encounters. Do we welcome them, or do we marginalize them?

6. How might a childlike faith help adults treat children better?

7. Identify one or more situations in which you recently saw adults treating children or youth poorly. What could the adults have done better?

8. What are the most crucial ways in which our society needs to learn to treat the young in more Christlike ways?

Take Action

How can we become champions for children? We can start by acting toward children—and toward attempts to marginalize them—as Jesus would.

9. Think about the kinds of interactions you expect to have with children in the near future. How would Jesus speak and act in those situations?

CHAPTER 13: WHEN "FOLLOW THE LEADER" ISN'T CHILD'S PLAY

Bring the Chapter into Focus

Are children the church of tomorrow or God's instruments today? In chapter 13, Stafford offers examples from the Bible and recent church history to argue that children are instruments in God's hands right now.

1. Review the story under the heading "Needed: An Evangelist in the Village (Ecuador 2004)," beginning on page 226. Why do you suppose the adults in this story were so surprised by the number of children this young evangelist led to Christ?

2. Describe what you believe to be the typical expectations for children in the Western church.

Go Deeper into the Word

Read 1 Corinthians 1:26-31. As Stafford explains, children are often considered foolish, weak, lowly, and despised—and that is probably why God uses them for his purposes.

3. What kind of situation may have existed in the Corinthian church to elicit this outpouring by the apostle Paul?

4. Do you agree that children fit into the categories of people whom Paul describes as being ripe for use by God? Why or why not?

5. What makes children and youth effective as God's agents?

6. How might God use children to "nullify the things that are" (verse 28) in our day?

Apply It

Stafford concludes this chapter with a call to respect the children around us because they are often more willing servants of God than adults.

7. Think about the examples of children as God's agents in this chapter. Describe the common character traits you see in those children.

8. Describe a child or youth in your own life who is an agent of God. Explain your choice.

9. How have you seen adults stand in the way of children who are willing to be used by God?

10. What will it take to overcome adults' hesitancy to see children as agents of God?

Take Action

Chapter 13 offers a sound rationale for keeping children in mind as we look for signs of God's activity in our world.

11. What attitudes might you need to overcome in yourself if you are to be looking for children to act as agents of God in the world?

12. What can you do to help other adults see children as God's agents or to help children see themselves in this way?

CHAPTER 14: IMAGINE...

Bring the Chapter into Focus

Chapter 14 lays out a vision for what could be if children were properly valued in our world. The author brings the vision to the international, national, community, church, and family levels.

1. What part of the author's vision do you find most compelling? What part challenged your thinking the most?

2. Do any of the ideas for action that Stafford presents in this chapter seem impossible to you? If so, explain why.

Go Deeper into the Word

Read Proverbs 22:6: "Train a child in the way he should go, and when he is old he will not turn from it."

3. What elements combine to make up the training of a child?

4. What does it mean to direct a child in the way he should go?

5. Do you think we should consider this proverb an ironclad promise or a general statement of truth? Explain.

6. What hope does this proverb give you about the future of children if adults were to take their responsibility toward children more seriously?

Apply It

Growing up can be a complex and difficult process. That's why a child needs an environment that supports his or her growth.

7. Of all the changes that Stafford imagines taking place in the treatment of children, which do you see as most important?

8. Which of the levels (international, national, and so forth) can ordinary people have the most impact in? Why?

9. Recall the author's illustration of a cement block all but preventing the growth of a wildflower (page 239). What are the top two "cement blocks" in the world of children that need to be removed? Explain your choices.

Take Action

Stafford offers a list of action items for child advocacy on several fronts.

10. Where do you see yourself fitting into the effort to make this vision a reality?

11. What is one thing you are willing to do this week to make the environment of the children you influence more suitable for their growth?

CHAPTER 15: "JUST" CHILDREN: A CALL TO ARMS

Bring the Chapter into Focus

As *Too Small to Ignore* concludes, Stafford encourages us to become child advocates—those who will speak up for children.

1. Discuss your reaction to the statement: "A church begins to die when it says, 'They were just children.' "

2. What signs do you see that the children in your life need advocates?

Go Deeper into the Word

Read Jesus's statement in Luke 12:48: "From everyone who has been given much, much will be demanded; and from the one who has been entrusted with much, much more will be asked."

3. Do you feel like you've been given or entrusted with much? Explain your response.

4. What do you think might be demanded or asked of you by God in relation to children?

5. Given your social, intellectual, financial, and spiritual resources, what might be the most significant thing you can offer as a child advocate?

Apply It

The role of child advocate is not always appreciated. Yet the benefits that an advocate can bring to children are too significant to ignore.

6. Describe what you believe it means to be a child advocate.

7. As you grew up, which adults stood out as advocates for children in your community? What can you learn from their example?

8. What are some of the challenges awaiting someone who decides to become a child advocate? What are some of the rewards?

Take Action

The book's final chapter is a call to action. Will you respond?

9. If you were to become a lifelong child advocate, what might that look like? How can you begin today to make that a reality?

10. In one or two sentences, summarize what you have gained from reading *Too Small to Ignore* and using this study guide.

NOTES

Introduction: The Great Omission

1. The Council of Bishops of the United Methodist Church, *Children and Poverty: An Episcopal Initiative* (Nashville: United Methodist Publishing House, 1996), 1.
2. United Nations Food and Agriculture Organization, "State of Food Insecurity in the World 2002," www.fao.org/docrep/005/ y7352e/y7352e00.htm.
3. United Nations Food and Agriculture Organization, "Agriculture and Food Security," World Food Summit, Rome, November 13–17, 1996, www.fao.org/ documents/show_cdr.asp?url_file=/DOCREP/x0262e/x0262e05.htm.
4. *The State of the World's Children 2005: Childhood Under Threat* (New York: UNICEF, 2004).
5. Barna Group, "Evangelism Is Most Effective Among Kids," October 11, 2004, *The Barna Update*, www.barna.org.

Chapter 2: Building Castles in the Clouds

1. Dorothy Law Nolte, "Children Learn What They Live," 1972. Used by permission.
2. Steve Brearton, "Fatherhood by the Numbers," TodaysParent.com, www.todaysparent.com.

Chapter 3: It Really Does Take a Village

1. Dean Merrill, "Not Married-with-Children," *Christianity Today,* July 14, 1997, 34–36.

Chapter 4: Getting the Full Picture—Body and Soul

1. E. Stanley Jones, speech to the 1970 Good News Convocation in Dallas, Texas, later condensed in *Good News* magazine, www .goodnewsmag.org.

Chapter 6: When Is Enough…Enough?

1. Kids' Money, "Kids' Allowance Stats," www.kidsmoney.org/allstats. htm#Amt.
2. Linda Kulman, "Our Consuming Interest," *U.S. News & World Report,* July 5, 2004, 59.
3. Marianne Szegedy-Maszak, "Where Size Matters," *U.S. News & World Report,* July 5, 2004, 60.

Chapter 7: When Triumph Is Disaster

1. "Response to a Serenade," in Roy P. Basler, ed., *The Collected Works of Abraham Lincoln* (Piscataway, NJ: Rutgers University Press, 1953), 8:96.
2. George B. Leonard, "Winning Isn't Everything," *Intellectual Digest,* October 1973, quoted in George B. Leonard, "Winning Isn't Everything," *Faith at Work,* June 1974, 8–9, 32–33.
3. Donald P. McNeill, Douglas A. Morrison, and Henri J. M. Nouwen, *Compassion: A Reflection on the Christian Life* (Garden City, NY: Doubleday, 1982), 6.

Chapter 9: Breaking the Silence

1. C. B. Widmeyer, "Come and Dine," © 1907 S. H. Bolton, © 1914 Thoro Harris. Owner: Lillenas Publishing Co.

Chapter 11: Why Doesn't Poverty Just Go Away?

1. U.S. Census Bureau's Small Area Income and Poverty Estimates, Annie E. Casey Foundation, www.aecf.org/kidscount.
2. *The State of the World's Children 2005: Childhood Under Threat* (New York: UNICEF, 2004).
3. United Nations Food and Agriculture Organization, "Agriculture and Food Security," World Food Summit, Rome, November 13–17, 1996, www.fao.org/documents/show_cdr.asp?url_file=/DOCREP/x0262e/x0262e05.htm.
4. Keepkidshealthy.com, "Calorie Requirements," www.keepkidshealthy.com/nutrition/calorie_requirements.html.

Chapter 12: The Children's Champion: A Righteous Rage

1. See country-by-country epidemiological charts at www.unaids.org.

Chapter 15: "Just" Children: A Call to Arms

1. Barna Group, "Evangelism Is Most Effective Among Kids," October 11, 2004, *The Barna Update,* www.barna.org.

Afterword: The Rest of the Story

1. Dennis Jernigan, "You Are My All in All," (Muskogee, OK: Shepherd's Heart Music, Inc., 1991, administered by Word Music, Inc.).

ABOUT THE AUTHORS

Dr. Wess Stafford, president of Compassion International, is an internationally recognized advocate for children in poverty. Wess's life experiences have uniquely prepared him for this role. While he has earned degrees from Moody Bible Institute, Biola University, and Wheaton College, and a PhD from Michigan State University, Wess often says, "Everything I really need to know to lead a multinational organization, I learned from the poor while growing up in an African village." As the son of Ivory Coast missionaries, Wess was one of the village children who were watched over by a wise and loving African "extended family." But his young heart was often broken when African friends died from the cruel ravages of poverty.

In 1977 Wess joined the staff of Compassion International, one of the world's largest Christian child-development agencies, partnering with more than sixty-five denominations and thousands of local churches to serve more than six hundred thousand children in twenty-three countries. He has worked with the ministry, both overseas and at headquarters, for twenty-eight years and has served as president since 1993.

An avid outdoorsman and committed family man, Wess lives on a little ranch near Colorado Springs, Colorado, with Donna, his wife of twenty-five years. They have two daughters, Jenny and Katie—the two children in the world for whom Wess is the greatest advocate of all.

Dean Merrill is a former magazine editor for *Campus Life, Leadership Journal,* and *Christian Herald* and has served as the editorial director for David C. Cook and Focus on the Family. He has written seven books and co-authored twenty-one others. In addition to this recent collaboration with Wess Stafford, Dean has written with Hobby Lobby entrepreneur David Green, Philippine missionary survivor Gracia Burnham, and Brooklyn Tabernacle pastor Jim Cymbala. Two of these books won Gold Medallion awards, and another was the Christian Book of the Year. Dean is a graduate of Christian Life College–Chicago and Syracuse University. He and his wife live in Colorado Springs and have three children and four grandchildren.